The Semantics of Desire

CHANGING MODELS OF IDENTITY

FROM DICKENS TO JOYCE

The Semantics of Desire

CHANGING MODELS OF IDENTITY
FROM DICKENS TO JOYCE

Philip M. Weinstein

PRINCETON UNIVERSITY PRESS

PRINCETON, NEW JERSEY

For Penny

Preface

SEMANTICS and desire, signification and force, cultural value and natural impulse: the interplay of these paired terms helps to stabilize human identity. No self is likely to be imagined free of one member of the pair, composed wholly of its opposite. This book seeks to show that the protagonists of mid-Victorian fiction cluster as near to one pole as the protagonists of Modernist fiction locate at the other. From Dickens and George Eliot through Hardy and Conrad toward Lawrence and Joyce, the protagonistic self becomes less a figure defined by semantics, signification, cultural value, and more one defined by desire, force, natural impulse. The immaculate self—self-withholding and self-aware—gradually cedes place to the incarnate self—sexualized and immersed beyond self-knowing in experience.

All subjects, fictional and otherwise, are in bodies. I think I first conceived my book when I realized that different novelists—and the different cultural sanctions they express—attend in vastly different ways to the bodies of their subjects. David and Arthur, Maggie and Gwendolen, Tess and Jude, Jim and Nostromo, Birkin and Connie, Stephen and Bloom: all of these figures seek to enact their freedom (to express their desire), and the shape of their career is inseparable from their own and their creator's imaginative attitudes toward the body. To move from Dickens to Joyce is to encounter a virtual revolution in which the body's propensity and the mind's restraint exchange roles as primary indices of identity. A reverse of focus occurs. Identity becomes less and less legible in the mind's dominion over bodily desire. Rather, it begins to emerge in desire's evasion of the mind's inapplicable injunctions.

Semantics opposes desire; semantics is also inflected by desire. Words acknowledge openly; they also intimate unknowingly. Suspended between culture and nature, value and impulse, the human subject's language simultaneously signifies a situation and insinuates an orientation. Our language always means more than we think it does, and imaginative language does so supremely. An attempt is made in the following pages to read both what six novelists acknowledge and what they intimate: to read their imaginative productions imaginatively.

Acknowledgments

THIS BOOK has been in process for twelve years; one accumulates many debts over that amount of time. I am most immediately indebted to Philip Fisher and Richard Ludwig. The one my oldest friend since graduate school, the other my first undergraduate teacher and advisor, they have read this book more than once and counseled me at every stage of its composition.

I have also been lucky in my home institution. Swarthmore College has provided me with sustaining colleagues, demanding students, and a generous leave policy that permits, every four years, not only a time for personal work but also a breathing space in which to ponder the work's hidden assumptions and its further implications. John Hinchey, Craig Williamson, Mary Poovey, and Peter Schmidt have read various chapters of my study and served as a critical and sympathetic resource for its knottiest problems. Thelma Miller, my departmental secretary, has typed and retyped this manuscript with unfailing patience and grace.

An NEH Fellowship in 1974-1975 allowed me to study further the development of irrational thought—from Schopenhauer to Freud—that underlies this book. And a Mellon grant in 1978-1979 enabled me to draft over half of its chapters while on sabbatical leave at Cambridge University. At that time Tony Tanner generously read and commented on the Hardy chapter, and Calvin Bedient interrupted a busy schedule to attend to my chapter on George Eliot.

The book's roots extend farther back. There are four men who taught me most as an undergraduate and graduate, and whose voices are never far from my mind when I attempt to write. I would have liked for Lawrance Thompson, Laurence Holland, R. P. Blackmur, and Reuben Brower to be able to read this book: I could not have written it without their example.

My brother Arnold Weinstein and I have been discussing literature together ever since I can remember; his influence on this book is diffuse but considerable. Robert Bell, an old friend since graduate school, read the manuscript and offered shrewd advice. Three other colleagues at Swarthmore—Robert Roza, Bernard Smith, and Lee Devin—contribute so much to the convivial/intellectual atmosphere in which I live and think that they too have left their imprint on my work.

The remaining influences are the most pervasive. For the past twelve years my Swarthmore classes and seminars have joined in the unpremeditated rehearsal of this book; the role played therein by students is incalculable. My mother and her support, my father who is no longer here, my children Liz and Katie, who have been growing up as this book was being written: there is not a word in it directly attributable to them, but they are the given conditions that have accompanied its genesis and inflected its shape. Finally, my wife Penny has enabled this book in utterly specific ways that show up on each page: a revised transition, an altered phrase, a deleted or appended paragraph. She has also enabled it—and me—in ways that are too profound to tell, and for which I can only express my gratitude.

An earlier version of the *Lady Chatterley's Lover* discussion appeared in *Modern Language Quarterly*, Vol. 43, No. 3, September 1982

A Note on Bibliographical Procedures and Primary Texts

A LIST of Works Cited appears at the end of this study and supplies all requisite bibliographical information. The notes are therefore substantive and are carried at the foot of the relevant page.

I have quoted from the following editions of the primary texts under discussion:

Charles Dickens, *David Copperfield*, ed. Nina Burgis (Oxford: Clarendon Press, 1981)

———, *Little Dorrit*, ed. Harvey Peter Sucksmith (Oxford: Clarendon Press, 1979)

George Eliot, *The Mill on the Floss*, ed. Gordon Haight (Oxford: Clarendon Press, 1980)

———, *Daniel Deronda*, ed. Barbara Hardy (Harmondsworth, England: Penguin, 1967)

Thomas Hardy, *Tess of the d'Urbervilles*, New Wessex Edition (London: Macmillan, 1975)

———, *Jude the Obscure*, New Wessex Edition (London: Macmillan, 1975)

Joseph Conrad, *Lord Jim*, ed. Thomas C. Moser (New York: Norton, 1968)

———, *Nostromo* (Harmondsworth, England: Penguin, 1963)

D. H. Lawrence, *Women in Love* (New York: Viking, 1960)

———, *The First Lady Chatterley* (Harmondsworth, England: Penguin, 1973)

———, *John Thomas and Lady Jane* (New York: Viking, 1974)

———, *Lady Chatterley's Lover* (New York: Bantam, 1968)

James Joyce, *Ulysses* (New York: Random House, 1961)

Contents

CONTENTS

The Semantics of Desire

CHANGING MODELS OF IDENTITY

FROM DICKENS TO JOYCE

You shall become who you are.
—Nietzsche, *The Gay Science*

... on ne se réalise que successivement ...
—Proust, *La Prisonnière*

Introduction

If the fool would persist in his folly he would become wise.—Blake, *The Marriage of Heaven and Hell*

THIS STUDY explores the changing relation between desire and value, as they affect the protagonists' identity, in English novels between 1850 and 1928. I examine the imaginative predilections of two mid-Victorians, two late-Victorians, and two Modernists. Each chapter seeks to identify the novelist's characteristic stance toward desire by interrogating in detail a pair of his novels.[1] The study moves from narratives of repression and disguise in Dickens and Eliot to narratives of release and celebration in Lawrence and Joyce.

Seen synoptically, my book inquires into the novelistic imagination of freedom. It does so by examining a range of protagonists' capacities to accommodate and turn to creative personal use the givens of nature and culture. To be in a body is to experience desire and to be inscribed in the natural world of space and time. To have a mind is to inherit attitudes toward desire because one is inscribed in the cultural world of sanctions and prohibitions. Since no one creates either his body or his mind, all embodied thinking subjects—all protagonists—achieve their freedom in the measure that they come to terms with these matrical systems of nature and culture.[2]

---

[1] My discussion of Joyce centers on the major novel, *Ulysses*.

[2] I realize that there are other and more spectacular forms of freedom, especially those that involve a risk of one's being in behalf of a chosen ideal. This is the domain of heroism proper. I have chosen to focus on a more obscure (though omnipresent) realm of freedom, that involved in a subject's relation to his inalienable given conditions.

Allegiance to nature and culture is involuntary. The character of the allegiance alters, however, and that alteration is the subject of my book. At its most schematic, the argument goes like this: the mid-Victorians privilege culture; they imagine the protagonist becoming himself—achieving freedom—by subordinating the givens of his natural body. The Modernists, by contrast, privilege nature; they envisage the protagonist's freedom and self-enactment in his capacity to affirm desire and to resist, ignore, or simply endure his culture's injunctions. Freedom is possible in both of these positions. For the novelists who come between mid-Victorian and Modern, however—for Hardy and Conrad—neither culture nor nature is privileged. Both systems are in limbo. The cultural scripts within the protagonist have lost their force but may not be discarded, while his natural propensities wreak havoc with his goals but may not be sanctioned. Hardy and Contrad cannot imagine self-discovery in terms other than self-rupture. Split between nature and culture, their protagonists rarely achieve identity or freedom.

This development has considerable formal consequences. We begin with the mid-Victorian plot of a cohesive protagonist moving through public space and time and, eventually, either achieving the social career that he has personally willed or failing (for carefully documented reasons) to do so. This is the plot of Dickens and Eliot in which an unruly self grows up. His freedom is enacted as his capacity to realize—through his will—the prescriptions of his culture: as Freud would say, to live up to the requirements of his superego. The late-Victorian plot of Hardy and Conrad characteristically accepts these societal terms but cannot make good on them. Tess and Jude, Jim and Nostromo, want to love, work, and succeed exactly as their culture prescribes, but the prescription is becoming chimera-like, beckoning yet unrealizable. Something at the core of the protagonist insists on or cannot evade the sabotage of aspirations.

The novels of Lawrence and Joyce exploit this element of sabotage. Their early Bildungsromane elaborate the acculturation plot in all of its impossibility. Neither writer can imagine the subjective experience of freedom in its terms. Lawrence and Joyce both conceive a protagonistic self in opposition to this model, a self that is not performed through the exercise of will, and not interested in a career defined by lengthy apprenticeship to and eventual mastery over culturally approved forms of work. Their great novels formally abandon or parody the plot of social integration. Lawrence imagines identity and freedom elsewhere; Joyce (in *Ulysses*) reconceives them here, within culture, but in terms that would perplex or scandalize his Victorian predecessors.

I shall argue in Part One that in the fiction of Dickens and Eliot the subject is conceived as transcendentally pure, established prior to cultural or natural constraints. Unlike the rebellious Romantic version of this subject, the transcendental Victorian subject chooses acculturation; he joins up. This orderly conception is of course disseminated by Victorian society; it is one of its foremost conventions. Thoughts and behavior that continue to transgress this normative convention may not be sanctioned in the protagonist; his career unfolds in the form of his gradual, often painful, assimilation of this norm.

Such a career may exact a considerable price, for it insists on a subject fully capable of altruism, discipline, and earnestness: a subject who subordinates his own concerns to those of others, who controls his body's impulses, and whose consciousness is capable of self-knowledge. My study begins at those moments when this subject starts to become unimaginable. That is, those occasions on which Dickens and Eliot are unable to imagine the protagonist fulfilling his prescription because other elements, just glimpsed in the self but somehow exigent, seem to require another denouement. In Dickens and Eliot these are only occasions because their imaginations are usually on good terms with their culture's protagonistic norm. Indeed, they never knowingly violate this norm. The panorama of characters unlike the protagonist usually permits the lateral siphoning off of illicit energies. At times, however, something does go wrong. The writer's imagination, uncoercible, shows signs of apostasy. It apprehends as subjectively desirable a course of actions or cluster of feelings that the dictates of conscience must abjure.

In Hardy and Conrad the cultural allegiances that make up conscience remain in place, but the writer's immediate apprehension of his subject's thoughts, desires, and probable behavior has become further thwarted. He cannot imagine the free development of a protagonist in terms that intersect his culture's norms, and he cannot endorse a development that violates those norms. I think of these novels as "tragic encounters" because the incarnate subject is embarked, increasingly, on a career conceived in terms that ensure disaster. His culturally enjoined identity—the sanctions by which he recognizes, orients, and evaluates himself—is losing its purchase on the immediate data of thought and feeling. He finds himself experiencing what he is incapable of accommodating; his culture has led him to propose for himself projects which he has no means of achieving. The scripts of legibility through which the culture licenses its models of identity are becoming for him inapplicable, but he will cancel himself through suicide rather than repudiate those scripts. His creator can imagine no exit from this dilemma.

Lawrence and Joyce begin to demythologize these scripts. Both writers overtly recognize (rather than merely imply) the injurious effects of culturally licensed norms of identity, aspiration, and career. The subject can be imagined as free again, because the relation between the subject and the myriad elements that compose and constrain it has been reconceived. The self no longer yearns to be transcendentally prior to the natural world (its incarnate grounding, the locus of its desires and actual possibilities), nor does it seek a perfect fusion with the cultural world (its ideological grounding, its human inheritance). The narratives that contain these newly conceived subjects are likewise redesigned to accommodate their newfound freedom. No plots of societal career that presuppose shared societal norms, likewise no plots of achieved escape that pre-suppose a transcendental self free of societal traces: in fact, little plot at all, for the freedom of these embodied subjects is largely constituted by their moment-by-moment movement in time, essaying (sometimes whimsically, sometimes ecstatically) their conditional possibilities.

❧

SUCH, in summary form, is the argument of this book. I need now (at the risk of re-inventing the wheel) to identify the literary and philosophical premises that have made the argument possible. These premises, everywhere operative though often un-stated, cluster about the following terms: freedom, protagonist, plot, subject, self and society, transcendental and contingent, identity, and (above all) imagination.

The question of freedom provides the rationale for this study's focus upon the career of the central figure(s), the protagonist(s), as well as for its considerable attention to the shape of plots. The protagonist is the character through whom the creative writer tends to imagine most intimately the experience of freedom. It is true, of course, that novelists project their sense of inner pos-sibility into the whole of their created canvas—its range of char-acters, its cluster of plots, its typical movement, its setting, its syntax. But preeminently they convey their own subjective reality (what it feels like to be alive, responsive, and desiring in a world of others) through the creation of protagonists.

Protagonists enact, however, a dual allegiance. If they house their creator's psychic investment, they also testify to the nor-mative stresses of the society within which their creator moves. This crossing of subjective energy and societal constraint defines, for my study, their peculiar interest. Becky Sharpe, for example, accommodates her creator's shrewdest sense of reality, but Thackeray has not treated her as a protagonist: he has not sought to align her energies within the web of her society's norms. In-deed, she may be defined as the power of illicit energies on the other side of the norms. In the Victorian novel the protagonists must move, in good faith, in the daylight of their culture's sanc-tions, however shaped they may be, simultaneously, by the noc-turnal energies of their creator's imagination. (This tension be-tween sanctioned forms of expression and wayward energies seeking release is the recurrent focus of Parts One and Two of this study. In Part Three the tension alters, as the Modernists call into question the sanctioning process itself.)

The range of movements that these protagonists desire to make exists in a dialectic relation to the movements that they are actually empowered to make. The shape of this dialectic is the plot. To discuss the plot is to register the variety of non-subjec-tive elements that affect the career of the protagonists: their ca-pacity for freedom.

Paradoxically, this opposition—protagonist versus society—
is at the same time an equation: protagonist-and-society. The self
that desires and the society that restrains are interpenetrative terms.
The romantic opposition of self (unscripted, pure) versus society
(scripted, maculate, corrupting) is, on scrutiny, untenable—untenable because it assumes that self is transcendentally prior to
society. If we reject this metaphysical assumption, we must conclude that "self" and "society" answer to opposed optics on a
common spectrum of phenomena, for how could self be constituted if not from the materials—family, school, church, law, customs, etc.—of society? And how could society be conceived apart
from its status as a historically descended commonwealth of selves?

The materials are common but the optics are opposed. This
simple point has considerable implications. Self can neither van-
quish society nor be merged into it: their difference is as inextinguishable as it is incomplete. An entity located in society, in every
respect composed of elements common to society, self is nevertheless not society. Or, to put it more precisely, self refers to no
entity at all—for entity implies object—but rather to the characteristic mode of relations that an individual *as subject* sustains
with himself and with the social world in which he lives.

For the writer as writer, that mode of subjective relation is
imaginative: we arrive thus at one of the governing concepts of
this study, imagination. Imagination is the writer's preeminent
faculty, a power of perception that has no transcendental status,
is at all times conditioned, but is nevertheless unpredictable. It
carries the writer's identity for, unlike his conscience, it is not
the property of his culture's norms. Not that it is exclusively his
own property either, to be shaped at will. "Perception is not
whimsical but fatal," says Emerson, and imagination is that ineluctable manner of seeing things that marks the writer's ineluctable identity (156). Operative within consciousness but not coe-
qual with it, shaped through the pressure of conscience by cultural
sanctions but equally a mode of responding to and deploying
those sanctions, gradually and unconsciously formed over the years,
a writer's imagination is his signature. It expresses (with whatever internal fissures) his inclusive way of reading his world.[3]

[3] For a shrewd discussion of how a writer's conflicted psychology creates

The point is important because it carries the issue of the writer's freedom (and by extension that of his characters). To be conditioned is not to be unfree; to be shaped by societal paradigms is not to be deprived of self. Self is authenticated through the deployment of materials not self-originated. The presence of ineradicable societal traces within a writer's imagination only means that his freedom is constituted by his relation to those traces: by what he does with and through them. The evolving dialectic between a writer's imagination and his given conditions (both inner and outer)—a dialectic as unpredictable as it is unrepeatable—finally *is* his creative freedom. Meditating on this dialectic, Proust states the case succinctly:

> Moreover this reaction of locally procured materials on the genius who utilises them and to whose work their reaction imparts an added freshness, does not make the work any less individual, and whether it be that of an architect, a cabinet-maker or a composer, it reflects no less minutely the most subtle shades of the artist's personality, because he has been compelled to work in the millstone of Senlis or the red sandstone of Strasbourg, has respected the knots peculiar to the ash-tree, has borne in mind, when writing his score, the resources, the limitations, the volume of sound, the possibilities of a flute or alto voice. (I:682)

The authority of individual achievement (and thereby the creator's identity) depends not on the myth of a transcendental subject working within the vacuum of its self-chosen terms and instruments. Rather, Proust indicates, it emerges through the performance of a contingent subject operating under the pressure of innumerable restrictions, and actualizing himself through those restrictions. Such a performative model of identity accommo-

---

fissures within the writing itself, see the essays Frederick Crews has collected in *Out of My System*. Crews candidly discusses the appeal and the pitfalls of a psychoanalytic approach to literature. See also Julia Kristeva's *Desire in Language: A Semiotic Approach to Literature and Art*. Kristeva locates the problematics of language in both the artifice of the sign and instinctual drives that skew any straightforward communication of meaning. Mikhail Bakhtin very suggestively reads Dostoevsky's entire corpus as an interplay of conflicting subjective voices, none subordinated to a single commanding design.

dates both authors and their protagonists; it underlies in a number of ways the argument of this book.

With respect to authors, the model suggests that their power is inseparable from their receptivity—to the bias of their imagination, to the exigencies of their medium, to the constraints of their culture. The writer's imagination, even as it eludes his would-be-sovereign will, records the stresses of his situation. He may truck with his imagination, abuse it, exploit it, but he cannot commandeer its testimony. (The latent quarrel within this faculty between the press of nature and the restraint of culture [between the unconscious and the superego] animates my chapters on Dickens and Eliot. This same quarrel, become overt, animates my chapters on Hardy and Conrad. The attempt to heal the quarrel animates my chapter on Lawrence and Joyce.)

Insofar as the Proustean model accommodates protagonists, it focuses attention less on their intrinsic properties than on their mode of relations with the world they inhabit. Freedom and identity emerge in the subject's transactions, in his capacity, not to create new conditions, but to realize himself by accepting and energizing his given conditions. Throughout, of course, these given conditions are nature and culture, bodily desire and societal constraint. They have been addressed first in terms of my book's argument, next in terms of its premises. They may now be approached in terms of its methodology.

෨

THE SEMANTICS of desire: my title comes from Paul Ricoeur. In the opening pages of his study of Freud, Ricoeur speaks of "the semantics of desire, a semantics that centers around a somewhat nuclear theme: as a man of desires I go forth in disguise—*larvatus prodeo*" (6-7). A man of desires is opaque—to himself, to others. To be understood, he must be subjected to a hermeneutical scrutiny that will unravel his utterance by locating the kernel of unacknowledged desire that is serving as its orientation. Ricoeur goes on to identify Marx, Nietzsche, and Freud as the three master critics of a school of suspicion that specializes in the art of unmasking. In their work the testimony of subjective consciousness becomes systematically suspect, for consciousness is everywhere blind to its own strategic biases. Conditioned by an economic system that dictates his ideology, a libidinal system that controls his erotic choices, and a will to power that predisposes him to the exploitation of others, the mystified subject nevertheless manages to think of himself as transcendentally free, guileless, and self-knowing. "Beginning with [Marx, Nietzsche, and Freud]," Ricoeur writes, "understanding is hermeneutics: henceforward, to seek meaning is no longer to spell out the consciousness of meaning, but to *decipher its expressions*" (33).

In order to assess properly the subject's hidden conditionality, this study will supplement its literary analysis by drawing (especially in the chapter on Dickens) on Nietzsche and Freud. Both thinkers subvert a nineteenth-century model of the subject as innocent and autonomous. Nietzsche seeks to dislodge this model of the subject by exposing the concealed presence of an amoral will to power within its discourse and behavior, while Freud's hermeneutic charts the disowned movement of unresolved (and likewise amoral) sexual energies within the same discourse and behavior. For both thinkers, the subject is essentially unaware of his own motives.

A critical methodology rigidly shaped to the contours of the Freud-Nietzsche model has, however, its limitations. Put simply, such a model is too suspicious; it assumes, programmatically, that consciousness is opaque to all of the subject's deeper intentions. The point is important because Marx, Nietzsche, and Freud—in their common premise of a mystified subject—have served as a *point de répère* for recent interpretive theory. The shared premise is that an initiated observer with a privileged hermeneutical lens can identify those ideological crossings that the author himself has absorbed but not understood, and which have actively produced his text.[4] Terry Eagleton writes:

[4] The contemporary makers of this argument are legion. For an excellent overview, see Josue V. Harari's "Critical Factions/Critical Fictions." A handful of representative works that explore or expound this premise include Jonathan Culler's *Structuralist Poetics,* Paul de Man's *Blindness and Insight,* Terry Eagleton's *Criticism and Ideology,* Michel Foucault's *Les mots et les choses* and *L'ordre du discours,* Frank Lentricchia's *After the New Criticism,* and Edward Said's *Beginnings.*

Criticism is not a passage from text to reader: its task is not to redouble the text's self-understanding, to collude with its object in a conspiracy of eloquence. Its task is to show the text as it cannot know itself, to manifest those conditions of its making (inscribed in its very letter) about which it is necessarily silent. It is not just that the text knows some things and not others; it is rather that its very self-knowledge is the construction of a self-oblivion. (43)

To an extent I have followed this shrewd (and in its way irresistible) advice: the author begets but does not own his text. Ineradicably stained by ideology himself, how could he fail to produce a text that says more and other things than it knows itself saying? The critic's job is not to cooperate with the text but to expose it. Explain, don't interpret: so runs the current axiom. The stance is deliberately neutral if not hostile. The text must be approached from a standpoint as insistently external to the text's own self-understanding as possible. This argument is buttressed by the sophisticated awareness that no text can be fully entered on its own subjective terms anyway: and if the critic is irremediably outside, let him make a virtue of his foreignness.

At this point the price that a hermeneutics of suspicion pays for its insight comes into view. The subject is transformed into the object. Since it cannot be grasped in its self-understanding, since, moreover, it has no access to its own deepest implications, it must expressly undergo a tactics of alienation. It becomes, in the current critical act, an entity foreign to itself and foreign to its observer.[5] Insofar as my deepest epistemological conviction is that we understand only those human objects whose inner subjectivity we can imagine, I draw back from this model of the alienated object. It needs to be counter-balanced by a model of the coherent subject.

This counter-model is phenomenological in two respects. It reads the work of art as expression, as a complex imaginative

[5] Roland Barthes' *S/Z*, in its dismantling and reconstruction of an inconspicuous tale by Balzac, is probably the *terminus ad quem* of this methodological model. Barthes' interest in the tale, and his capacity to find the tale interesting, are remarkable. What is generally missing, however, is Balzac.

gesture toward wholeness and self-discovery on the part of the author who created the work. And it proposes, as the task of criticism, the most intimate relation possible to the creative voice at the heart of the work.[6] This intimacy, like all intimacy, depends upon a critical surrender to the entity being approached. My book seeks, therefore, to approach the self-understanding of the novelistic universe in question, to identify its nodal and enabling assumptions, those creative premises that have generated its characteristic shape and concerns and that intimate what can and cannot be achieved within its contours. I do not claim to have entered the subjective voice of each novelist, and it may be that my attempt to approach that voice is, ultimately, indefensible (because, the Derridean argument runs, there is no voice to be approached). In any event, I remain persuaded that the writer's imagination does shape such a voice, and that deliberately to ignore it amounts to a denaturing of the object under scrutiny.

Edward Said discusses the issue of the writer's command over his own meanings in terms of authority and molestation. Authority refers to the related notions of begetting, continuing, controlling, and possessing that are bound up in the master idea of an empowering creative subject. Molestation refers to the ob-

---

[6] Within the practice of literary criticism, phenomenology means, most generally, those methodologies that seek to locate in a writer's work (indeed in all his utterances) the hidden movement of his subjective consciousness in search of its own wholeness. This search necessarily traverses the entire world of objects within which the subject lives: for the riddle of subjective identity is inscribed precisely in his manifold relations with the objective world. Practitioners I have learned most from are Georges Poulet, Jean-Pierre Richard, and (in their earlier work) Leo Bersani, Geoffrey Hartman, and J. Hillis Miller. See Georges Poulet, *Studies in Human Time, The Interior Distance, The Metamorphoses of the Circle*; Jean-Pierre Richard, *Littérature et sensation*; Leo Bersani, *Marcel Proust: The Fictions of Life and Art*; Geoffrey H. Hartman, *Wordsworth's Poetry: 1787-1814*; J. Hillis Miller, *Charles Dickens: The World of His Novels; The Disappearance of God: Five Nineteenth-Century Writers; Poets of Reality: Six Twentieth-Century Writers*; and *Thomas Hardy: Distance and Desire*. Sarah Lawall discusses many of these critics and their interpretive models in her *Critics of Consciousness*. As a philosophical movement, Phenomenology derives from the work of Edmund Husserl. Nonspecialists will find a more accessible presentation of the major premises in Maurice Merleau-Ponty, Paul Ricoeur (*Le conflit des interprétations*), and Vincent Descombes.

stacles to authority, "a consciousness of one's duplicity, one's confinement to a fictive, scriptive realm, whether one is a character or a novelist" (84). The terms are necessarily dialectical, for all non-transcendental authority emerges within the impersonal and inhibiting conditions that make up molestation.

I have approached my six novelists as simultaneously instances of this dialectic and writers about it. Their sovereign control rewards a phenomenological movement of submission, even as their failures of authority—their susceptibility to molestation—solicit a critical model of suspicion. Each chapter regulates in its own fashion the ratio of trust to suspicion. Indeed, as each fictional world is composed in its own distinctive terms, so the approach varies to accommodate the specific tenor of those terms. For example, the Dickens world invites sustained attention to a wide range of relationships, all keyed to an ambiguous emotional dynamic. By contrast, the Eliot, Hardy, and Conrad novels focus more narrowly on protagonistic quests. Analysis of these latter writers is therefore briefer and more strictly attentive to the reasons why such quests are ill-conceived or foredoomed. When I reach Lawrence, I encounter a radically different kind of career from any earlier examined; my chapter attends in detail to the contours of that career in both his life and art. Career itself—the idea of disciplined progress toward an established goal—becomes a comic notion in *Ulysses*; thus that huge novel is approached not as a field of developing life-histories, but rather as a resonant universe, bristling at any given moment with its constituent patterns and discontinuities, but going nowhere.

The approach may vary, but, to use Lawrence's phrase, I keep my eye on carbon. The focus in every chapter remains on the identity-bearing encounter between desiring subject and restraining context. These discrete assessments are throughout related to the larger dimensions of the writer's enterprise, with increasing emphasis upon relevant connections among the six novelists. Yet this study's first allegiance is to the movement of embodied protagonists through a single writer's landscape of inhibiting conditions. Each novelist imagines this movement in his own way. I prefer to run the risk of an apparently uncentered discourse rather than force each fictional world to fit the frame of a univocal vocabulary (mine) and to serve as objective in-stances that bear out an unvarying argument (also mine).

Nietzsche and Freud remain *éminences grises* in this book. (Radical trust in the text's self-knowledge is as limiting a premise as radical distrust.) The contexts of molestation they clarify are, on the one hand, the imperious pressures of the body on thought and behavior, and, on the other, the increasingly disabling char-acter of cultural scripts of identity and aspiration. As this study reaches its third phase (the Modernists), many of these molesta-tions have themselves become auctorially assimilated. Lawrence and Joyce endow their protagonists with an awareness of the body's nature and the culture's artifice that had to enter my ear-lier writers' work either surreptitiously or with tragic conse-quences.

A more sustained focus on molestation would call even more deeply into question the authority of the subject. (Desire itself has its societal models,[7] and there remain to be assessed those cultural and economic factors discussed by the Marxists.) I con-tinue, however, to believe in a coherent subject (though neither transcendentally posited nor perfectly self-knowing), and I con-tinue to believe it possible to approach the imaginative voice at the center of that subject's discourse. Structuralists would remind me that such approach can be conducted only through language and is therefore a chimera: language being an empty system con-stituted by differences and therefore hostile to qualitative notions of voice and identity. My provisional defense against this form of molestation (and against others that would wholly unseat the idea of authority) is to repeat a statement made earlier in this introduction: to be conditioned is not to be unfree; to be shaped by societal paradigms is not to be deprived of self. To the body

---

[7] For the cultural inflection of desire, see René Girard, *Deceit, Desire, and the Novel: Self and Other in Literary Structure*. Girard would reject my governing assumptions since he sees desire as an entirely culture-determined phenomenon: imitative, deceitful, and worthless. He assesses European novelists according to the rigor with which, in his view, they expose and excoriate desire. I find his book provocative, though it proceeds from assumptions and arrives at conclu-sions considerably opposed to my own.

and mind that we have not created ourselves must be added the language whose systemic organization is also not of our own making. Yet our freedom, like our authority, consists exactly in what we achieve with and through our conditional body, mind, and language.

PART ONE

Mid-Victorian: Constraints and Masquerades

THE CHAPTERS on Dickens and Eliot move, in their respective ways, laterally and downward. They seek to convey the imaginative geography of each writer's world—its norms of characterization, plot sequence, and setting—as well as to identify within each world, beneath the surface, a cluster of latent confusions. I attend to Dickens and Eliot in the measure that their work reveals an internal resistance to its own premises. Indeed, one formulation of Dickens' more capacious achievement is that his work manages (as Eliot's does not) to assimilate—by outmaneuvering, by disguising, by blinking—its own fissures.

To be more specific: Dickens and Eliot both invoke societal norms of altruism, discipline, and earnestness, but it is only Dickens who can accommodate (without direct recourse to punitive measures) a varied sense of life shaped inwardly by other forces—passion, anger, an irrational self-squandering or self-imposing. He accommodates these forces, often, by not acknowledging them, whereas the fineness and the limitation of Eliot's imaginative world is that she must acknowledge—weigh and assess—all traffic within its borders. She constantly patrols her own terrain. Maggie and Gwendolen, in their role as protagonists in whom Eliot has heavily invested herself, are submitted to a catechistical scrutiny that has no counterpart in Dickens.

The chapter on Eliot is correspondingly narrower, briefer, and more diagnostic. *Middlemarch* is omitted on the obvious grounds that it is too accomplished—too harmonious, too resolved—to serve my purposes. I want to examine the imaginative dilemmas of a great novelist, and these are best observed when least resolved, when the greatness and the dilemma are equally prominent. *The Mill on the Floss* and *Daniel Deronda* are conspicuous choices. The careers of Maggie and Gwendolen sufficiently illustrate the quarrel within George Eliot between subjectively imagined desire and culturally sanctioned norms of restraint.

The discussion of Dickens focuses on two novels that, though only seven years apart, represent widely different techniques and procedures (Uriah Heep is as unimaginable in *Little Dorrit* as Arthur Clennam is in *David Copperfield*). Nevertheless, Dickens is an unruly giant whose career exhibits more variety than this commentary can readily embrace. Insofar as *David Copperfield* reveals an imaginative weave largely unaware of its own problematics, my generalizations may extend (in some degree) to the other early, less self-conscious masterpieces. *Little Dorrit*, by contrast, is the work of a formidably self-aware artist; there I have mainly followed his own leads, hoping to shed some light as well on the more deliberately meditated novels between *Hard Times* and *Our Mutual Friend*. The chapter attends in considerable detail to the local workings of two novels—how they deploy and assess their materials—but it also seeks the synoptic shape of Dickens' imagination, an imagination at once social and personal, responsible and rebellious, maturely bonded and restively unappeased.

One &. The Nocturnal Dickens

As OFTEN, he was suffering from insomnia. Restless, certain that sleep would not come before morning—if at all—he dressed quickly, pocketed his notebook and pencil, and headed toward the river. Perhaps he would come across the inspector, and together they could survey the sinister traffic on the water that night. He was making his way briskly along the empty streets when, to his surprise, he came upon a young prostitute standing in the middle of the road about fifty yards away, alone and energetically swearing. Curious, he listened to the unbroken stream of oaths, and he began to smile on hearing some choice phrases unknown even to him. Out came the notebook and pencil; he swiftly jotted down each unfamiliar curse. The girl paused for a moment, looked at him with a mixture of confusion and anger. "Go on, go on," he encouraged her, and she resumed her volley of oaths. At this moment there appeared on the road—probably returning late from the club and a little tipsy—just such a benevolent old duffer as had so often peopled his fiction. The duffer stared at the strange scene before him and, though he could never have said what was wrong, he knew, from the shiver along the back of his neck, that something was wrong. "Stop that immediately!" he commanded the girl, and "You, sir! What do you think you're doing?" he charged the man intent on note-taking. The notetaker looked evenly at the duffer, drew himself unhurriedly into a posture of unassailable authority, and responded, "Sir, I am Charles Dickens." Pencil in hand, he then turned to the prostitute and said curtly, "Swear!"

This vignette captures the Dickens who is the subject of the following essays. I first heard it in a graduate seminar, and I hereby exonerate the seminar instructor from all responsibility for its accuracy as fact, its accuracy in my retelling, or its accuracy in the uses I shall make of it. In my reading of Dickens during the seventeen years since that seminar at Harvard, the restless figure of the vignette has deepened in complexity and interest, and I now see that there is something of the essential Dickens, not just in the sinister authority figure, but in the benevolent duffer and the humiliated child/prostitute as well. The story seems ideally true, whatever its factual status, and it suggests, *in nuce*, the following: that Dickens is a restless man, in search of further outlets for an energy he finds it difficult to contain; that his devotion to the dictates of his art may momentarily cross moral barriers without a qualm; that he has a penchant for scenes that hover between the conventional and the illicit, and can draw publicly on the resources of the one, while tapping secretly those of the other; that behind the figure of mercy is a figure of power, and his power is not to be gainsayed; that the different facets of his genius are in dramatic conflict with each other, rather than serenely integrated; and that his fiction, without being hypocritical, is enigmatic and compelling to the extent that, along with his other gifts, he also exploits the "nocturnal," the demonic within him. *Larvatus prodeo*: as a man of desires I go forth in disguise.

A PALIMPSEST OF MOTIVES IN *DAVID COPPERFIELD*

The following pages explore an unresolved tension between Dickens' involuntary imaginative vision and his moral assessment of that vision. In the Dickens world appropriation, overpowering, and imposition are inevitable effects of a thrusting human will. The frame of cultural values within which Dickens reads his world, however, centers on selfless, unaggressive discipline and cannot accommodate such effects except as the attributes of villainy. A restless and overpowering man, he makes little conceptual room for restlessness and the release of power in his fictive world. To use a phrase of Nietzsche's, Dickens falls into "sentimental weakness" when he burkes the implications of his imaginative insight, when he cloaks the hardness of his perception within a soothing interpretative framework. Cloaks, not eradicates; the imaginative insight leaves its indelible trace, making for a palimpsest of contradictory scripts. The imaginative texture seems to mean something other than what is claimed for it. In interpreting such instances, I shall follow D. H. Lawrence's dictum and trust, not the artist, but his tale.

The world limned by the tale (rather than the one asserted by the artist) answers in several respects to some common tenets of Nietzsche and Freud. In their writings energy is the primary human datum; repression and self-evasion are inevitable corollaries. At our core, says Philip Rieff (describing the Freudian psyche), "we are, first of all, unhappy combinations of conflicting desires. Civilization can, at best, reach a balance of discontents" (377). Paul Ricoeur writes in *Freud and Philosophy*: "Because the adult remains subject to the infant he once was . . . because he is capable of archaism, conflict is no mere accident which he might be spared by a better social organization or a more suitable education; human beings can experience entry into culture only in the mode of conflict. Suffering accompanies the task of culture like fate . . ." (196).

That our destiny has its source in our conflicting desires, that these desires are more or less permanently in conflict with each other, that the price of entry into culture is the suffering of instinctual repression—these are Freudian tenets creatively broached or flirted with in the Dickens world, yet rarely acknowledged. Nietzsche's superb advice, "You shall become who you are," is not adopted by the Dickens protagonist. Becoming who you are means probing the gap between cultural platitudes and conflicting desires, and then, insofar as possible, centering the self on its native and embodied resources. To become who you are requires neither abnegation nor metamorphosis, but an act of self-exploring and self-forming usually absent from the Dickens world. More often, the protagonists for whom he claims development end by "leaping" into their desired identity—or magically attaining it after a mysterious illness—and these are as different from becoming who you are as self-evasive idealism is from Nietzschean realism.

Reading Dickens' fiction in a light he could neither have intended nor accepted has been going on at least since Edmund

Wilson's seminal essay. More recently, Raymond Williams writes that Dickens "works more finely than anyone in his time the tension—often the unbearable tension—between orthodox ideas, the ratifying explanations of the world as it was, and the tearing, dislocating, haunting experience which the ideas, in majority, were meant to control." Williams goes on to say: "It is easy to show him, intellectually, as inconsistent, but my final point is that these deepest ideas and experiences tore at him, profoundly, in ways that make one see not inconsistency—the analytic abstraction—but disturbance—the creative source" (87, 98). Creative disturbance, not rational inconsistency, results from the tension between his imaginative grasp of passion and disorder and the conceptual framework of altruism and discipline within which he sought to control the passion and disorder.

A few words are in order on *David Copperfield*'s present disrepute. Its surface serenity attracts scant attention in a critical climate that still finds in *Dombey and Son* the first masterpiece, then jumps to *Bleak House* and the subsequent darker novels. When assessed, *David Copperfield* tends to elicit brief and condescending comments, if not an occasionally outright dismissal: "Surely, for all its extraordinary, almost revolutionary analysis of childhood thoughts," Angus Wilson says, "the most false of all his major books" (209).

In the present-day estimate, the novel accommodates only too well Gwendolyn Needham's earlier influential thesis about "the undisciplined heart of David Copperfield." Needham was the first to claim that the disciplining of the heart is the central activity of the novel: "The good heart must have no 'alloy of self,' must love humanity as well as persons. It must be self-reliant and possess constancy and fortitude . . ." (86). If these platitudes were appropriate, then the novel would indeed be a complacent exercise that deserves its present critical oblivion. I want to argue, however, the opposite case: that the novel merits attention because it imaginatively overflows the limits of its conceptual framework. *David Copperfield* "creatively disturbs" insofar as it surreptitiously reveals the wayward heart overpowering the inadequate ideas of discipline and altruism meant to unify and tranquilize it.

❧

THE "UNDISCIPLINED heart," as Needham claimed, is the major organizing concept of the novel. The careers of Clara Copperfield, Little Em'ly, Annie Strong, Dora, and David are all articulated within this framework. If we unpack the concept of the "undisciplined heart" and probe the unpersuasive resolutions of discipline asserted in its name, we can identify the novel's more interesting achievement: its expression of "conflicting desires," desires unacceptable, repressed, and yet legible nevertheless. The first of four sets of relationships keyed to this dynamic—simultaneously clamoring to be read in the light of renunciation, yet revealing less high-minded motives—is the triangle of Dr. Strong, Annie, and Jack Maldon.

> The Doctor was sitting in his easy-chair by the fireside, and his young wife was on a stool at his feet. The Doctor, with a complacent smile, was reading aloud some manuscript explanation or statement of a theory out of that interminable Dictionary, and she was looking up at him. But, with such a face as I never saw. . . . Distinctly as I recollect her look, I cannot say of what it was expressive. . . . Penitence, humiliation, shame, pride, love, and trustfulness. I see them all. . . . My entrance . . . roused her. It disturbed the Doctor too, for when I went back . . . he was patting her head, in his fatherly way, and saying he was a merciless drone to let her tempt him into reading on; and he would have her go to bed.
> But she asked him, in a rapid, urgent manner, to let her stay—to let her feel assured . . . that she was in his confidence that night. And, as she turned again towards him . . . I saw her cross her hands upon his knee, and look up at him with the same face, something quieted, as he resumed his reading. (210-11)

This scene, like the entire relationship between the Strongs, is imagined in conflicting ways; it gives mixed signals. With his "complacent" smile, reading from his "interminable" Dictionary, the Doctor *is* a "drone." He is resolutely blind to his wife's quandary, but the narrative intelligence which upbraids David for being "blind, blind, blind!" refuses to censure the Doctor. Rather it benignly portrays Strong's blindness as one of his virtues, a sign of his incorruption. Nevertheless, our awareness that he will never complete the Dictionary, and that no one actually listens as he reads, is reinforced by the presentation of Mr. Dick writing his interminable, meaningless Memorial. Dick becomes, with unexpected swiftness, a fast friend of the Strongs, and if he and the Doctor walking together in the garden appear in one light as a brain-damaged man listening to a masterful savant, what we also see is a pair of good-natured, ineffectual duffers. Unsentimentally assessed, Dick and Strong exemplify virtue as impotence. Will-less themselves, free of desire, they exist as a kind of passive ideal, touchstones of others' aggression or kindness. If Dickens' presentation of them is complex—a blend of sympathetic and satirical perceptions—his assessment of them (especially of Strong) is monotonously sentimental. It is to that smugly befuddled side of Strong and Dick that a Nietzschean reading applies; they nicely anticipate Nietzsche's corrosive equation of virtue and stupidity in Christian society. Analyzing Christian morality as a species of "slave morality," Nietzsche argues that the fearful "slave" begins by defining "evil" as those traits of mastery and power which he does not possess. The "slave" then goes on, reflexively, to identify as "good" his own incapacity:

> . . . the good human being has to be *undangerous* in the slaves' way of thinking: he is good-natured, easy to deceive, a little stupid perhaps, *un bonhomme*. Wherever slave morality become preponderant, language tends to bring the words "good" and "stupid" closer together. (*Beyond Good and Evil*, 397)

Well-intentioned, pure of heart, ineffectual, "a little stupid perhaps"—no one would dream of so characterizing Charles Dickens, but these traits dominate in those benign duffers that people his fiction.[1] Such traits seem to define evil as the danger

---

[1] Noting the reversal of initials, Jerome H. Buckley sees David as Dickens'

of power itself and good as the sweetness of incapacity. My point is that Dickens' text treats these traits ambivalently. Even as David rhapsodizes over the ineffectual Strong, the novel insinuates a Nietzschean valuation of the Doctor in numerous ways: by implicitly equating him with the grotesque Mr. Dick, by emphasizing the forty-year difference between his age and Annie's, by drawing attention to Annie's guilt-ridden interest in Jack Maldon.

It is a curious fact that, during the first half of the novel, readers are as persuaded of her liaison with Maldon as of Miss Mowcher's demonic character. Eventually, we become "undeceived" on both issues; we are told that Annie Strong labors under unjustified suspicions, and that Mowcher has a maligned heart of gold. We learn from Edgar Johnson's biography, however, that our first sinister impressions of Mowcher were not ill-founded. She was originally to be an evil figure and was drawn as such; but the real dwarf who served, unawares, as her model recognized herself in the early chapters, complained to Dickens, and caused his revision (never persuasive) of the character in later scenes (Johnson, II, 674-75). Analogously, Dickens "knows," in that involuntary part of his imagination that acknowledges energy and the will to power, that Annie is implicated with Maldon because he "knows," in the same region of the imagination, that Strong is an inert, inadequate husband for a young wife as intense as she is repressed. He may be said to "know" this because his novel has been insistently, compellingly expressing her guilty gestures until Chapter 45.[2] At that point we discover Annie's innocence, and we hear the impassioned speech about her "undisciplined heart."

"counterpart rather than his double; he is as quiet, serene, gentle, and self-effacing as Dickens was passionate, excitable, and aggressive" (33). The purpose of my discussion is to reveal within David the latent double beneath the manifest counterpart.

[2] Although he makes no case for repression, Milton Millhauser identifies precisely the same malaise in Dickens' handling of the Annie/Strong/Maldon triangle: "The sense of something disagreeable going on just beneath the surface . . . is wonderfully conveyed. . . . Perhaps not, ultimately, January and May, but not quite Griselda either" (340-41).

"If I were thankful to my husband for no more, instead of for so much, I should be thankful to him for having saved me from the first mistaken impulse of my undisciplined heart. . . . I do not hope that any love and duty I may render in return, will ever make me worthy of your priceless confidence; but . . . I can lift my eyes to this dear face, revered as a father's, loved as a husband's, sacred to me in my childhood as a friend's, and solemnly declare that in my lightest thought I have never wronged you; never wavered in the love and the fidelity I owe you! . . . Do not think or speak of disparity between us, for there is none, except in all my many imperfections. . . . Oh, take me to your heart, my husband, for my love was founded on a rock, and it endures!" (564-66)

Not only does this passage unpersuasively "revise" the earlier guilt-ridden gestures, but—with its florid language, its strident tone, its blank-verse rhythms—such prose represents Dickens at his worst. The asserted emotion and the expressed emotion are hardly the same. Humility and devotion are asserted, but a near shameless self-exoneration is expressed. The lineaments of the real Dr. Strong disappear beneath his wife's operatic outpouring, as husband, father, teacher all unite into perfection itself. The ideological paradigm of the faultless father-husband and the reverent daughter-wife reveals itself. Annie's language turns religious, her husband appears divine, and her love, like Christ's church, is "founded on a rock."

The stridency and excess seem meant by Dickens to persuade the reader that Annie is (and knows herself to be) ideally situated in her marriage. Beneath Annie's rant one thus glimpses a disquieting proposition (latent here, enacted with Emily): that her desire represents a trap she may perish in, not a faculty she is entitled to, and that her elderly husband represents a sanctuary of passionless benevolence for which she should feel grateful—a protection from "the first mistaken impulses of an undisciplined heart." Her marriage may be superficially assessed by Dickens as a disciplining of the passions, but it is more punitively imagined as a retirement from them.[3]

To Dickens' credit, this scenario dedicated to Annie's self-immolation bristles with inconsistencies. Here, as with Emily and Mr. Peggotty, the asserted meanings fail to persuade. Q. D. Leavis characterizes the Strongs' marriage as "almost shockingly perverse," and she concisely assesses the Strongs themselves, "neither of which Dickens at bottom found appealing, we can see, for he can't make them either attractive or plausible" (65). Needless to say, I find them interesting for this reason. Their relationship is suggestively suspect; any problems of the "undisciplined heart" it is meant to resolve remain problematic. Likewise problematic will be the relationship whose meaning is obviously keyed to the curious scene just examined: the relationship between David and Agnes.

꿏

LIKE "Dame Durden" in *Bleak House*, Agnes emerges, even as a child, as a mature housekeeper. Magically escaping the anger and terror that threaten David's childhood, Agnes is disciplined and

---

[3] In the two paragraphs just written I encounter one of the vexing problems of a Freudian criticism. At what point does one cease talking about a character and begin talking about the author? Is Annie Strong operatic and self-deceived, or is Dickens? Frederick Crews suggests the following: "What psychoanalytic criticism needs . . . is not an injunction against seeing arrested development in literary heroes, but a vocabulary for describing a work's implied psychological pattern without mistaking that pattern for the hero's case history. Hamlet may not have an Oedipus complex, but *Hamlet* does" (15). It seems clear to me that the traits defined above are expressed in the text, and they are not meant to be there. Therefore I shall maintain that the contradictions within Annie Strong are contradictions her creator typically broaches when he is imagining the Annie Strong situation. Later, when discussing Peggotty's feelings for Little Em'ly, I shall again assume that the gap between asserted and expressed meanings is to be ascribed to the creator's imagination whenever it focuses on a relationship that is simultaneously parental and erotic. In closing this note, I should say that E. D. Hirsch's vigorously argued *Validity in Interpretation* denounces the entire concept of unintended verbal meanings (see especially 19-23, 51-57). Ultimately, disagreement with Hirsch involves a different model of the creative act: one that sees its meanings as partly—but inherently—unchosen.

harmonious from birth on. She seems to have emerged full-grown from her mother's portrait, and she radiates "home" wherever she goes. Her religious presence brings tranquility to David's baffling passions; she makes him feel unified.

> "Whenever I have not had you, Agnes, to advise and approve in the beginning, I have seemed to go wild, and to get into all sorts of difficulty. When I have come to you, at last . . . I have come to peace and happiness. I come home, now, like a tired traveller, and find such a blessed sense of rest!". . .
> Whatever contradictions and inconsistencies there were within me . . . whatever I had done, in which I had perversely wandered away from the voice of my own heart; I knew nothing of. I only knew that I was fervently in earnest, when I felt the rest and peace of having Agnes near me. (484)

Like Dr. Strong for Annie, Agnes represents for David a welcome shelter from the contradictions of his own passional experience.[4] In a reliable Victorian paradigm, she is what he comes home to; home is where he retires. For a tired, inconsistent, and undisciplined man, Agnes is a visionary figure in whose presence all such irascibles are bypassed, not resolved. In the presence of Agnes David feels himself to be—not what he is—but what he would like to be—an earnest, self-respecting, Victorian gentleman.

"Earnestness" is so often advocated as to be one of the leitmotifs of the novel: it is what the original David Copperfield and Clara both lack, what Betsy Trotwood recommends again and again to young David, what Agnes' presence bestows upon him, what characterizes David's eventual artistic success ("I have always been thoroughly in earnest" [518]), what even redeems Martha the prostitute when Mr. Peggotty reposes his trust in her. By coordinating the self's energies in the prosecution of self-

[4] Alexander Welsh's *The City of Dickens* abounds in insights about the more than human role that Victorian men required their idealized wives to play. See 141-95.

transcending socially esteemed work, earnestness is a means of generating and maintaining self-respect. It is David's most cherished virtue, the beacon by which he makes his way in the dark.

David is not fully entitled, however, to the earnestness he claims. Too many energies within him are ignored, not coordinated or disciplined, in his quest for emotional unity. At rare moments David may speak of "the sharp consciousness of many talents neglected, many opportunities wasted, many erratic and perverted feelings constantly at war within [my] breast, and defeating [me]" (518). But no sooner is this admitted than he returns to the praise of earnestness as a means of quelling internal dissension: ". . . there is no substitute for thorough-going, ardent, and sincere earnestness. Never to put one hand to anything, on which I could throw my whole self . . . I find, now, to have been my golden [rule]" (518).

Such protestations notwithstanding, neither David Copperfield nor *David Copperfield* exhibits a golden rule for success; both teem with unacknowledged psychic transactions in which we find, not the "whole self" earnestly applied, but, metaphorically, one hand covertly placed. "Erratic and perverted feelings constantly at war," Freud claims, are intrinsic features of the human psyche, not momentary aberrations; and Dickens manages to reveal them *as* intrinsic even though they are assessed as aberrations.

When David's "erratic feelings" are wholly ignored, we come upon scenes beneath whose insistent and highminded earnestness we trace the unacknowledged single hand of other motives at work. This is especially true in the courtship scenes with Agnes, late in the novel. So long as David's desire was directed toward Dora, his reverent feelings for Agnes were, if monotonous, at least imaginatively coherent. But when he returns to Agnes at the end, Dora conveniently laid to rest, Dickens' language must bridge desire and reverence: what results is, to borrow Raymond Williams' phrase, a "creative disturbance."

> "And you, Agnes," I said, by-and-by. "Tell me of yourself . . ."
> "What should I tell?" she answered, with her radiant smile. "Papa is well. You see us here, quiet in our own home;

our anxieties set at rest, our home restored to us; and knowing that, dear Trotwood, you know all."

"All, Agnes?" said I.

She looked at me, with some fluttering wonder in her
face.

"Is there nothing else, Sister?" I said. . . .

I had sought to lead her to what my aunt had hinted
at [that Agnes has a "lover"]; for, sharply painful to me as
it must be to receive that confidence, I was to discipline my
heart, and do my duty to her. I saw, however, that she was
uneasy, and I let it pass. (719)

Agnes has "nothing else" to tell because, in the imaginative
economy of *David Copperfield*, she has only two roles: to be a
housekeeper for her father and to love David selflessly. David's
solicitude, under the guise of "disciplining" his heart and en-
couraging her love for "another," is in effect a singleminded campaign to make Agnes yield up her secret. Between these assaults
disguised as tender inquiry, both Agnes and David avoid the
actual make-up of their feelings by indulging in fantasies of
regression and transcendence.[5] Agnes tells David that she has
"found a pleasure . . . while you have been absent, in keeping
everything as it used to be when we were children. For we were
very happy then, I think" (719). Riding back to Betsy's, David
also savors his situation: "I was not happy; but, thus far, I had
faithfully set the seal upon the Past, and, thinking of her, pointing upward, thought of her as pointing to that sky above me,
where, in the mystery to come, I might yet love her with a love
unknown on earth, and tell her what the strife had been within
me when I loved her here" (723). His language, like Annie
Strong's, is suggestively specious. The "Past," far from being sealed,
has been broached and will soon be broached again; the imme-

---

[5] David insists on calling Agnes "Sister" (Arthur Clennam will call Amy
Dorrit "my child"). Albert Guerard notes, in this regard, that brother-sister relations recur as often as father-daughter ones within a suggestive context of illicit
sexuality: "The fondest forbidden game would appear to be imagined marriage
with an idealized virgin: all the more forbidden because she might be daughter
or sister or sister-in-law. Is there any way, a number of plots seem to ask, to
legitimize these longings?" (*The Triumph of the Novel*, 71)

diate future (rather than the "mystery to come") is already being cultivated. By fantasizing a "love unknown to earth," by imagining his behavior as renunciatory, transcendent, and sublime, David disguises the unrelenting courtship he is presently waging. He returns to offer further "sympathy":

> "You have a secret," said I. "Let me share it, Agnes."
> She cast down her eyes, and trembled.
> "I could hardly fail to know, even if I had not heard . . . that there is some one upon whom you have bestowed the treasure of your love. Do not shut me out of what concerns your happiness so nearly! If you can trust me, as you say you can, and as I know you may, let me be your friend, your brother, in this matter, of all others!"
> With an appealing, almost a reproachful, glance, she rose from the window . . . put her hands before her face, and burst into such tears as smote me to the heart.
> And yet they awakened something in me, bringing promise to my heart. . . .
> "Let me go away, Trotwood. I am not well. I am not myself. . . . Don't speak to me now. Don't! Don't!" . . .
> "Agnes, I cannot bear to see you so . . . My dearest girl . . . if you are unhappy, let me share your unhappiness. . . . If you have indeed a burden on your heart, let me try to lighten it. For whom do I live now, Agnes, if it is not for you!"
> "Oh, spare me! I am not myself! Another time!" was all I could distinguish.
> Was it a selfish error that was leading me away? Or, having once a clue to hope, was there something opening to me that I had not dared to think of?
> "I must say more. . . . For Heaven's sake, Agnes, let us not mistake each other after all these years. . . . If you have any lingering thought that I could envy the happiness you will confer; that I could not resign you to a dearer protector, of your own choosing; that I could not, from my removed place, be a contented witness of your joy; dismiss it, for I don't deserve it! I have not suffered quite in vain. You have

not taught me quite in vain. There is no alloy of self in what I feel for you." (736-37)

The scene strikes me as profoundly ambivalent. Ostensibly offering selfless sympathy, a bit like the governess in "The Turn of the Screw," David closes in on Agnes: the violation is manifest. She trembles, looks reproachful, weeps, and cries repeatedly: "I am not myself . . . I am not myself." Passion wracks her, and she suffers the same humiliating "contradictions and inconsistencies," the same painful sense of self-alienation that David had suffered from his "undisciplined heart." Suddenly she is for the reader a credible human being, a creature of "conflicting desires" whose momentary display of feelings serves—for the only instance in the book—to transform her admirer into a lover.[6]

Her entreaties to be spared fall on deaf ears; David's desire fastens on those traits in Agnes' distracted behavior that give her away. He cannot afford noble discretion at this juncture; aroused, he intensifies his campaign: "For whom do I live now, Agnes, if not for you?" As she relents, he presses on, and even after he glimpses that there may be "something opening" up to him, he insists on his utter altruism. He is pleading, he claims, for another, not himself; he has learned to "discipline" his heart: "There is no alloy of self in what I feel for you." Such words, it seems clear, screen his motives and further his attack.[7]

After this display of will, finely calculated to penetrate Agnes' defenses and solicit the sweet words of reward, "I have loved you all my life!" after the rigor of this pursuit and exploitation, this *imposition* of his desire upon Agnes, David blinds himself to all but the surface of his motives. In Nietzschean terms, he denies what he is, his incarnate complexity and the force and direction of his desire; he insists upon what he would like to be: a discarnate figure of sublime selflessness. The exploitation of others attendant upon the will to power and the drive toward self-fulfill-

[6] I owe this point to the undergraduate thesis of Christopher Cornog, Swarthmore College, Class of 1975.

[7] It is worth recalling that Needham hammers her thesis home by quoting this phrase whose meaning is rather dubious within its context. "The good heart must have no 'alloy of self,' must love humanity as well as persons. . . ."

ment is an unacceptable component of the Dickens protagonist's sense of himself. We see an overpowering, but we hear of a renunciation.

David writes after his wedding: "Clasped in my embrace, I held the source of every worthy aspiration I had ever had; the center of myself, the circle of my life, my own, my wife; my love of whom was founded on a rock!" (740) Courtship over, the inconsistent has become magically harmonized, the undisciplined disciplined. David attains "maturity" by retiring to the tranquilizing circle of Agnes' security. His exalted love, "founded on a rock," is as solemn and religiously idealized as Annie's is for Dr. Strong.

❧

I TURN briefly to David's relationship with Dora. Despite the praise of contemporary critics, that relationship seems quite unevenly imagined. It becomes compelling only in its later stages as, significantly, it moves into pathos. Consider the tone of their first meeting:

> We turned into a room near at hand . . . and I heard a voice say, "Mr. Copperfield, my daughter Dora, and my daughter Dora's confidential friend!" It was, no doubt, Mr. Spenlow's voice, but I didn't know it, and I didn't care whose it was. All was over in a moment. I had fulfilled my destiny. I was a captive and a slave. I loved Dora Spenlow to distraction! (333)

This fluffy, "light-hearted," comic mode recurs with little variation. Tonally limited, such a mode soon becomes monotonously exuberant. Despite David's repeated "What an unsubstantial, happy, foolish time it was!" it is hard to believe in David's affection for Dora. Dickens has not found the language which would express the bittersweet, foolish reality of that young love affair. David chuckles and exaggerates; his ardor is asserted rather than expressed within the novel. By contrast, in *Great Expectations* Pip's courtship is precisely and movingly rendered. In the later novel the boy's feelings are painful but profoundly imagined; in the earlier novel they are whimsical but shallow. And that David's feelings are shallow presents a problem unresolved by his later discovery that Dora was an ill-chosen object for them.

In only one respect is this relationship persuasive—in its rendering of Dora's abortive love for David and the pain of his insufficient response. Almost from the beginning she has grasped her limitations; she knows before David does that Agnes is a better match and she says after her wedding: "Are you happy now, you foolish boy? and sure you don't repent?" (541) As David begins to learn what Dora already knows, how compromised he is by this commitment, we read:

> The old unhappy feeling pervaded my life. It was deepened, if it were changed at all. . . . What I missed, I still regarded—I always regarded—as something that had been a dream of my youthful fancy; that was incapable of realisation; that I was now discovering to be so, with some natural pain, as all men did. . . . Sometimes, the speculation came into my thoughts, What might have happened . . . if Dora and I had never known each other? . . . I always loved her. What I am describing, slumbered, and half awoke, and slept again, in the innermost recesses of my mind. There was no evidence of it in me; I know of no influence it had in anything I said or did. . . .
>
> "The first mistaken impulse of an undisciplined heart." Those words of Mrs. Strong's were constantly recurring to me, at this time; were almost always present to my mind. . . . For I knew, now, that my own heart was undisciplined when it first loved Dora; and that if it had been disciplined, it never could have felt, when we were married, what it had felt in its secret experience. . . . I had endeavoured to adapt Dora to myself, and found it impracticable. It remained for me to adapt myself to Dora; to share with her what I could, and be happy; to bear on my own shoulders what I must, and be happy still. This was the discipline to which I tried to bring my heart, when I began to think. It made my second year much happier than my first; and, what was better still, made Dora's life all sunshine.
>
> But, as that year wore on, Dora was not strong. . . . (594-96)

36

This is a passage of appealing self-analysis; yet it reveals, when probed, David's incompatible motives. His desire for some finer happiness is rendered simultaneously as a growing awareness of Dora's inadequacy (here it signals maturity) and as the mutterings of an "undisciplined heart." A mature, disciplined heart would either have chosen flawlessly, or have willed itself later into not feeling regret. The cluster of inadequate ideas behind "discipline" emerges here, for "discipline" entails either a fantasy of foolproof emotional decisions in the first place, or a fantasy of magic repression afterwards, whereby we think ourselves into not feeling (or at the least, never showing) what we feel. The inalienable risk and danger in all feeling is what both fantasies serve to minimize. David does not like these feelings of inconsistency and contradiction, these "conflicting desires": as always he seeks the highminded emotional unity that he calls earnestness.

The sustained analysis of a sympathetic but bad marriage, here approached, is beyond Dickens' aim in *David Copperfield*. David retreats from his own unsettling perception, tries the conventional wisdom of internally gritting his teeth, and waits for results. Dora's life is turned into sunshine, and then she starts to die.

This seems to me to be having it both ways: a simplistic therapy of discipline—simply repressing the bad thoughts—is claimed to be successful. The radiant patient, however, dies during the cure; and David, unlike Lydgate in *Middlemarch*, is no longer required to bear the burden of his discipline. His ostensibly abandoned "youthful fancy" of a flawless love can now be surreptitiously rejoined. Dickens transforms a potentially complex relationship into melodrama. Dora gives up trying to be an adult, regresses to her original child-identity, and is lavishly (because briefly) adored by David. The recalcitrant reality of a flawed marriage is evaded, first by the fantasy of a child-wife perfected in death and, second, by the culturally shared platitude of an all-reconciling housekeeper, Agnes.

It is hard not to see in the denouement of this marriage a shadowy repetition of the denouement of Clara Murdstone's marriage. There a cold disciplinarian tampered with a loving child-wife until he broke her heart and she died. Here, a gentle disciplinarian tampers briefly with his loving child-wife, pulls back in horror at his behavior, is stalemated. At this point the *deus ex machina* descends, and—no gentle disciplinarian he—does the requisite dirty work. David is putatively disciplined, but the plot surreptitiously inflicts the real discipline on Dora. She is stricken with a mysterious mortal disease, and David is permitted to escape from his prison, with his highminded idealism still intact, free to marry Agnes. In each case the insufficiently loved woman *does* die, but only in the earlier case is blame ascribed. Given the way David both applies an inadequate notion of discipline and is simultaneously released from the price of its application, it is difficult to see his relationship with Dora as a persuasive study in successful self-control. Such confusions attain their acme in the most egregiously misassessed altruistic relationship in the novel, that between Mr. Peggotty and Little Em'ly.

ፈ

NOT ACCIDENTALLY, David and Steerforth burst in upon the Peggotty home at the portentous moment when Emily's engagement to Ham is being announced. Announced, however, not by Ham—who is rarely articulate—but by Mr. Peggotty. And it turns out that Mr. Peggotty has also done Ham's proposing for him: "Well! I counsels him to speak to Em'ly. He's big enough, but he's bashfuller than a little un, and he don't like. So *I* speak" (268). The scene that unfolds is massively dominated by Mr. Peggotty. Neither his niece nor his nephew initiates now, nor initiated earlier, any proposition. Instead, Ham and Emily have courted each other through the old man, as he negotiated Ham's wavering offer and Emily's initial refusal, and finally ratified her acceptance. He coordinates, narrates, and registers the emotional significance of their courtship. We cannot but perceive it as *his* courtship.

The upshot is that, while the nominal fiancé is Ham, the scene is so imagined by Dickens and conveyed to the reader that the voice of overriding affection belongs to Mr. Peggotty. All troths are plighted to him. An underlying logic in the novel almost requires that the male most profoundly betrayed by Steerforth should be Peggotty, not Ham. The pattern resonates: the first David Copperfield, Wickfield, Dr. Strong, Mr. Peggotty are all older men uneasily doubling as fathers and husbands. Unable to abandon or endorse this fantasy-desire, Dickens insistently shadows these father/husbands with their potential betrayers: Murdstone, Heep, Maldon, and Steerforth.

Whether it reflects his unquenched feeling for the adolescent Mary Hogarth or some other blockage in his imaginative make-up that prevents him from providing his young heroines with sexual partners their own age—whatever the reason, Dickens is obsessed (as many critics have noted) with the older man playing this double role. One may hazard that the screen afforded by the doubleness appealed to his imagination. As ostensible father, the older man nobly transcends those passions which, as latent lover, he may surreptitiously indulge. Successfully mislabeled, his passion bypasses awareness and can be released without hindrance. Old Peggotty is the extreme instance of a figure whose milder incarnations include Nell's grandfather, John Jarndyce, Arthur Clennam, Joe Gargery, and Eugene Wrayburn.[8] Dickens' imagination finds this configuration alternately menacing and seductive; the younger man may appear as either a rescuer or a betrayer. The constant is the scenario itself.

Only after Emily runs off with Steerforth does the old man's double identity become clamorous. We see that if he is ostensibly a father, he is more profoundly a betrayed lover. His extraordinary design—to track her down and bring her back—is instantaneously adopted and embarked on:

> "I'm a going to seek her, fur and wide. If she should come home while I'm away,—but ah, that ain't like to be!—or if I should bring her back, my meaning is, that she and me shall live and die where no one can't reproach her. If any hurt should come to me, remember that the last words I left for her was, 'My unchanged love is with my darling child, and I forgive her!' " (403)

[8] One of the many reasons why the unfinished *Mystery of Edwin Drood* marks a further stage in Dickens' art is that finally, in John Jasper, parental benevolence and erotic obsession are eerily and (on Dickens' part) consciously fused. He seems to have recognized what he had been suggesting all along: that Quilp and Nell's grandfather are two facets of the same psyche.

When Faulkner's Quentin wishes he could flee with Caddy and "isolate her out of the loud world" (220) of experience, the wish is explicitly identifiable as a fantasy of incest and escape. Mr. Peggotty's scenario is equally pathological, though never so assessed. The entire world gets reduced in it to a hiding ground for Emily; and the world's inhabitants are reduced to himself as forgiving God, Emily as errant creature, all others as helpful, harmful, or indifferent spectators.[9] As Q. D. Leavis says, "While Mr. Peggotty seems at first sight to offer the pattern of disinterested devotion to the winning child he had fostered, what emerges is a horribly possessive love that is expressed characteristically in heat, violence and fantasies, impressing us as maniacal" (79).[10] If Freudian diction be permitted, rarely has the id more spectacularly passed itself off as the superego.

Incisively, Dickens juxtaposes Peggotty's suspect sweetness toward Emily against Rosa Dartle's authentic anger. This passage occurs one page before Peggotty's just quoted speech and nicely silhouettes it:

> "I would have her whipped! . . . I would have her branded on the face, drest in rags, and cast out in the streets to starve. If I had the power to sit in judgment on her, I would see it done. See it done? I would do it! . . . If I could hunt her to the grave, I would. If there was any word of comfort that would be a solace to her in her dying hour, and only I

[9] Mr. Peggotty's descriptions to David of his journeys throughout Europe in search of Emily bear the mark of rampant fantasy. Cf. the following:
"By little and little, when I come to a new village or that, among the poor people, I found they know'd about me. They would set me down at their cottage-doors, and give me what-not fur to eat and drink, and show me wheer to sleep; and many a woman, Mas'r Davy, as has had a daughter of about Em'ly's age, I've found a-waiting for me, at Our Saviour's Cross outside the village, fur to do me sim'lar kindnesses. Some has had daughters as was dead. And God only knows how good them mothers was to me!" (499)
The passage is shaped, not by the requirements of plausibility, but by those of a fantasized universe of loving parents and lost children. It reminds one of Blake's poems of lost children in the *Songs of Innocence*.
[10] Leavis differs from me in believing that Dickens knows what he is doing here, and that the portrait of Peggotty is meant to express "morbid states and the strange self-deceptions of human nature" (80).

40

possessed it, I wouldn't part with it for Life itself." (402-403)

Excessive, we say to ourselves, and indeed her words are insanely vindictive. They carry anger without alloy, just as Peggotty's claim to carry forgiveness without alloy. The imaginative wholeness of the novel—its elaborate network of covert single hands and interconnected "nervous ganglia"[11]—surreptitiously join both responses, showing them to be mirrors of each other, both actuated—one entirely, the other in part—by ferocious jealousy. Thus when Emily is finally found, Dickens permits Peggotty to rescue her only after Rosa Dartle has administered a tongue-lashing so corrosive and elaborate that it fills up four pages of text.

Inexplicably, David remains hidden and silent; he refuses to interfere. In a sympathetic attempt to justify David's behavior in the novel, Janet Brown points to this scene and claims that the reader accepts David's passivity: "He is to be present, that is all. He is prepared for nothing more." Nevertheless, she concedes that his silence imposes "an outrageously unjust penalty on Emily" (201).

What seems clear is that Dickens *is* granting Rosa the "power" she requested: "to sit in judgment on her . . . See it done? I would do it!" When she is finished doing it, having reduced Emily to a quivering mass of repentance, Peggotty is finally allowed to enter:[12]

---

[11] The phrase is Dorothy Van Ghent's, quoted from her superb essay, "On *Great Expectations*," 132. The context is as follows: "A universe that is nervous throughout, a universe in which nervous ganglia stretch through both people and their environment."

[12] The scene was on first conception even stranger. In the manuscript version Dickens actually has Peggotty accompany David to the room in which Rosa is lambasting Emily. When David is moved by pity to intervene, Peggotty forcibly holds him back. The manuscript concludes: "Mr. Peggotty waited until she [Rosa] was gone, as if his duty were too sacred to be discharged in such a presence, and then passed into the room" (MS IIB, 34). There is reason to believe that Dickens scented the perverse odor emanating from Peggotty's behavior here: within the week that intervened between the manuscript version and the printed galleys for this number, he decided massively to revise the episode. He simply removed Peggotty from the encounter until the very end, thereby

"Uncle!"

A fearful cry followed the word. I paused a moment, and looking in, saw him supporting her insensible figure in his arms. He gazed for a few seconds in the face, then stooped to kiss it—oh, how tenderly!—and drew a handkerchief before it.

"Mas'r Davy," he said, in a low tremulous voice, when it was covered, "I thank my Heav'nly Father as my dream's come true! I thank Him hearty for having guided me, in His own ways, to my darling!" (618)

"His own ways" is a rich phrase. Insofar as we are meant to assent to it—and the corroborative context suggests that we are—it conveys Dickens' attempt to assess the treatment of Emily in his culture's terms of Christian forgiveness. It serves, as well, as a screen for inadmissible, passionate motives. "His own ways" involve a blistering attack upon Emily, a full venting of outrage at her sexual misconduct. This anger, once expressed in the narrative design of the novel, however, is scrupulously ignored by David, Peggotty, and Dickens. It is passed off as a mere irrelevance in a larger scenario that is labeled divinely beneficent. Emily is indeed forgiven, but the form of forgiveness—a corrosive tongue-lashing followed by permanent exile with Peggotty—serves also as a disguised punishment for Emily, an illicit reward for Peggotty.

Once he has found Emily, old Peggotty takes further steps to realize his fantasy. Australia now enters the novel as the never-never land where what fails in England is finally granted success. When David asks Peggotty if he and Emily are going to Australia "quite alone," he is told:

"Aye, Mas'r Davy!" he returned. "My sister, you see, she's that fond of you and yourn ... that it wouldn't be

attenuating David's motive for passivity but, more importantly, keeping Peggotty's highmindedness intact. Still, the jealousy/outrage motives are deep-seated and ineradicable; they manage to surface even in the revised scene, and they are manifest elsewhere. (I wish here to express my gratitude to the Victoria and Albert Museum for permission to consult the Forster Collection of Dickens Manuscripts.)

hardly fair to let her go. Besides which, theer's one she has in charge, Mas'r Davy, as doen't ought to be forgot."

"Poor Ham!" said I.

"My good sister takes care of his house . . . and he takes kindly to her. . . . He'll set and talk to her, with a calm spirit, wen it's like he couldn't bring himself to open his lips to another. Poor fellow! . . . theer's not so much left him, that he could spare the little as he has!" (624)

The talk moves to Mrs. Gummidge; Peggotty explains his plans for taking care of her as well; and David reflects: "He forgot nobody. He thought of everybody's claims and strivings, but his own" (625). His own "claims and strivings," I hope it is clear by now, are supremely well served. The "love unknown to earth" that David fantasized over with respect to Agnes is granted to Peggotty in Australia. In having his Little Em'ly to himself, he has what he wants: the stunning instance of a man whose claims and strivings are forgotten is not Peggotty but his nephew Ham.

The emotional dynamics involved in this obscure trade-off can only be guessed at. Emily's stain in effect kills off Ham and rejuvenates Peggotty. As fallen woman, Emily cannot be married; for any legitimate lover she is "damaged goods." For an unadmitted lover, however, she is now available, all implicit charges of Peggotty's selfishness being annulled by her stain. She is perfectly free, and only free, to live an exiled life with a father-figure now doubling as a husband-figure. So the old man's sister moves to the waning young man, and the young man's fiancée moves to the vigorous old man. That Peggotty could in good conscience thus replace his nephew, that Ham could be as resolutely and unresistingly killed off as Dora was—these fantastic transactions characterize an imaginative world in which "His own ways" are Dickensian but hardly godlike: that is, they are anything but persuasively disciplined, unified, and altruistic.

Annie and Strong, David and Agnes, David and Dora, Peggotty and Little Em'ly—these four relationships bristle with unintended meanings. Beneath their self-renunciatory resolutions, one repeatedly detects not the earnest whole self but the covert single hand, the play of disallowed desires moving along the ubiquitous "nervous ganglia" of this novel. *David Copperfield*'s authenticity—its status as a flawed masterpiece—has less to do with the successful "discipline" of a wayward heart than with the compelling imagination of feelings not only undisciplined, but unrecognized. This covert semantics of desire creatively disturbs the authorized script of sublime motives. Together they make something richer than mere coherence: they make a palimpsest that expresses both a mid-Victorian ideal and the gathering forces that ideal was meant to keep at bay.

&

I ALLUDED to Nietzsche earlier in this discussion, and I can commence its speculative conclusion by returning to him. Nietzsche writes in *Beyond Good and Evil*:

> But today . . . don't we stand at the threshold of a period which should be designated . . . as *extra-moral*? After all, today at least we immoralists have the suspicion that the decisive value of an action lies precisely in what is *unintentional* in it, while everything about it that is intentional, everything about it that can be seen, known, "conscious," still belongs to its surface and skin—which, like every skin, betrays something but *conceals* even more. (234)

Nietzsche's assertion, penned nearly forty years after Dickens wrote *David Copperfield*, posits a psychology of conflicted motives, of deluded consciousness, as foreign to mid-Victorian self-confidence as it is congenial to twentieth-century self-distrust.

Like Freud, Nietzsche takes none of the givens of consciousness at face value. Both thinkers posit a godless world in which asserted values and metaphysical designs serve to disguise behavior that would be more properly designated as extra-moral, as an unconscious strategy drafted for orientation and survival. They both define man as a bodily creature housing energies. This creature can "become who he is" on condition that he come to terms with his own incarnate nature: to that extent he may create himself. Such an act of self-assumption must necessarily (according to Nietzsche and Freud) transgress the Sermon on the Mount, for Christian morality imposes a set of inherited constraints, convictions, and goals, based on an inadequate psychology, that keep the man-creature from ever maturing into his own man-creator. As long as God is the Father, then man's licensed identity is as His child, a creature who cannot become his own creator, whose final discovery must be his dependence upon sanctions set up by the Other. As a child, he continues to take his values, purposes, and identity as metaphysically given; and he judges himself, therefore, according to Christianity's essential dualism: the good, reasonable, obedient soul, on the one hand, and the evil, energized, appetitive body, on the other. This is exactly the opposition that Blake mockingly formulates in *The Marriage of Heaven and Hell*:

> From these contraries spring what the religious call
> Good and Evil. Good is the passive that obeys Reason.
> Evil is the active springing from Energy.
>   Good is Heaven. Evil is Hell.

Nietzsche, Freud, and Blake, are not digressive figures in an essay on *David Copperfield*. They are, in a significant measure, the psychic company Dickens unwittingly keeps. Dickens is a Christian moralist whose imagination is not only Christian but Blakean, Nietzschean, and Freudian as well—not wholly but ineradicably so. He is a writer obsessed with energy and unequipped (by his culture) with a moral framework to legitimize this obsession. His mind suspects that "Evil is the active springing from Energy," but his imagination knows that "Energy is the only life, and is from the body." Dickens' moral paradigms are Christian and transcendental, but his imaginative psychology is Blakean in its concern with embodied energy, Nietzschean in its concern with embodied power, Freudian in its concern with somatic guilt and repression. He thus writes a fiction whose meanings often elude his focal terms of value—earnestness and altruism—a fiction in which, recurrently, "the decisive value of an action lies precisely in what is unintentional in it."

By the time of Lawrence and Joyce, Proust and Gide, Mann and Kafka, such conflicts have become paradigmatic. In Modernist writers a Freudian model has largely replaced (in its essentials, if not its terminology) a Christian one as a more revealing key

to motives. It has almost become axiomatic that the nobler altruistic motive will serve as a screen, and that the lower motive
will be repressed from consciousness. As Rieff says, "The psychoanalytic expectation is of the sinister; the signposts all point
downward, into the dark" (84).

Dickens is all the more intriguing, then, because—unlike the
Modernists—his imagination is simultaneously Christian and
Freudian. In this essay I have stressed only the latter more brutal
element, an element as present as it is disowned. Yet Dickens'
canvas has its authentic Christian sweetness as well. The death
scenes of Dora in *David Copperfield* and Jo in *Bleak House* may
appear sentimental, but few would thus criticize the poignant last
scenes between David and his mother, or the powerful sequence
in which Esther Summerson draws near to and finally touches
the face and body of her mother, now "cold and dead." These
scenes, quietly narrated in what Albert Guerard calls Dickens'
grave, interior voice, render the bond of feeling in the human
family: its original oneness, its resistless sundering, the pain of
orphanhood. Like Dostoevsky and like no one else, Dickens succeeded as a Christian novelist in imagining humanity as truly
orphaned and yet truly interrelated, as creatures who did not and
cannot create themselves, creatures whose well-being is inextricably dependent upon the concern of others, and of an Other who
seems to brood over them all. Behind the welter of malefactors
and benefactors one senses (at least up to *Drood*) a sanctioning
Authority, the writer as God's shadowy delegate, who protects
his child-creatures in the measure that they find the humility to
accept their own vulnerability and interdependence.

The co-presence of this Christian paradigm with the drama
of an irrepressible will to power makes Dickens' fiction a "creative disturbance" of the highest order. In his work we find, abun-
dantly, the child-creature, errant yet sanctioned, earnest, altruistic, and successfully acculturated. We find as well, though less
easily "placed," the restless man-creator, unsponsored, aggressive, a figure of conflicting desires and insistent will: a man of
powerful self-assertion.

This latter figure, a robust staple of romanticism, appears
during the mid-Victorian period, perforce, as somewhat de-

formed and tinged with villainy, for the threat of embodied, demonic power (which he houses, in however degraded a form)
runs athwart the age's ideology of selfless, virtually discarnate
behavior shaped to patterns of societal harmony. Such a figure
must remain more or less simplistically villainous so long as self-
interested actions are seen as chosen, consciously one's own, and
therefore evil. This scenario alters, however, as the assumptions
behind it alter. The introduction into behavior of unconscious
motives, of unacknowledged impulses stronger than one's restraining will, spells the clouding of consciousness, the loss of
moral certitude, and the end of villainy.[13] Uriah, Rigaud, and
Orlick are evil hypocrites, but is John Jasper? With Jasper—and
a fortiori with the obscure, embattled, and self-deceived protagonists of Hardy and Conrad—we enter a fiction in which character is opaque to itself, unable to decipher its own motives.
Desire and impulse are now glimpsed—by the reader, not the
character—as ingrained, ineradicable, no longer obedient to the
dictates of the conscious will. Egoistic desire may now appear
anywhere, even within the noblest protestations of the protagonist: earnestness is not enough.

Once earnestness is recognized as an insufficient moral
touchstone, then the strange antics on which this chapter has
focused—the complicit dance of desire beneath the conscious assertion of duty—can begin to take on the interconnected wholeness which Freud will claim for them at the beginning of our
century: the enduring drama of the conflicted human animal
seeking to realize his normative image of himself, to become (in
his own eyes and in those of others) a human being. That drama
may have grown exceedingly complex, but it is never anything
but obvious in the novels of Eliot, Hardy, and Conrad. In *David
Copperfield*, however, its lineaments are almost invisible, until they
have been teased into silhouette against the more manifest drama
of earnest and altruistic discipline.

[13] Not quite the end of villainy. Conrad retains his evil grotesques—Don-
kin, Cornelius, Brown, Nikita, Jones, Ricardo, etc.—even as, in his imagination
of protagonists, he employs a psychology of embattled and opaque consciousness
that is incompatible with the conventions of villainy.

ENIGMAS OF POWER AND IMPOTENCE: *LITTLE DORRIT*

Little Dorrit is one of Dickens' most tightly woven and problematic masterpieces. Unlike *David Copperfield*, its very coherence makes more salient its internal conflicts. On the one hand, it is Dickens' most penetrating study of the plight of impotence. Abusive parents (figurative and literal) abound in *Little Dorrit*—the Circumlocution Office, Marshalsea Prison, Casby, Mr. Dorrit, Mrs. Merdle, Mrs. Gowan, Mrs. Clennam. The novel patiently scrutinizes the injurious relation between such parents and their children—the Dorrits and the other jailbirds, the Plornishes, Edmund Sparkler, Henry Gowan, Flora Finching, Maggy, Arthur Clennam. These children all suffer from damage to the will.[1] They have been either abandoned or prematurely molded, coerced away from their own center of feeling (literally: made eccentric) by the impress of impersonal and uncaring authority. Their capacity for desire—their ability to explore their own feelings, to shape them purposely, to identify themselves *as* creatures of feeling—has been tampered with.[2] In no other novel is Dickens more sympathetically attuned to the affective plight of the dependent child.

Yet, in no other novel are the sources of liberating power—institutional, familial, and personal—rendered with such suspicion. Even benign sources outside the self stifle more than they

---

[1] Following Rollo May, I use the word "will" not in its Victorian sense of the faculty "which is based upon our capacity to force our bodies to act against their desire" (222), but rather in the broader, if more elusive, sense of "intentionality." "Will" refers, that is, to the entire cluster of feelings and attitudes (partly conscious, partly unconscious) with which a subject attends an object. (See 223-45).

[2] In his Introduction to the Penguin edition John Holloway accounts brilliantly for this underrated aspect of Dickens' genius: "The point is that, in the usual case, Dickens' caricaturing *is* characterization: it presents us with the elaborate, colourful, ridiculous *persona* with which a living soul has come to confront the world. What Dickens presents in caricature is not, usually, some arbitrary and meaningless *tic* of outward conduct: it is the fantastic eddies, if you like, that experience has forced from the flow of the individual personality, so that, somehow or other, that personality may continue to flow in spite of all" (25). (I here acknowledge a general debt to Holloway's sensitive reading of the novel.)

nurture, and the resources within the self are so thoroughly disguised and muffled that Arthur Clennam and Amy Dorrit (as muted a couple as Dickens ever created) emerge as the novel's appropriately undemanding hero and heroine. An air of paralysis haunts *Little Dorrit*. The effect of the narrative, as H. M. Daleski says, "is of a movement that is constantly checked, of flight that is frustrated—in a word, of arrest" (197). Energetic rebellion against unjust authority appears in a bleaker guise—is shown as ultimately more repressive—than the authority itself. Dickens has imagined a multitude of prisons that need escaping, but he endorses no credible exits.

I begin by exploring some of the novel's enigmas of power, analyzing three figures—Meagles, Amy, and Clennam—in whom the issue of power (strength benevolently exercised over others, resources within oneself that are expressed or repressed) appears most problematic. Thereafter a broader reading can be offered of the Dickens world as a drama of repressed feelings and disguised motives. Children unloved, humiliated, and unable to express directly their own feelings; parents and parental structures abusive but able through screens to disguise their abuse; desire everywhere disowned even as it connects the most disparate members of society—in a word, Dickens' theatrical world in which interdependence is denied and false powers are proudly paraded. The chapter concludes by examining one of the more virulent forms of false power in the novel, the phenomenon of patronage.

୬ଛ

IN AN EARLIER nóvel Meagles would have appeared simply as a solid paterfamilias. Next to Clennam, however (with whom we first meet him), Meagles' outspokenness seems strident, his assurance arrogant. Naively complacent, he knows no foreign languages.[3] He casually disparages the Marseillais in statements that are dogmatic and absolute: "When these people howl, they howl

---

[3] Eight years later Dickens will fully develop the negative potential of this character: Podsnap in *Our Mutual Friend*. Other critics have noted the complexity of Meagles, but few have found this problematic. Robert Garis speculates that Dickens may have intended in Meagles a portrait of greater nuance that his "theatrical" techniques permitted (178).

to be heard. . . . I mean the French people. They're always at it. As to Marseilles, we know what Marseilles is" (15). He puts his hands in his pockets and rattles his money, but even this reassuring sign of an unhampered will does not assuage the anxiety caused by the quarantine.

The suspicion of illness bothers him more than illness itself. Thoroughly English, he likes his distinctions neat—one either has the plague or is free of it—and he can hardly bear this ambiguous state of arrest and suspicion. Accustomed to expressing his will without hindrance, he has architected his domestic world to reflect the clarity he requires. He has named his family as though they were appendages of his own will—Mrs. Meagles is Mother, the daughter is Pet, and the maid is Tattycoram. Clennam inquires into the latter's history; and we learn that, with impeccable motives, he has acquired Tattycoram as (in part) a delicate toy for his living daughter and a replacement for his dead one. His first words to Tattycoram, like his last some nine hundred pages later, are authoritative and proprietary: "Tattycoram, stick you close to your young mistress" (16).

Because he is inadequately aware of the nature of those he manages, because his paternal wisdom rarely exceeds the advice to "count five and twenty," Tattycoram rages under his management. Dickens shows us immediately, in Miss Wade, an image of how far Tattycoram's wrath could take her. Sullen, brooding, with dark hair and heaving breasts, Miss Wade, Tattycoram, and (later) Fanny Dorrit are as unmistakably the same type—robust, passionate, full-grown—as Pet and Little Dorrit, with their slim builds and timid souls, are the same type—unassuming, unaggressive, childlike. The childlike ones forgivingly absorb injury, but the passionate ones do not. Once free from quarantine, the jovial Meagles burbles out: "But I bear those monotonous walls no ill-will now. One always begins to forgive a place as soon as it's left behind; I dare say a prisoner begins to relent towards his prison, after he is let out." Miss Wade crisply rebuts him, whereupon he "cheerily" rejoins, "Oh! . . . Dear me! . . . But it's not natural to bear malice, I hope?" Miss Wade responds: "If I had been shut up in any place to pine and suffer, I should always hate that place and wish to burn it down, or raze it to the ground. I know no more" (21-22).

I have followed this scene at some length because one of the novel's enigmas of power is here sketched out. Surrounded by Clennam and Wade, Meagles' thickly aggressive good cheer cannot but appear provincial. His benevolent intentions notwithstanding, he emerges as the beaming creator/jailor of his domestic circle. His strength translates into others' restraint. Both Pet and Tattycoram will escape from this circle; he will treat each exit as tragic. Dickens, however, neither undermines this critical reading of Meagles nor supports it consistently. Tattycoram does escape, but she eventually returns, penitently and voluntarily and with Dickens' apparent approval, to an even more paternalistic Meagles. Likewise, Pet escapes, but to a marriage so complex in its failings that Dickens, unable to endorse and unwilling to explore, mainly averts his attention from it.

Most important, Meagles' dramatic opposite in the quoted scene, Miss Wade, appears (in her compulsion to be free of all restraining authority) more deformed and deforming than Meagles at his worst. To bolt from his cheerful restrictiveness is to fall into bondings that are more repressive yet. Self-liberation, insofar as it exists in *Little Dorrit*, must involve a procedure more complex than overt release. Despite his limitations, Meagles is the most benign instance of parental strength Dickens provides; and Meagles is as dubious as he is inescapable.[4] The novel centers not on how to escape from prison—and less yet on how to "raze it to the ground"—but on how, and at what cost, to become free within it.[5] With this context of power sketched in, we can approach Little Dorrit.

"Little" is the key to everything: Amy requires no space.

[4] Doyce is of course the model most to be emulated in *Little Dorrit*, but he remains curiously undeveloped. Lacking Meagles' moral complexity, unburdened by a family, unrooted in any social framework, Doyce flits through the novel and is not related to others densely enough to be considered an important figure of authority.

[5] Holloway points to several instances of liberation (27-29), but these are superficial escapes, to my mind, when compared with the enduring forms of repression in the novel.

Her name suggests not only that she is small, childlike, unaggressive; it also cloaks her sexuality. (The reader first encountering this novel does not know if Little Dorrit is to be male or female, or indeed a toy, a house, or a village in England.)[6] This form of address (and she insists upon it) keeps her, as it were, on the near side of puberty, protecting her from the conditions of adult sexuality. "Little" goes further and suggests a repudiation of the body altogether. The physical robustness of Tip and Fanny and the psychic swollenness of Mr. Dorrit and Mrs. Clennam account figuratively for the diminution of Amy Dorrit. Her humility is the ground of their excesses; she has grown thin in making them fat. Dickens' introduction of her in Chapter 3 underscores these qualities:

> "Affery [Clennam is speaking], what girl was that in my mother's room just now?"
>
> "Girl?" said Mrs. Flintwinch in a rather sharp key.
>
> "It was a girl, surely, whom I saw near you—almost hidden in the dark corner?"
>
> "Oh! She? Little Dorrit? *She*'s nothing; she's a whim of—hers." It was a peculiarity of Affery Flintwinch that she never spoke of Mrs. Clennam by name. "But there's another sort of girls than that about. Have you forgot your old sweetheart? Long and long ago, I'll be bound."
>
> "I suffered enough from my mother's separating us, to remember her. I recollect her very well."
>
> "Have you got another?"
>
> "No."
>
> "Here's news for you, then. She's well to do now, and a widow. And if you like to have her, why you can."
>
> "And how do you know that, Affery?"
>
> "Them two clever ones have been speaking about it."
> (39-40)

[6] Only the free-associating Flora Finching is permitted to share Dickens' humorous awareness of Amy's odd name: ". . . and of all the strangest names I ever heard the strangest, like a place down in the country with a turnpike, or a favorite pony or a puppy or a bird or something from a seed-shop to be put in a garden or a flower-pot and come up speckled" (265).

Little Dorrit may be muted, but it is densely woven. This interchange takes place in a conversation saturated in the unnaturalness of marriage—the monstrous imposition of Jeremiah upon Affery ("a Smothering instead of a Wedding"), the desired but abortive marriage between Clennam and Flora, and behind these both the bond between Mrs. Clennam and her deceased husband, a bond so injurious that the dying Mr. Clennam's last impulse was to make reparation. Marriage appears as an arrangement that cuts athwart desire, and the passage makes clear that the thwarting arrangers are Jeremiah and Mrs. Clennam. They made the one marriage, she put asunder the other; they now consider reversing that earlier ban. Into this context of failed unions and marriage brokers, of feelings abused and thwarted, Amy Dorrit enters the novel without a name—at first a "girl," then "Little Dorrit . . . *she*'s nothing." The reader has not seen her before this moment, and Dickens artfully conveys her "invisibility," her weightlessness. A "whim" of others, Amy appears as a cog in their designs, a slight, unknown element within a skein of ruined marriages.

Her next appearance is equally laden with implication. Summoning his courage, Arthur informs his mother of his father's inarticulate remorse and of his own suspicion that someone has been wronged. Mrs. Clennam responds furiously: "By a swift and sudden action of her foot, she drove her wheeled chair rapidly back to [the bell-rope] and pulled it violently—still holding her arm up in its shield-like posture, as if he were striking at her, and she warding off the blow. A girl came hurrying in, frightened. 'Send Flintwinch here!' " (47-48)

Flintwinch comes; Mrs. Clennam places her hand upon the Bible, and she tells Arthur, with satisfying rancor, that in the Old Testament parents have renounced their children forever, when they behaved as he has just behaved. The ironies are heavy, for this threatened repudiation took place years ago, and in her indifferent reception of him after a twenty-year absence, it is taking place again. A greater irony is concealed in Dickens' way of showing us, even as she spurns Arthur's charge, the measure of her offense. It is in those six words: "A girl came hurrying in, frightened." Mrs. Clennam may passionately defend herself, but

Dickens reveals—unknown to Arthur, unknown to the beginning reader—the injured party. In the frightened, dependent, ignored, childlike figure of Little Dorrit we see an image of the frightened, dependent, ignored child that was Arthur Clennam. We see that this woman's sin, whenever it will be revealed, is a sin against children.

Incapable of nurture, she stunts, bends, and manipulates those she touches. She systematically undermines their will to live; she opposes their essential bodily exuberance. Human desire she takes as her implacable enemy. Unable, until the end, either to break free of her self-enforced aridity or to forgive others for the lovelessness of her life, Mrs. Clennam is the closest approximation in all of Dickens to Nietzschean *ressentiment*:

> . . . here rules a *ressentiment* without equal, that of an insatiable instinct and power-will that wants to become master not over something in life but over life itself, over its most profound, powerful, and basic conditions; here an attempt is made to employ force to block up the wells of force; here physiological well-being itself is viewed askance, and especially the outward expression of this well-being, beauty and joy; while pleasure is felt and *sought* in ill-constitutedness, decay, pain, mischance, ugliness, voluntary deprivation, self-mortification, self-flagellation, self-sacrifice. All this is in the highest degree paradoxical: we stand before a discord that *wants* to be discordant. . . . (*On the Genealogy of Morals*, 553-54)

The entire truth of this description notwithstanding, Mrs. Clennam—like Miss Havisham—has involuntarily inflicted the greatest damage upon herself. Her last speeches testify poignantly to the pain she suffers in being Mrs. Clennam. Beneath her justificatory Old Testament prose, one hears the outraged voice of a woman wounded in her identity as a feeling and dependent creature. The discovery of her husband's love for another woman has not destroyed her capacity to move and be moved, but it has deformed that capacity and made it inaccessible.

If Mrs. Clennam is the ultimate repressive Dickensian parent, Amy appears to be the ultimate repressed Dickensian child.

In her one finds an almost saintly reduction of personal aspiration, and another of the novel's enigmas of power and impotence comes thus into focus: is that reduction the sign of psychic malnourishment or of psychic health? To explore this paradox—how Amy can strike the reader as both affectively deformed and radiantly uninjured—is to follow up a fundamental contradiction in Dickens' imagination. How is it that, in a novel saturated in the baneful effects of repressive power, one is asked to admire a girl who has so restricted the scope of her desires that she can tranquilly accept conditions of tyranny? The question begins to receive an answer when one notices that Amy is not quite emotionally imprisoned. She does express desire, but only indirectly, through the agency of two psychic phenomena often operative in the release of desire within Dickens' protagonists: sublimation and disguise.

These phenomena are most prominent in her relationship with Arthur Clennam. Their first extended scene together occurs when, trembling with gratitude for his "anonymous" aid to Tip, Amy comes to see Clennam. They immediately establish their discourse on a father/daughter basis (". . . let me call you Little Dorrit" "Thank you, sir, I should like it better than any name" [161]), and Amy begins to vent her feelings:

> "And what I was going to tell you, sir," said Little Dorrit, trembling in all her little figure and in her voice, "is, that I am not to know whose generosity released him—am never to ask, and am never to be told, and am never to thank that gentleman with all my grateful heart! . . . And what I was going to say, sir, is . . . that if I knew him, and I might, I would tell him that he can never, never know how I feel his goodness, and how my poor good father would feel it. And what I was going to say, sir, is, that if I knew him, and I might—but I don't know him and I must not—I know that!—I would tell him that I shall never any more lie down to sleep without having prayed to Heaven to bless him and reward him. And if I knew him, and I might, I would go down on my knees to him, and take his hand and kiss it, and ask him not to draw it away, but to leave it—O to leave

it for a moment—and let my thankful tears fall on it, for I have no other thanks to give him!" (161)

The passage is remarkable. Amy knows her benefactor is Clennam, and Clennam knows she knows. The pretence of anonymity is a transparent screen through which both parties see; yet it serves its purpose. Permitted to speak of "him" rather than "you," slipping into a father/daughter rather than bachelor/maiden framework, Amy avails herself of these distancing and legitimizing formulations. She triangulates the scene, postulates a fictive third party, and waxes eloquent.[7] Indeed, she pours her heart out, as Dickens falls into one of those operatic set pieces that recur in his scenes of protestation and mar their illusion of spontaneity. As long, however, as the feelings of speaker and listener for each other remain technically unexposed, Amy's outburst is consistent with her modesty. In all, it is a rather intricate scene, emotionally devious, and representative—in its very "innocence"—of a kind of relationship one rarely finds expressed in a post-Freudian literature. Critics have often dismissed Amy as incapable of amatory feeling. It is more accurate to say that she is incapable (until the end of the novel) of direct expression of that feeling.[8]

Consider, in this light, her story of "the little princess." John Holloway rightly notes that this vignette is not merely sentimental. "To be a story-teller is, for a moment, Little Dorrit's *persona* (a mask, a 'surface'). She adopts it so that she can both vent, and conceal, her feelings" (25). One can take Holloway's point further. A "story-teller" is an apt description of her behavior in the previous scene as well. She can release her feelings only through

[7] In a cogent and suggestive article Janice M. Carlisle identifies recurrent "instances in which characters create 'fictions' to hide the 'reality' of their feelings or social positions" (198). Carlisle makes it clear that, beginning with her name and ending with the folded paper she has Arthur burn, Amy Dorrit is a mistress of fictive appearances.

[8] Robert Garis notes that the Trilling interpretation of Amy (as saintly rather than womanly) ignores Dickens' discreet (if, for Garis, unpersuasive) insistence on her womanhood: "The end of the novel simply says that Arthur Clennam learns that Little Dorrit is not a child but a woman, and my view is that the reader doesn't believe it" (185).

the "circumlocutionary" disguise of selfless anonymity. Although Dickens is tender toward Amy's strategies, he does counterpoint, through Maggy, some of her ethereal excess. To Amy's sentimental scenario, "there was a cottage in which there was a little tiny woman who lived all alone by herself," Maggy retorts energetically, "An old woman" (284); and we measure the prematurity of Amy's imagined retirement from life. Throughout Amy's dreamlike narrative Maggy supplies comic relief. Indeed, when Amy's masochistic scenario reaches its delicious climax—the death of "the tiny woman"—Maggy responds unerringly, "They ought to have took her to the Hospital . . . and then she'd have got over it" (286). The implication is delicate but firm: the tiny woman need be neither so tiny nor so doomed to ethereal renunciation. At the Hospital they would have fed her "Chicking" and all would be well. Through Maggy's comments, and even more through Maggy's insistent corpulence, Dickens gently balances Amy Dorrit's urge toward self-extinction.

If Amy tends to imagine herself pining away, Arthur Clennam is even more firmly attached, as critics have noted, to the scenario of barren old age. I quote the following speech less for its fiction of decrepitude than for the way that fiction screens the release of other feelings:

"If, in the bygone days when this was your home and when this was your dress, I had understood myself (I speak only of myself) better, and had read the secrets of my own breast more distinctly; if, through my reserve and self-mistrust, I had discerned a light that I see brightly now when it has passed far away, and my weak footsteps can never overtake it; if I had then known, and told you that I loved and honoured you, not as the poor child I used to call you, but as a woman whose true hand would raise me high above myself, and make me a far happier and better man; if I had so used the opportunity there is no recalling—as I wish I had, O I wish I had!—and if something had kept us apart then, when I was moderately thriving, and when you were poor; I might have met your noble offer of your fortune, dearest girl, with other words than these, and still have blushed to touch it. But, as it is, I must never touch it, never! . . ."

He took her in his arms, as if she had been his daughter. (739)

This is, precisely, a declaration of love that Clennam can make only through his fiction of its being too late for such a declaration. His operatic outburst, released by the exquisite sensation of martyrdom (he entered the novel wanting to repay a debt through renunciatory suffering, and he has now managed to do so), echoes the one by Amy quoted earlier. Both speeches exploit the father/daughter frame of reference (Clennam's rhetoric uses it, pretends to discard it, and then uses it again to legitimize the concluding embrace). Both speakers rely on fictions of selfless non-reciprocation in order to communicate their unacknowledged burden of feeling to their listener.

Speaking directly from the heart rarely occurs in Dickensian love-relations. A cluster of fictive and legitimizing postures is required to sanction the release of feelings that would otherwise remain impermissibly egotistic. (Note how, in earlier scenes of intimacy with Clennam, Amy requires the duenna-like presence of Maggy to triangulate the interchange—though Maggy says little or nothing—and thus ease her utterance.) Dickens enjoins a certain deviousness of thinking and speaking when it is a matter of eros. His timid lovers are more comfortable in not recognizing their motives.

Arthur Clennam works hard to consider his feelings for Pet those of "Nobody."[9] He would prefer to remain entirely ignorant of himself as a man of desire, and this is another way of saying that Mrs. Clennam has left her mark upon him. His inability to own his desire is bound up with his inability to conceive a present identity or a future career, for, as Rollo May puts it, "It is in intentionality and will that the human being experiences his identity. 'I' is the 'I' of 'I can'" (243). Beneath Clennam's "cannot," as beneath Amy's "will not," there breathes, as I have

---

[9] Ronald Librach persuasively assesses this self-labelling as a desire for extinction: to become "a character emptied, so to speak, of his own psychological substance" (543).

shown, a repressed "can" and "will." These predicaments of blocked desire and disowned motive are patently generalizable, and they invite some broader considerations of the Dickensian social world as a world keyed to the dynamic (best described by Freud) of repression and disguise.

ᕦᕤ

FREUD writes of hysteria:

> All these experiences had involved the emergence of a wishful impulse which was in sharp contrast to the subject's other wishes and which proved incompatible with the ethical and aesthetic standards of his personality. There had been a short conflict, and the end of this internal struggle was that the idea which had appeared before consciousness as the vehicle of this irreconcilable wish fell a victim to repression. . . . (11:24)

The cultural paradigm of identity, the civilized self sanctioned by the age and dominant among Dickens' protagonists, is a composite of "ethical standards" enforced by the superego but rarely conformable to the psyche's inmost experience. The ensuing repression of "irreconcilable wishes" fails, however, to banish them; it only (and unsuccessfully) ignores them. Philip Rieff expounds the connection between memory and repression:

> Memory, for Freud, is not a passive receiver whose performance can be measured quantitatively; it embodies a moral choice, a sequence of acceptances and rejections. Forgetting is active; it is not the absence of an action, something dropped out of the container mind. Freud felt his way down into the container until he found its false bottom, repression; below this memory really begins. (40)

Freudian man's behavior intimates continuously the impress of those past events and present wishes that he can neither bear to remember nor manage to forget. Doomed to be and to want what he cannot endorse being and wanting, he disguises himself, tries to pass himself off (to himself as well as to others) as decent, even if the result be "paid for" (as with Mrs. Clennam) by self-paralysis. The repressed elements beat upon the periphery of consciousness, issuing out, deviously, into his dreams, his jokes, his gestures, his slips of the tongue, setting the unconscious tone of his conscious behavior. A world filled with such figures is nervous, ambiguous, and above all theatrical. The extravagance of Dickensian characterization is not least due to the parade of false motives and mixed signals, on the part of actors who egregiously and operatically misunderstand themselves.

They misunderstand themselves and they systematically remain misunderstood. Dickens is unsurpassed in his ability to frame discourse that denies communication. This use of words—in which non-relationship and autonomy are perpetually asserted—seeks mainly to deny the underlying complicity of the Dickens world.[10] Asserting the fiction of unaided strength, it disguises the interdependence of everyone upon everyone else, even though one set of characters march to their death defiantly crying, "Don't know ya! don't know ya!" or sedately insisting, "It never does . . . it never does." Estella is the daughter of a convict; Rigaud makes his way into Mrs. Clennam's house. No one's life has its meaning apart from the life of others he finds it demeaning to acknowledge. Here is Mrs. Merdle rejecting Fanny Dorrit:

> "I pointed out to your sister the plain state of the case; the impossibility of the Society in which we moved recognizing the Society in which she moved—though charming, I have no doubt; the immense disadvantage at which she would consequently place the family she had so high an opinion of, upon which we should find ourselves compelled to look down with contempt, and from which (socially speaking) we should feel obliged to recoil with abhorrence." (236)

If the hidden condition of human nature in Dickens is interdependence, we see here the "circumlocutionary" fiction by means of which Mrs. Merdle has denatured herself. Relying on that fiction of immaculate exclusiveness, Mrs. Merdle passes off the contempt that fills this scene as not her own but dictated by Society. She feels morally obliged to despise Fanny Dorrit. She

[10] Societal interdependence is a commonplace of Victorian thought. I am interested in how this fundamental fact of complicity cuts athwart the character's vain attempt to maintain an autonomous identity.

has coaxed herself into a position in which, like Mrs. Gowan with the Meagleses, her rudest remarks slip through the censor of propriety.[11]

The extreme instance of inauthentic theater is Mrs. General, a woman who has so successfully indoctrinated herself that she seems to take the fictions of Society as reality itself. She acknowledges only what the censor has approved. Her eyes have no expression; her mind has no opinions; she is such a cancellation of the unvarnished private life of desire that Dickens imagines her sleep to be free of dreams—that is to say, free of all unwanted intrusions: the ultimate state of successful quarantine.

Dickens' plots insist, however, on unwanted intrusions. The humble and humiliated are joined to the vengeful and powerful by the bonds of kinship denied, of responsibility repudiated, of desire hushed up. The Dickensian narrative unfolds a sort of Freudian map of London: the pretence of autonomous edifices above the surface, the reality of interconnected desires underneath. Whether released or repressed, desire (in the later novels especially) is the binding force of Dickens' society, and desire hushed up is an acceptable definition of most Dickensian secrets. In its strictest form, as here and in *Bleak House*, such a secret is the box of love letters on which the plot of the novel hinges.

More broadly, all the rickety structures in *Little Dorrit*—the Circumlocution Office, Marshalsea Prison, Casby's house, Mrs. Clennam's house—are ill-conceived edifices shaped to constrict, exploit, and penalize feeling: they give off continuously the stench of the secrets they are supposed to keep contained. Deforming their clientele, both those they partially hold in and those they partially keep out, such unfit structures must collapse. They cannot maintain the fiction of autonomy, of successfully hushed up feeling.

The river flows to the sea in every Dickens novel, and that flow images the dynamic of his imaginative world. The temporal paralysis of a Miss Havisham or Mrs. Clennam and the spatial separateness of a Mr. Dorrit or Mrs. Gowan are a kind of willful

[11] Mrs. Gowan is one of Dickens' small masterpieces. She radiates false theater wherever she goes, and her artfully sadistic posturing reduces Meagles more than once to sententious floundering. See 504-509 for one of the most incisive brief portrayals of class prejudice in Dickens' work.

quarantining meant to forestall (through the fiction of immunity) the common liabilities of feeling, contact, and dependency—ultimately of mortality itself. As Alexander Welsh has noted, the verb in the last sentence of *Little Dorrit* is "passed along" (118). Nothing retains its exclusive pose of autonomous strength and permanence.

Whatever his aloofness, whatever his age, the Dickens adult harbors within himself a sentient child, and this child (though permanently repressible) constitutes his core of instinctively social being. (A charming instance of the child hiding in the man is Pancks playing leapfrog over the solemn back of Rugg [379]; a spectacular instance is the rejuvenated Scrooge.) The underlying society in Dickens, as many critics have implied, is a community of interdependent children of all ages. The fulfillment of their desires is mutual—their strength is a common strength—and the role of parental institutions can only be to rationalize and nourish these common bonds.

The institutions regularly fail at this role. They tyrannize or abandon, and life in common becomes an isolated maze instead of a reciprocal community. Yet life in common remains in common: the orphans have parents, however truant they be. Abandoned by the Circumlocution Office, the Dickens children cannot fall out of society. They are caught up by the Circumlocution Office's mirror institution, the debtors' prison. Shunted from one institution to another, exploited or ignored, the Dorrits and Plornishes and Chiverys of the world tend toward one of two polar attitudes toward the parental society: they come to terms with their social impotence or they rebel.

The prudent and modest ones come to terms. They accept their victimization, and they withdraw into discrete pockets on the periphery of institutional power. Here one finds Daniel Doyce, John Chivery, the Plornishes, Arthur Clennam, Frederick and Amy Dorrit: humble figures who have assimilated their own orphanhood. Their acceptance of estrangement constitutes their authenticity and permits them to grow up. They are sometimes grotesque, but, compared to the vindictive and enraged ones, they are only mildly damaged.

Those children of society who cannot accept the terms of

their orphanhood rebel. They entertain great expectations of storming society at the center; they will either defeat society or become society. These are the malcontents—Tattycoram, Miss Wade, Rigaud, Fanny Dorrit, her father—figures of Nietzschean *ressentiment* who have been crushed and who spend their lives in fantastic scenarios of revenge. Such scenarios propose, not the mutual strength of community, but the invidious strength of exclusion. They are scenarios in which the malcontent's injured and orphaned ego plots its apotheosis: that moment when the self-annihilating insult of others is transformed into self-reconstituting envy by others.

Old Dorrit's deepest desire is to reverse his present degradation and to return to a fantasized youth in which "I was accomplished, I was good-looking, I was independent—by God I was, child!—and people sought me out, and envied me. Envied me!" (221.) Personally nullified, permanently "uncentered," he measures his worth by the eyes of others; he is rich only so long as he is envied. His scenario accommodates but one actor (he who is now envious and who would be envied by others), and the actor's apparent authority is a mask for his inner emptiness. This peculiar condition of inner humiliation parading as outward power is one of the keys to perhaps the most widespread parody of strength in the novel: the phenomenon of patronage.

PATRONAGE (though on occasion genuinely benevolent) is usually in Dickens (and especially in the later Dickens) a theatrical means by which one who is secretly self-doubting and dependent may pass himself off as admired and immune. If the strength of true paternity be defined as the power to father forth and nurture, the capacity to create community, to share the scene with those one nourishes and to take pleasure in their burgeoning strength, then patronage appears as the theatrical counterfeit of true paternity. The Dickens world is peopled with children, but it has (in the sense defined above) few authentic fathers.[12]

[12] Although Daleski does not consider the gap between patronage and paternity, his reading of patronage in *Little Dorrit* is richly suggestive.

Rigaud, for example, tirelessly proliferates patronizing screens which keep at bay an awareness of his true impotence and vileness. (Clennam correctly perceives him as a coward when unsupported by the filched secrets of others.) At the Marseilles prison he ritually defines himself as the gentlemanly patron of John Baptist; later he patronizes the company of the Break of Day Inn; later still he patronizes Flintwinch and tries to patronize Arthur and his mother. In all these scenes he requires others' weakness in order to summon a sense of his own power.

More subtly, Henry Gowan patronizes Rigaud. By insisting on being seen with Rigaud, Gowan mocks the convention of "gentleman," mocks those who must put up with Rigaud, and "strokes" himself as well, through the ever-displayed comparison of himself with an impostor. Figuratively orphaned by his uncaring mother, Gowan betrays beneath his pretence of superiority (as F. R. Leavis observes) "an underlying consciousness of nullity . . . he feels that if he doesn't assert, as something that doesn't need his asserting, his intrinsic superiority—the 'reality' of which is the recognition it gets—he is nothing" (*Dickens the Novelist*, 232-33). Empty himself, he maintains, beneath his casual air, an undeviating project: to create emptiness in the human world that surrounds him.

Similarly, Fanny Dorrit patronizes Amy (even to the extent of calling her Pet). Silhouetted by Amy, Fanny will appear in her superior force and breeding. Amy is necessary for supportive contrast, lest Fanny doubt the wisdom of her audacious project.[13] Fanny's patronage of Mrs. Merdle is more obvious and virulent. Although she is marrying Edmund Sparkler, Dickens suggests that the deeper (and monstrous) intimacy is between the two women, each preparing for an endlessly patronizing embrace/clash.

Patronage in gentler form (still egotistic, but no longer sadistic) occurs in Meagles' treatment of Tattycoram and Doyce,

---

[13] Like Mrs. Clennam, Fanny is more complex than my argument may suggest. She requires Amy's company; equally she dreads being equated with her. One surmises that the shame Fanny projects upon her sister has its source in herself. Fanny resembles her father in nothing more than her incapacity to delude herself entirely.

and the gentlest patronage of all is that which Mrs. Plornish bestows upon John Baptist. Suddenly expert in Italian, she sports him as a measure of her capacious heart and intellect. When he is unaccountably silent, she implores, "Peaka Padrona!" (561)

Perhaps the most aggressive patronage in the novel is that radiated everywhere by Miss Wade. One of Dickens' brilliantly sinister creations, she reveals in "The History of a Self-Tormentor" a voice uncannily similar to that of the Underground Man whom Dostoevsky would create some nine years later. Her confession shows how intolerable the reality of Dickensian interdependence can be. As in Dostoevsky, human vulnerability is an affront to individual pride that can be borne only through love. Unloved at birth, Miss Wade is incapable of love, and likewise incapable of perceiving it in others. She thus distorts every loving relationship into the secretly resentful power play of patronage. Alienated from her own center of feeling, she incarnates the raging force of despised and despising self in Dickens: the force that insists on orphanhood, that resists all possibility of community. Her fixed and impoverished life is enslaved to a single memory and a single desire—the memory of having been psychically crippled by patronage, the desire to regain strength by inflicting that fate on others. She is one of Dickens' most haunting figures, and it is right that we should meet her when we meet Meagles. Her authentic isolation measures nicely what is problematic and superficial in his blustery assertions of family.

There are other patronizers in this novel, but they pale before the supreme case, Old Dorrit. In him patronizing attains the nuance of a fine art. Uncentered by his Marshalsea imprisonment, Dorrit is permanently humiliated, and this humiliation never softens over time into self-accepting humility. Rather, upon being reduced to a helpless child, he responds with the fiction of a revered father. He will not own that figure of impotence he knows himself to be. Dickens delicately shows the "Collegians" corroborating this deception; eventually they take it for the truth. To sustain Dorrit's fictive posture is in a small measure to dignify their own. The prison collaborates in their humane version of Mrs. General's varnishing. They repress knowledge of the more brutal elements of their incarceration; they put a good face on it; they "circumlocute."

Dorrit goes further. His forced exclusion becomes the voluntary reclusiveness of royalty; his dependence on others, their "Testimonial" to his greatness. Throughout his performance he manages—in the figures of Frederick Dorrit and John Edward Nandy—to project away (to foist upon them) his irrepressible awareness of his own impotence. Their decrepitude guarantees his precarious strength. Immured in his fantasy he would become psychotic, were it not that he always glimpses the fictionality of his fiction. The truth he cannot tolerate is always, and only, half-repressed. Eventually, at the Roman banquet near the end of the novel, his egg-shell pretence gives way. In that sublime scene Dickens shows that, as Freud puts it, "Our hysterical patients suffer from reminiscences" (11:16). The mark of the past is inescapable, and either one chooses one's necessity, like Amy, or one is overwhelmed by it, like her father.

> She was hurrying to him, unobserved, when he got up out of his chair, and leaning over the table called to her, supposing her to be still in her place:
>
> "Amy, Amy my child!"
>
> The action was so unusual, to say nothing of his strange eager appearance and strange eager voice, that it instantaneously caused a profound silence.
>
> "Amy, my dear," he repeated. "Will you go and see if Bob is on the lock?"
>
> She was at his side, and touching him, but he still perversely supposed her to be in her seat, and called out, still leaning over the table. "Amy, Amy. I don't feel quite myself. Ha. I don't know what's the matter with me. I particularly wish to see Bob. Ha. Of all the turnkeys, he's as much my friend as yours. See if Bob is in the lodge, and beg him to come to me."
>
> All the guests were now in consternation, and everybody rose. . . .
>
> He looked confusedly about him, and, becoming conscious of the number of faces by which he was surrounded, addressed them:

"Ladies and gentlemen, the duty—ha—devolves upon me of—hum—welcoming you to the Marshalsea. Welcome to the Marshalsea! The space is—ha—limited—limited—the parade might be wider; but you will find it apparently grow larger after a time—a time, ladies and gentlemen—and the air is, all things considered, very good. . . . Those who are habituated to the—ha—Marshalsea, are pleased to call me its Father. I am accustomed to be complimented by strangers as the—ha—Father of the Marshalsea. Certainly, if years of residence may establish a claim to so—ha—honourable a title, I may accept the—hum—conferred distinction. My child, ladies and gentlemen. My daughter. Born here!"

She was not ashamed of it, or ashamed of him. . . . She was between him and the wondering faces, turned round upon his breast with her own face raised to his. He held her clasped in his left arm, and between whiles her low voice was heard tenderly imploring him to go away with her.

"Born here," he repeated, shedding tears. "Bred here. Ladies and gentlemen, my daughter. Child of an unfortunate father, but—ha—always a gentleman. Poor, no doubt, but—hum—proud. Always proud. It has become a—hum— not infrequent custom for my—ha—personal admirers— personal admirers solely—to be pleased to express their desire to acknowledge my semi-official position here, by offering—ha—little tributes, which usually take the form of— ha—Testimonials—pecuniary Testimonials. In the acceptance of those—ha—voluntary recognitions of my humble endeavours to—hum—to uphold a Tone here—a Tone—I beg it to be understood that I do not consider myself compromised. Ha. Not compromised. Ha. Not a beggar. No; I repudiate the title! At the same time far be it from me to— hum—to put upon the fine feelings by which my partial friends are actuated, the slight of scrupling to admit that those offerings are—hum—highly acceptable. On the contrary, they are most acceptable. In my child's name, if not in my own, I make that admission in the fullest manner, at the same time reserving—ha—shall I say my personal dignity? Ladies and gentlemen, God bless you all!" (625-29)

I have quoted the scene at length because, prepared by several earlier eating scenes (scenes also of pretence and tears), it renders Dorrit in all his trembling dignity and ridiculousness. Beneath his authoritative patronizing we hear the plea of a suppliant in need. For the first time Amy is proudly and lovingly introduced. He almost grasps that she has made his life possible. A testimonial to her, a self-exposing confession to his audience, a self-ratifying performance to himself, Dorrit's speech both gives him away and reasserts his fictive delusion. Dorrit has become his fictive delusion, and Dickens seems to respect the fiction, even as he deplores the delusion. By sheer linguistic power, language unsupported by reality, William Dorrit has affirmed his identity. His speech is saturated in the vocabulary and syntax of self-esteem. If he is a fraud, does he not "reserve—ha—shall I say my personal dignity?" Not quite unsupported by reality, for Amy's loving forbearance is the enabling condition of her father's final performance. One harsh word from her would pierce his gossamer delusion. To the end she collaborates in the enterprise, half-comic, half-tragic, of sustaining William Dorrit's dignity.

From a no-nonsense Freudian perspective Old Dorrit is a cautionary disaster. He reveals the price of fantasy, he commits the cardinal Freudian sin of not being present in his own life. Yet Dorrit is something more than this failure. In a sense, the Marshalsea was the making of him. Without it he would have been a nonentity; because of it he became a tragi-comic fraud. The self he performs is grounded in deceit, but the force that energizes his performance can only be his own anguish. One can be charitable to him, if only because he never succeeds in fully duping himself. Humiliated, annihilated, he has, in the most suggestive way, followed the path of his once-prison-shadowed and humiliated creator. He has generated his dignity through the power of his own words. Rescuing himself from prison through the restorative fictions of language, he has salvaged his sanity by both believing in those fictions and yet not believing in them altogether. At a great price to others and to himself, he has made a life of it. It is an uncomfortable solution, but then it was an uncomfortable dilemma. A measure of Dickens' triumphant sanity lies in the generosity with which he delineates both the achievement and the deformity of such a life as Dorrit's.

The old man is taken up the narrow stairs. He dies soon after, and Frederick's death follows hard upon his. The chapter concludes: "The two brothers were before their Father; far beyond the twilight judgments of this world; high above its mists and obscurities" (632). Only in the afterlife, Dickens seems to hope, will the antics of all the orphans, patronized and patronizing, be replaced by what Freud could never believe in: the unimaginable care and strength of true paternity.

Meanwhile, life below will continue in its "misty" conditions. Most patrons will patronize rather than nurture. And the children will be lucky if, rather than attempt to raze their prison, they manage (like Arthur and Amy) to tap their obscure resources and to release their disguised and inhibited desire for each other. Through the art of circumlocution these two have found a way to (but not named) their own center of feeling. Obeying the Carlylean numerator of their lives—the realm of outward limitation—they will regulate the denominator of demand. Patronizing no one and pretending to no powers—wanting little and that mainly in their possession already—they embody the only wisdom *Little Dorrit* can muster: that it is better to accept the culture's various modes of restriction than to seek, with impotent rage, to remove all limitation. Burdened with the paradoxical conviction that desire can be neither successfully quarantined nor overtly released, Dickens cannot resolve the enigmas of power and impotence which his novel explores. The best he can imagine is to learn, circumlocutiously, to live in one's prisons in such a way as to cease being a prisoner within them. Why must the means of liberation be so meager?

ஐ

IT MAY, in conclusion, be possible to shed light on Dickens' dilemma by briefly contrasting his imagination of desire with Blake's. In Blake desire begins in the body and is self-delighting. It is experienced simultaneously as outer possibility and inner receptivity, as power and feeling: the capacity to move, and be moved by, others. The strong man endorses his own desire and nurtures it in others. Vice is, precisely, the hindering of act in self or other, for the Blakean imagination of desire is simply an advocacy of "the Staminal Virtues of Humanity," an unambiguous sanction (at once personal and societal) of energy in the entire human family (590). And Blake is willing to take this sanction to its radical extreme: the reconception of human society, in which all incarnate desire is realized.

By contrast, the conflict in Dickens' imagination of desire emerges as an endorsement of personal feeling, but an opposing. fear of power, of the acts of passion to which the release of (originally balked) feeling may lead. He is in the awkward position of sympathizing spontaneously with the frustrated child, yet sharing his culture's cautionary fear of that child's attempts to redress his situation. Desire remains a dusky phenomenon in Dickens—he has such a fine eye for its welling up, such a suspicious eye for the damage to self and other its release can cause. For desire is of the body and its slides easily into irrational passion, threatening those altruistic norms of identity by which the protagonist recognizes himself in Dickens' world. In those norms is inscribed the society's securest defense against the motives (equally powerful in his work) to tear it down. Consequently we find in Dickens no vision of Blakean promise in which, as every man might enact his "leading propensity," feeling would move into desire and thence into action. We tend to find instead a polarized world in which energies are simultaneously endorsed and opposed, moving and arrested, a world in which, on the one hand, those with a profound awareness of others' feelings forbear to realize (in both senses of the word) their own desire, and, on the other, those with a developed will to power lack (or have repressed) the capacity for sympathetic feeling. We find what this essay has focused on, two recurrent scenarios, both eccentric: the scenario of feeling separated from personal power (the assertion of selfless devotion to others), and the scenario of power separated from personal feeling (the assertion of an immune self, molding through patronage the destiny of others).

The first scenario is obviously superior to the second. Feeling (which may be more precisely defined as receptivity, the capacity to be moved and hurt) is the moral center of Dickens' novels. At the core of his imagination (as many critics have noted in other contexts), there is a vulnerable and helpless child. Dickens is nowhere more opposed to Blake and Nietzsche than in his underlying allegiance to this passive child who cannot help himself and who must be helped. This allegiance entails pity for the creature rather than admiration for the creator: power is too often in Dickens' world the injury an unfeeling (or outraged) adult can inflict on a sensitive child.

Power opposes feeling; in Dickens' sinister figures it asserts itself as freedom from feeling. If an Arthur Clennam seeks release from the stresses of feeling in the harmless fiction of "Nobody," others take more drastic steps. Developing fictions of superior exclusiveness, they seek to eliminate their own interdependency, to stop up their springs of responsiveness. They will avenge their capacity to be hurt by humiliating those around them. These are Dickensian versions of Blake's Satanic figures, the accusers of sin. Self-evading patronizers whose strength is posited on others' weakness, they remain as distant from the exuberant models of Blakean and Dionysian power as do Dickens' repressed protagonists, Arthur Clennam and Amy Dorrit.

The latter, however chastened, are figures of hope. The only way to the modicum of genuine strength available in Dickens' mature world is through abasement and an acceptance of our common destiny as incomplete and feeling creatures. Arthur and Amy have traveled this way; humiliated, they have become humble. Recognizing the slightness of their power and the fullness of their vulnerability, they thus acknowledge what is for Dickens the moral center of their character. Their desire, as I have shown, is something more than they quite acknowledge, but they survive through their ability modestly to tap it, if not to name it.

The umbrella beneath which they can move from an overt "no" to a covert "yes" is of course Circumlocution. Circumlocution is in Dickens the genius of language itself, the intricate thread by means of which, as Nietzsche knew, human beings go about reconciling their culturally enjoined dilemmas with their incarnate desire.[14] Through language they somehow survive in-

---

[14] The best study of "circumlocution" in Dickens is Garrett Stewart's *Dick-*

tact, covertly acting upon the stresses of their embodied state as they navigate between the requirements of an altruistic conscience, on the one hand, and the humiliating impasse of societal negation, on the other. If in Old Dorrit circumlocution verges on psychosis, and in Casby and Mrs. Merdle it has only the attributes of self-aggrandizing egotism, in Arthur and Amy circumlocution is that necessary screening device, that protean inner resource on which two dutiful children draw to endorse each other's hidden promise, to become adult lovers, and to set to work transforming their prison into a home.

---

ens and the Trials of Imagination. Stewart has only passing commentary on *David Copperfield* and *Little Dorrit*, but his general field of inquiry—the variety of relations that obtain between a character's (or author's) imaginative language and the non-verbal situations to which that language refers—is akin to mine, though his purposes are quite different.

Two ❧ George Eliot and the Idolatries of the Superego

THE FOREGOING chapter has sought to address two of Dickens' novels on their own terms, and this has occasioned two somewhat differing analyses. The *David Copperfield* commentary centers on the phenomenon of misnaming: the movement, beneath the univocal rubric of the earnest whole self, of discrepant and disowned psychic energies. Four of the novel's major relationships reveal the implicating play of desire (or the traces of desire repressed) even as they clamor to be seen in terms of altruistic discipline.

Little Dorrit, by contrast, is abreast of its own transactions; yet these remain sharply conflicted. This novel is Dickens' most probing exploration of "mind-forged manacles," but (unlike Blake's work) it refuses to envisage liberation. Desire finds its outlet— desire hushed up and then released characteristically moves the Dickens plot—but it emerges ignored, resisted, or penalized at every stage. The power to nurture, to affirm others' capacity for growth, appears to be as muted, when genuine, as it is proclaimed, when false—in its parodistic form of patronage.

George Eliot's fictional world is more tightly governed than Dickens' by the sanctions of conscious scruple. For this reason it has elicited V. S. Pritchett's harsh but accurate phrase, "the idolatries of the superego" (211). An effect of this unremitting control is that when Eliot's imaginative sympathies stray beyond their own normative premises, they have nowhere to go. She is too judicious a reader of her own imagination to permit the lateral movements, the creative misnamings by means of which the

73

Dickens narrative can satisfy the demands of desire and censorship at the same time. If normative behavior is impossible and apostasy unacceptable, the narrative has no choice but to subvert its own impetus, to choke on its own motives. This dilemma, writ large in *The Mill on the Floss* and writ small in *Daniel Deronda*, serves as the focus of my chapter on George Eliot.

BODY BRUISED TO PLEASURE SOUL: *THE MILL ON THE FLOSS*

Those critics who find this novel both great and greatly flawed seem to me persuasive. The flaws are especially manifest in "the final rescue" of the flood, though latent throughout Book VI. What is for this study most interestingly in question are two issues: the nature of Maggie's desire and the implications of that desire. Eliot has so complicated the first issue, and so curtailed the second, that commentary on this novel—as opposed to *Adam Bede* and *Middlemarch*—is not likely ever to agree on the most fundamental matters. Is Maggie a Feuerbachian model of self-transcendence or a victim of adolescent and swooning daydreams? Is she actually in love, or merely infatuated, with Stephen Guest? Is she heroic or self-deceived in rejecting Stephen and returning to St Ogg's? Is she a figure of ennobling "passionate sensibility" (*The Mill on the Floss*, 211) or of destructive, even demonic enchantment?[1] There is impressive textual support for

[1] Perhaps because the novel is such a problematic masterpiece, it has elicited a wide range of excellent criticism. F. R. Leavis' *The Great Tradition* and Bernard J. Paris' *Experiments in Life* put forth the classic polar positions concerning the novel: that the later Maggie succumbs to her author's recurrent bouts of vague and adolescent sentimentality (Leavis), or that the later Maggie develops into an ideally self-renouncing Feuerbachian heroine, having gained "a sense of religious orientation in the cosmos" (Paris, 168). Michael Steig's "Anality in *The Mill on the Floss*" shrewdly and tentatively approaches the narrative from a Freudian perspective; and, less circumspectly, Elizabeth Ermarth confronts "Maggie Tulliver's Long Suicide," erring only in attributing her incisive analysis of Maggie's morbidity to Eliot herself. Perhaps the most intriguing essay on the novel is Nina Auerbach's "The Power of Hunger: Demonism and Maggie Tulliver"; Auerbach makes headway against one's initial skepticism as she illuminates the cluster of "witchlike" traits associated with Maggie. Countering these three "subversive" readings are the poised and "reconciliatory" essays of John Hagan ("A

all of these views, and Eliot has ended the novel in such a way as neither to validate nor invalidate any of them. The flood forecloses all but resolves nothing. Before we attempt to sort out these issues, it will be helpful to identify some of the norms of presentation and assessment within Eliot's work, against which we can measure our confusions about Maggie and the waywardness of her drowning.

Eliot's typical stance toward her characters, as is well known, is the judicious extension of sympathy and judgment to every figure on the canvas, a stance supremely embodied in *Middlemarch*. "Realism, as Eliot conceives of it, involves the tactful unravelling of interlaced processes, the equable distribution of authorial sympathies, the holding of competing values in precarious equipoise" (Eagleton, 114). Her fiction is generally agreed to achieve excellence when a cluster of conditions is operative: when the action moves easily from subjective individual gesture to objective social response, from the immediacy of a momentary act to a clarifying and enlarged context of former acts and future hopes and consequences, from the vivid picture of sensuous experience to the reflective diagram of human motives understood and evaluated. At her best she is surpassed only by Tolstoy in her capacity to render experience in its manifold aspects—what it feels like at the moment and what it feels like in anticipation and in retrospect, how its inner meaning differs from the meanings it will have in others' hearts and minds, how it is both the issue of instantaneous free feeling and yet the product of one's emotional and intellectual history, a history in no small part molded by the pressure of external forces.

Middlemarch repeatedly renders this effect of unstinted sympathy and unbiased judgment, of life grasped momentarily and in the larger view, inwardly and outwardly; and *The Mill on the Floss* displays as well a good measure of Eliot's integrative genius. Maggie's episode with the gypsies, for example, effortlessly blends the realities of inner and outer perception. We follow Maggie running away from the Pullets' home, and Eliot makes us both

---

Reinterpretation of *The Mill on the Floss*,") and Barbara Hardy ("*The Mill on the Floss*," in *Critical Essays on George Eliot*).

see her gradually getting lost and feel her own ignorance of that fact. The gypsies are just what she had desired. Still, when she actually encounters them, "it was astonishing to herself that she did not feel more delighted" (94). Eliot narrates the scene with a deft focus on both gypsy facts and Maggie fantasies, and we have a persuasive instance of the educative aspect of new experience: ill-kempt, "brown" Maggie, who has just pushed Lucy into mud and cow-dung, wishes the gypsies "had not been so dirty" and anticipates the time when she will have "taught the gypsies to use a washing-basin" (94, 95). The scene is attentive to external setting—the description of the gypsy camp, their talking hurriedly among themselves, their calculated tone of deference to Maggie, their shrewd glances at her belongings—and to the subjective shifts of Maggie's feelings: her desire to be an amusing and instructive queen for these needy people, and—once she becomes thoroughly scared—her hope that some women accompany the men when they take her away, because "it would be more cheerful to be murdered by a larger party" (99). There is nothing better than this in George Eliot, but its excellence is of a kind that we find repeatedly. The inwardness of the experience is generously rendered, but not at the expense of its "public" context in space, time, and the interpersonal world of others.

Eliot's death scenes are masterful examples of the same poised attention to inner and outer. Featherstone and Casaubon in *Middlemarch*, old Tulliver in *The Mill on the Floss*—these characters do not exit in a dramatic flourish. Their dying is a matter of minute complicity between subjective and objective facts. They linger throughout the novels, not failing to die (as we and they expect), but not quite managing to do so at the optimal moment. Their deaths reveal the inclusive interplay of personal will and impersonal destiny, and they illustrate the habitual, incremental nature of determining experience in Eliot's fictional world. Against the authority of these deaths we measure how awry, how thematically uncontrolled, are the abrupt deaths of Maggie and Tom in *The Mill on the Floss* and of Grandcourt in *Daniel Deronda*.[2]

[2] To the well-known fact that Eliot researched the flood before beginning *The Mill on the Floss*—and thus the conclusion was no hurried afterthought—one

Another revealing instance of a momentary event set in the context of an overarching emotional history is Mr. Tulliver's abortive attempt to recover his loan to his sister and her husband. The chapter (I, viii) opens on a detached and admonitory note: "For Mr. Tulliver was in a position neither new nor striking, but, like other everyday things, sure to have a cumulative effect that will be felt in the long run" (67)—he is less well-off than supposed. Wisdom, in such a bind, might well consist in firming up one's resolve and securing one's loans, but the chapter goes on to show how impossible is this theoretical determination to be prudent. The scene (one of the finest in the novel) is immediate and, in its unexceptional way, overwhelming. The flesh-and-blood presence of his loving sister and her children touches the fibers of Tulliver's confused heart. Without quite knowing why, he reverses his decision and though he thereby deepens his own financial plight, he rides home "with the sense of a danger escaped" (74).

The "long view" thus appears rather problematic. In one sense, Tulliver betrays it, failing again to gain control over his financial actions and thus supervise their consequences. In another sense, though, he ratifies the "long view," for he has been subconsciously wrought upon by a chord of buried affection for his little sister, now a straitened and aging woman. This emotional accessibility—inconceivable in the Dodsons—is the mark of Tulliver's appeal, but it also makes him potentially vulnerable before the immediate plea of a loved one. At its extreme, such emotional accessibility approaches the spontaneous sympathy that characterizes the novel's germinal emblem of virtue itself: Ogg and the ragged woman in distress.

Ogg succors her because "it is enough that thy heart needs it," and she responds, "Ogg the son of Beorl, thou art blessed in that thou didst not question and wrangle with the heart's need, but wast smitten with pity, and didst straightway relieve the same" (102). The essence of Ogg's virtue is that he responds immedi-

---

may cite Barbara Hardy's comment: "What we are prepared for is the struggle between the energetic human spirit and a limited and limiting society: such struggles are not settled by floods" ("*The Mill on the Floss*," 47).

ately to the woman in need. He does not look before or after, does not rationally ponder the consequences. He is explicitly set apart from the other men who want assurances first: "Wherefore dost thou desire to cross the river? Tarry till the morning . . . so shalt thou be wise, and not foolish" (102).

In the condensed form of a stylized legend, this vignette crystallizes one pole of Eliot's moral ideal—the ideal of passionate generosity. But in the expanded form of a realistic novel it tugs uneasily against Eliot's other moral desideratum: the considered and rational assessment of consequences. Indeed, one way of formulating Maggie's sin is to say that she has responded to the compelling reality of the moment; she has been "foolish" and "not wise," not guided by earlier commitments that ought to inhibit her present act. Her passionate response in this case has been fueled by incarnate desire, by the clamorous pressure toward self-fulfillment. For this response the judgmental commitment in George Eliot to context and consequences requires, somewhat obscurely, that she shall die.

I hope my examples make clear that this is a conflict within the norms themselves of Eliot's fiction, a conflict between the ardent generosity of instant response and the controlled, self-inhibiting behavior that mediates between presence and absence, between the push of the actual moment and the tug of remembered commitments and imagined consequences. These two moralities—one of immediacy, the other of abstraction—are in a certain measure irreconcilable, and in her best fiction (as in *Middlemarch*) Eliot achieves unity by moderating the most stringent demands of each. This sense of unity is of course that seamless blend of attention to the near and the far, the inner and the outer, that I have discussed earlier; and I propose to examine the flawed ending of *The Mill on the Floss* as a symptom of these unreconciled moralities. What is missing in the affair of Maggie and Stephen is a temporally overarching context within which its full range of meanings—otherwise unconditionally immediate or apocalyptic—can be gradually unfolded and assimilated.

The flood serves to arrest—to wrest out of time—the opposed meanings of their passionate act. It aborts the event rather than delivering it in its fullness. And this is a problem in no way addressed by Eliot's lament that "the tragedy is not adequately prepared. . . . The Epische Breite into which I was beguiled by love of my subject in the first two volumes, caused a want of proportionate fullness in the treatment of the third, which I shall always regret" (Jones, *George Eliot*, 21). Ample detail is not what is lacking; I shall argue later that Book VI (which makes up three-fourths of the third volume) moves with an unprecedented slowness in Eliot's narrative world. What is missing is the fullness of conclusion: the unhurried exploration of Maggie's act in objective time, in the continuing lives of others, as well as in Maggie's own memory and understanding.[3] Failing this fullness of conclusion we have a melodramatic death scene which permits (but does not ratify) a range of contradictory meanings, from affirmation to suicidal defeat—a range of meanings, that is, which permits everything but the realistic stalemate in time which survival would probably have meant. The pace of time itself is excluded from the ending, and I turn therefore to that motif in *The Mill on the Floss* in which the relation between past and present time has struck readers as most confusingly handled: the motif of idyllic memory.

WE COULD never have loved the earth so well if we had had no childhood in it,—if it were not the earth where the same flowers come up again every spring that we used to gather with our tiny fingers as we sat lisping to ourselves on the grass. . . . These familiar flowers, these well-remembered bird-notes, this sky, with its fitful brightness . . . such things as these are the mother tongue of our imagination, the language that is laden with all the subtle inextricable associations the fleeting hours of our childhood left behind them. Our delight in the sunshine on the deep-bladed grass today, might be no more than the faint perception of wearied souls, if it were not for the sunshine and the grass in the far-off years which still live in us, and transform our perception into love. (36)

[3] Compare, for example, the reverberations that follow Hetty's liaison with Donnithorne, Bulstrode's "murder" of Raffles, Dorothea's unwise union with Casaubon, Gwendolen's with Grandcourt.

Critics have rightly pointed to the disparity between this nostalgic recall and the actual texture of Maggie's childhood experiences, a disparity with huge implications. The sanctities of the past, obedience to which largely dictates her return to St Ogg's, are hardly rendered in the novel as sanctities when experienced in the present. The quoted passage contains a further irony, for it speaks of a blessing denied to Maggie herself, the blessing of a lengthy retrospective vision. The voice we hear is the middle-aged and nostalgic one of a narrator who has survived the "hopelessness . . . of early youth, when the soul is made up of wants, and has no long memories, no superadded life in the life of others" (205).[4]

Pressed further, the passage suggests that even now the present would be felt as a burden, the sterile scene of "wearied souls," if we had not the inspiriting echo of former, childhood joys. If one notes that the unmediated present is in both cases a time of confusion and weariness, then the psychological process at work emerges. The past, no less than the present, is first experienced—in its immediacy—as laden with travail. It takes on its beneficent healing power only through the gradual balm of retrospect. This nostalgic passage celebrates, then, a fictive construct embroidered upon highly selective memories, a construct enabled by the pastness of the past, and meant to soothe the unresolved dilemmas of the present. It is a source of support conspicuously unavailable to Maggie Tulliver, whose past, when revisited, displays no signs of mellowing with time. Rather it displays all the brutality it possessed in the present:

> "Tom," she began, faintly, "I am come back to you—I am come back home—for refuge—to tell you everything."

[4] The voice of the survivor is obviously George Eliot's own. To Sara Hennell she writes in 1844: "Childhood is only the beautiful and happy time in contemplation and retrospect—to the child it is full of deep sorrows, the meaning of which is unknown. . . . All this dear Sara, to prove that we are happier than when we were seven years old, and that we shall be happier when we are forty than we are now. . . ." Indeed, nearing forty, Eliot writes in her Journal (in 1857): "Few women, I fear, have had such reason as I to think the long sad years of youth were worth living for the sake of middle age." Both passages are quoted in Ruby Redinger, *George Eliot*, 50.

"You will find no home with me," he answered with tremulous rage. (426)

This gap between the sharp-edged misery of immediate experience and the softened wisdom of nostalgic retrospect is writ large in the narrative. We see it in those wistful passages that end Books II and VII—"the golden gates of their childhood had for ever closed behind them" (168) and "the days when they had clasped their little hands in love, and roamed the daisied fields together" (459)[5]—and we see a version of it as well, I believe, in Eliot's tone of dignified bewilderment, as she responds to the *Times*'s appreciative yet critical review of *The Mill on the Floss*:

> I have certainly fulfilled by intentions very badly if I have made the Dodson honesty appear "mean and uninteresting," or made the payment of one's debts appear a contemptible virtue in comparison with any sort of "Bohemian" qualities. So far as my own feeling and intention are concerned, no one class of persons or form of character is held up to reprobation or to exclusive admiration. Tom is painted with as much love and pity as Maggie, and I am so far from hating the Dodsons myself, that I am rather aghast to find them ticketed with such very ugly adjectives. (Haight, *George Eliot*, 328)

There is no hypocrisy in this response. Rather, we hear in it only the judicious and measuring voice, the consequence-pondering voice. We do not hear the voice in which most of the Dodson part of the novel is written, a voice which—through immediate allegiance to Maggie's ardor—caricatures Dodsonian self-interest as comic, yes, but insufferably petty, smug, and blind. No reader would confuse the outrageous world of Pullets and Gleggs with the nuanced and dispassionately conceived one of Vincys or Gascoignes: the former is an *idée fixe* caricature of the

---

[5] Sara M. Putzell notes that the original form of three-volume publication stressed—more than does the present arrangement of seven Books—the pastoral relation between Tom and Maggie. Each volume concluded with a passage of lyrical reunion following separation between brother and sister. See the last paragraph of V, vii, as well as the passages I have quoted from the end of II, vii, and VII, v.

foibles of the latter. This gap between extreme and modulated assessment has a telling temporal dimension. In every case the excessive stance reflects the under-distanced perspective, so to speak, of Mary Ann Evans imaginatively reliving and suffering the moment-by-moment ordeal of Maggie Tulliver, whereas the even-handed poise reflects the detached perspective of an assured survivor—not Mary Ann Evans but George Eliot—who maturely surveys the whole scene.

Ultimately George Eliot will come to define personal identity itself in terms of this second, judicious voice. Personal identity appears in her fiction as one's incremental history in time, the record of one's social duration, one's cumulative impact on the lives of others. It is the register of the momentary challenges that one has persistently survived (or failed to survive). Who one is emerges in stepping back from the pang of immediate experience and perceiving the pattern available only in the middle distance—the pattern of habitual response in space and time and the continuous public world of others. In the light of these two unreconciled temporal perspectives—that emanating from passionate present experience and that arising from a judicious overview—we are now prepared to interpret the affair of Stephen and Maggie in Book VI.

ॐ

IF THE context proposed so far is persuasive, it should help to place one of the stranger aspects of Book VI, one that (I suspect) has struck more readers than critical comment on it would suggest. That is the extraordinarily slow pace and close-up perspective of Book VI, the sense of experience minutely rendered and moving virtually second by second. The scenes between Maggie and Stephen are justly praised as unique in Eliot's work, her single portrayal (in Barbara Hardy's phrase) "of sexual tension" (*The Novels of George Eliot*, 56). Again and again there is a close-up rendering of the movement and allure of two sentient bodies; and the physical notation of fingers, arms, eyes, hair, and voice is expressed with an attention, if not a delicacy, that recalls Henry James. We get "short views" so intensely presented as to seem dream-like, unevenly focused in public space and time. Rather than Eliot's typical interweaving of momentary event with over-arching context, of inner perception with outer fact, we find scenes virtually given over to the expression of amoral desire:

> Stephen laid down his hat, with the music, which rolled on the floor, and sat down in the chair close by her. He had never done so before, and both he and Maggie were quite aware that it was an entirely new position.
> "Well, you pampered minion!" said Stephen, leaning to pull the long curly ears that drooped over Maggie's arm. . . . It seemed to Stephen like some action in a dream, that he was obliged to do, and wonder at himself all the while—to go on stroking Minny's head . . . he only wished he dared look at Maggie, and that she would look at him—let him have one long look into those deep strange eyes of hers. . . . As for Maggie, she had no distinct thought—only the sense of a presence like that of a closely-hovering broad-winged bird in the darkness, for she was unable to look up, and saw nothing but Minny's black wavy coat. (356)

This scene is slower, the notation is keener, outwardly less is happening, than in anything earlier in the novel; and the determinant of this extraordinary pace is the momentary magic and danger of mutual desire. The scene is slow because it is fraught. Philip's body, Tom's, Bob Jakin's, Lucy's—these can be described more cursorily, their interest is only incidentally narrative or at best moral. Stephen's body, however, is alive with sexual potential; and its every dangerous motion is carefully noted, carefully interrelated with Maggie's responsive motion, the two bodies forming an odd, illicit, pre-Lawrentian ballet of desire:

> "Very well," said Stephen, dreamily, looking at her, as he rested his arm on the back of his chair. "Then we'll stay here."
> He was looking into her deep, deep eyes—far-off and mysterious as the starlit blackness, and yet very near, and timidly loving. Maggie sat perfectly still—perhaps for moments, perhaps for minutes—until the helpless trembling had ceased, and there was a warm glow on her cheek.

"The man is waiting—he has taken the cushions," she said. "Will you go and tell him?"

"What shall I tell him?" said Stephen, almost in a whisper. He was looking at the lips now.

Maggie made no answer.

"Let us go," Stephen murmured, entreatingly, rising, and taking her hand to raise her too. "We shall not be long together."

And they went. Maggie felt that she was being led down the garden among the roses, being helped with firm tender care into the boat, having the cushion and cloak arranged for her feet, and her parasol opened for her (which she had forgotten)—all by this stronger presence that seemed to bear her along without any act of her own will, like the added self which comes with the sudden exalting influence of a strong tonic—and she felt nothing else. Memory was excluded. (407)

These scenes are not only thematically illicit, they are formally illicit as well. They take the reader closer to the physical reality of the body and its powers than Eliot's reserves and beliefs normally permit. They seditiously imply, in their form as in their theme, a sense of identity that Eliot the moralist (and spokesman for her culture) must find anathema. Here the body is itself the inalienable locus of identity, the source of compelling sensations to which character and reader must attend; and attendance takes place perforce in the present moment. Identity is bound up with immediate impulse and incarnate desire; it inheres in a bedrock of affective propensity. It emerges directly, in the pressure of a given moment, rather than indirectly through the summarized script of incremental behavior accumulating over time. In the simplest terms, identity is what Maggie's affair with Stephen reveals. Identity as Eliot more typically renders it is what Maggie's affair with Stephen betrays.[6]

---

[6] Drawing on the suggestive phrase, "Memory was excluded" (437), Jerome H. Buckley makes the normative connection between cumulative memory and identity: ". . . her essential self is simply what she can remember; it is all that the past has made her" (111).

Maggie herself is quick to use Eliot's judgmental language in characterizing her passion for Stephen as a momentary aberration, an indulgence "in the present moment" (418). At her most succinct she declares:

> "Faithfulness and constancy mean . . . renouncing whatever is opposed to the reliance others have in us. . . . If we—if I had been better, nobler, those claims would have been so strongly present with me—I should have felt them pressing on my heart so continually, just as they do now in the moments when my conscience is awake—that the opposite feeling would never have grown in me, as it has done: it would have been quenched at once—I should have prayed for help so earnestly—I should have rushed away, as we rush from hideous danger. I feel no excuse for myself—none. I should never have failed toward Lucy and Philip as I have done, if I had not been weak, selfish, and hard—able to think of their pain without a pain to myself that would have destroyed all temptation." (417)

This passage rings with auctorial approval. In it we find a moral argument so armor-plated as to appear impregnable against stress. The long view, if imaginatively and emotionally held, is a shield against the worst temptations of the present moment. At least it is meant to be a shield: like David pondering his problem with Dora, Maggie cannot bear to imagine that unrelenting discipline might not extinguish unwanted feelings at their root ("it would have been quenched at once"). Such an argument, in its complete reliance on mediation, simply denies legitimacy to the stresses of actual experience. A fortified mind and heart will be proof against them. (No room here for the lateral, life-furthering evasions of David and Arthur and Amy: Maggie's options are honor or dishonor, nothing intermediate.) The model for such virtue, notwithstanding minor reservations voiced by Philip Wakem, is the crucified Christ of Thomas à Kempis, the figure of unrelenting self-transcendence.[7] Ardent Maggie Tulliver, with

---

[7] As many critics have noted, Philip Wakem identifies the element of desperation in Maggie's attempt at self-abnegation: ". . . you are shutting yourself up in a narrow self-delusive fanaticism. . . . Stupefaction is not resignation: and

her beautiful arms, her exquisite eyes, her luxuriant hair, is never granted a more generous morality than the rigorous extirpation of desire: "she saw it face to face now—that sad patient loving strength which holds the clue of life—and saw that the thorns were for ever pressing on its brow" (413).

Any yearning on her part toward physical gratification is perceived as a kind of dream-like vertigo, a potential dissolution of the self. The impulse to yield to Stephen "is attended with a less vivid consciousness than resistance; it is the partial sleep of thought; it is the submergence of our own personality by another" (410). If this cautionary passage about physical yielding is compared to the cheerful ones that contemplate physical self-sacrifice to Philip ("He was given to me that I might make his lot less hard" [419]), one sees that, for Eliot, an irreducible kernel of spiritual identity is ratified in the very act of bodily self-denial, whereas who can gauge the vertiginous transformations of self that might occur in physical fulfillment? Whatever the self may be, wherever it be "located," it knows itself and is assessed in Eliot's world only through its accumulating ledger of moral transactions—a ledger keyed to the paradigm of a self-subduing, virtually discarnate Jesus Christ.[8]

---

it is stupefaction to remain in ignorance. . . . *You* are not resigned: you are only trying to stupefy yourself" (288). Few critics go on to note the bleakness of Maggie's response: ". . . she felt there was some truth in what Philip said, and yet there was a deeper consciousness that, for any immediate application it had to her conduct, it was no better than falsity" (288). Maggie's response makes it clear that, whatever the theoretical limitations to either the posture of Kempis-like resignation or her grasp of it, she sees no other posture practicably available. Her creator certainly does not suggest any other. For a more general discussion of this dilemma from the perspective of Eliot's own dilemma as a woman writer— her simultaneous endorsement and repression of her heroines' incarnate impulses—see Sandra Gilbert and Susan Gubar, 443-535.

[8] Elaine Showalter shrewdly identifies Maggie's inability to own her desire as *hers*, and therefore to permit its force to enter the silent discourse of her self-understanding: "When Maggie *does* feel sexually attracted to a man, she has no vocabulary for her emotions and must define her physical excitement as 'love'; she must pretend that Stephen Guest has kidnapped her and that she is helplessly drifting away, when it is obvious that they are colluding in the elopement. Even after her awakening in the boat, when she makes the decision to resist Stephen, Maggie cannot move toward a purposeful construction of her life" (128).

If Maggie is most lovingly perceived by others in the language of metamorphosis, as a nymph or a Hamadryad, so much the worse, finally, for her; this moving and sensuous picture has no option but to fit the static moral diagram of renunciation.[9] "The great problem of the shifting relation between passion and duty is clear to no man who is capable of apprehending it" (437), Eliot tells us with superb liberality. But Maggie's paralyzing self-despair—her inability either to eradicate bodily desire or to forgive herself for this "failure"—seems to many readers to be presented less as a morally unclear instance of that "great problem" than as an exacerbated thumb-screwing to Thomas à Kempis:

> It was the practice of our venerable ancestors to apply that ingenious instrument the thumb-screw, and to tighten and tighten it in order to elicit non-existent facts; they had a fixed opinion to begin with, that the facts were existent, and what had they to do but to tighten the thumb-screw? (148-49)

❧

TO SUMMARIZE, then: *The Mill on the Floss* exhibits a cluster of formal and thematic incompatibilities. A morality of immediate generosity is at odds with one of prudent consideration. Further, certain experiences rendered and assessed in their immediacy differ widely from the same experiences viewed nostalgically, calmly, at a distance. The unconditional paradigm of Christ-like self-extirpation is pressed upon an emotional drama whose moment-by-moment enactment strongly resists that paradigm. Finally, there is the gap between a narrative thoroughly embedded in the convention of continuous public time and an apocalyptic conclusion that violates the narrative's established temporality. The wisdom of recollected time cannot be made to superimpose on either the urgency of instantaneous time or the fantasy of transcendent timelessness. In each case these incompatibilities reveal a breach between the sense of immediate ex-

---

[9] I owe this association of Maggie with the language of metamorphosis to Auerbach.

perience, on the one hand, and judicious paradigms of sanity and morality proffered by a more detached overview, on the other.

The flood, in conclusion, is the unpersuasive repudiation of the picture by the diagram. Unpersuasive because not rooted in the temporal moral dilemma which it comes to conclude; necessary because Eliot can find no vantage point within the realm of the probable to retreat to, in order to command a morally satisfying overview and so compose the ledger of Maggie's life. Those devastating love-scenes are sufficiently disruptive to prevent a thematic recuperation by the wise voice with the long view. The immediate experience has proved unassimilable, and Maggie's return to St Ogg's has been pure misery, despite desperate attempts to convert it into retrospective wisdom: "Surely there was something taught her by this experience of great need; and she must be learning a secret of human tenderness and long-suffering, that the less erring could hardly know?" (453) Her plea is answered only, and immediately, by the "startling sensation of sudden cold about her knees and feet: it was water flowing under her" (454).

A fully humiliated Maggie would succumb to suicide or a cheerless aftermath. A fully triumphant Maggie would retrieve the situation and manage to refresh the conditions that remain to her with her moral ardor. We find neither of these but a translation of realistic fiction into evasive fantasy, in which Maggie is simultaneously celebrated by the ardent George Eliot, scourged by the judicious George Eliot, and concealed from view by the single yet not unified George Eliot who contains both these others. The author can literally no longer imagine her heroine's life, and she thus fails to meet her own standards of validation: the credible aftermath of a decisive action, the reverberations it must inevitably make.

In place of aftermath and reverberations we find an "undoing." Point by point Maggie is permitted by Eliot to undo the staining effects of her earlier trial by water: she is "revirginized." This time the force she is irresistibly borne by is holy and spiritual rather than secular and bodily; the union it takes her to is the regressive and pastoral one with Tom rather than the adult and troubling one with Stephen. The vicissitudes of the flesh and

blood Maggie are no longer imaginatively sustained by her author. The novel ends with a lame overview of her that has imposed on no one: the image of Maggie fructifying (like Dorothea
later) in the continuing lives of Lucy, Stephen, and Philip. Surely
we want to know not this but something else: the adult life of
that impulsive and spendthrift child who pushed Lucy into the
mud and had the bad luck later on to fall passionately in love
with Stephen Guest. It is a story that George Eliot was never
able to tell. She came nearest, however, not in the sublimities of
Dorothea Brooke but in the iridescence of Gwendolen Harleth.

"A GREAT DEAL OF SLOW POISONING": *DANIEL DERONDA*

"Whatever uneasiness a growing conscience had created, was
disregarded as an ailment might have been, amidst the gratification of that ambitious vanity and desire for luxury within her
which it would take a great deal of slow poisoning to kill" (401).
Eliot's metaphor of poisoning points to one of the less discussed
problems in *Daniel Deronda*: the mode of Gwendolen Harleth's
moral education. If education is taken in its root sense of leading
out the spirit, then, whatever the chastening and reform of original impulse be required, the spirit is to be finally, in some measure, liberated. There should occur within the subject an increase—however painful the process—of personal resources. But
Eliot's notion of "a growing conscience" is posited upon a prior
violation; the metaphor of poisoning suggests a war upon the
subject's faculties, essentially an attempt to extirpate them. She
singles out "ambitious vanity and a desire for luxury" as the objects to receive "slow poisoning," but it is hard to identify any
of Gwendolen's faculties that Eliot exempts from this regime.
The following pages seek to explore the implications of an auctorial treatment of Gwendolen conducted under the somber banner of the novel's motto: "Let thy chief terror be of thine own
soul."[1]

[1] As long ago as 1885 Lord Acton noted, sympathetically but firmly, Eliot's
undeviating insistence on punishment: ". . . retribution is the constant theme and
motive for her art. . . . She was firmly persuaded that the postponement of the
reckoning blunts the edge of remorse, and that repentance, which ought to be

ↄ⤸

ALTHOUGH Deronda himself enters this argument only tangentially and toward the end, the "Gwendolen subject" cannot be understood without reference to the "Deronda subject." Since the subtle problems of the former are bound up with the gross problems of the latter, those larger problems must first be briefly established to orient the later discussion of Gwendolen. As will be clear, I join those critics who insist on the novel's indivisibility, as well as those who deplore the failures of execution (and partly of conception) in the Jewish strand of the novel. About these failures a great deal has been written, and it would be hard to improve on Barbara Hardy's remarks in her Introduction to the Penguin edition:

> The psychology and style of the Jewish characters, notably Mirah, Daniel, and Mordecai is simplified and idealized. The language of Mordecai is inflated and visionary, and the style of Mirah in every way sentimental. Daniel is a very interesting result of imaginative effort straining and almost, but not quite, succeeding. These ideal creatures are representative of a Semitic world placed in ideal contrast to a very sharply satirized world of English genteel and Gentile society. (15)

Having conceded this much, Hardy nevertheless goes on to compare Eliot with Tolstoy in her attempt to combine "philosophical and general writing with the vividness and movement of psychological realism" (25). The comparison is flattering to Eliot but unpersuasive. The historical pondering of Pierre or Andrew or Levin (unlike that of Deronda and, *a fortiori*, Mordecai) is seamlessly fused with their psychological reality. And the political career of Kutuzov—at once fictive and historical, private and public—is simply beyond Eliot's range. The point needs stressing because individual destiny and public history—though

---

submission to just punishment, proved by the test of confession, means more commonly the endeavour to elude it" (156). More speculatively, Jean Sudrann has argued in a recent essay that the theme of terror in *Deronda* expresses, not Eliot's complacent moralizing at the expense of her character, but their shared (and quite modern) dread of self-dissolution: the failure of the self to sustain, under pressure, its sense of identity, and thus its inevitable fall into alienation.

Eliot insists on their connection—remain insecurely integrated in *Daniel Deronda*. The private and the political elements neither stand alone nor are successfully interfused. A few passages—one from Eliot's 1856 review of Riehl, two from *Deronda* itself—may help to identify Eliot's normative position in this matter of public and private, as well as silhouette her divergence from the norm in her last novel. I begin with the review:

> He [Riehl] sees in European society *incarnate history*, and any attempt to disengage it from its historical elements must, he believes, be simply destructive of social vitality. What has grown up historically can only die out historically, by the gradual operation of necessary laws. The external conditions which society has inherited from the past are but the manifestations of inherited internal conditions in the human beings who compose it; the internal conditions and the external are related to each other as the organism and its medium, and development can only take place by the gradual consentaneous development of both. ("The Natural History of German Life," 287)

Critics agree that Eliot's conservative realism has nowhere been better glossed than in these comments. In their light we can specify what is lacking in the novel itself: the patiently articulated interweaving of action and reaction, gesture and response, ardent will and chastening context, that must characterize all political phenomena. Set against this sober passage, the Zionist strand of the novel appears in its true lineaments, as a romance that stresses the zeal of the "organism" while minimizing the "medium"—the social context—within which that organism has its reality.[2] Unwilling either to locate Mordecai's vision within its

---

[2] Leon Gottfried argues, in my view unanswerably, that the Deronda strand of the novel bears all the marks of romance. Thus the gap between the English and Zionist worlds is not only social, psychological, and moral; it is also generic: "But in his life apart from Gwendolen Deronda exists, like most heroes of romance, in a world governed by a prefigurative pattern of muffled births, secrets, omens, mystic talismans, clairvoyant recognitions, mysterious heralds, typological recurrence, ritual deaths, rebirths, initiations, and apotheoses" ("Structure and Genre in *Daniel Deronda*," 168).

larger European context or to ground it in its immediate English context, Eliot is reduced to rendering that vision as, mainly, fervent desire. Yet she excepts it from the critical scrutiny to which she elsewhere (and so tellingly) exposes fervent desire.

Within the novel itself the problematic intersection of a world-shattering destiny with the texture of humble, individual lives is directly addressed:

> But the fervor of sympathy with which we contemplate a grandiose martyrdom is feeble compared with the enthusiasm that keeps unslacked where there is no danger, no challenge—nothing but impartial mid-day falling on commonplace, perhaps half-repulsive, objects which are really the beloved ideas made flesh. . . . To glory in a prophetic vision of knowledge covering the earth, is an easier exercise . . . than to see its beginnings in newspaper placards, staring at you from a bridge beyond the cornfields. . . . (431)

This passage, occurring five pages before his introduction, is meant to prepare us for Mordecai, but the figure it point by point anticipates actually exists nowhere in the novel: a "commonplace, perhaps half-repulsive" man, immersed as unquestionably in his present-day London conditions as in the great historical event in the making. Such a figure is not Mordecai: a man the opposite of "commonplace," and one who may "repulse" us in ways more profound than any superficial ones of bearing intended by his author. Here is Deronda's first vision of Mordecai:

> But instead of the ordinary tradesman, he saw . . . a figure that was somewhat startling in its unusualness . . . the thought glanced through Deronda that precisely such a physiognomy as that might possibly have been seen in a prophet of the Exile, or in some New Hebrew poet of the medieval time. (436)

Mordecai never recovers from the romance of this description. Though she gives him a sister and a father and an English tongue, Eliot can succeed neither in dramatizing his identity as brother or son, nor in rendering his voice in credible English. She has obviously never "seen" him nor "heard" him speak. He

never budges from his uncommon role of consumptive prophet—
there is none else like Mordecai—and what this unfortunately
means for *Daniel Deronda* is that other destinies are judged to
succeed or fail by moral comparison with his. Moral issues must
approach Mordecaian sublimity or risk being dismissed as trivial
play. Thus the pious Mirah declaims to Mrs. Meyrick, "Is this
world and all the life upon it only like a farce or a vaudeville,
where you find no great meanings? Why then are there tragedies
and grand operas, where men do difficult things and choose to
suffer? I think it is silly to speak of all things as a joke" (257).
Only Hans Meyrick (and he gets upbraided for it) dares to take
Mirah with even a tinge of irony.[3] The implicit crudeness of her
moral world—its unnuanced polarization into either farce or
tragedy—is disturbingly in force throughout much of *Daniel Deronda*. In a word, despite Eliot's normative conviction that "commonplace . . . objects . . . are really the beloved ideas made flesh,"
the commonplace to be found in contemporary England is rendered as strictly barren, closed to moral fermentation.[4]

Gascoignes, Arrowpoints, Mallingers, Grandcourt—these
figures are superbly realized; yet, for better or worse, they remain
morally static. Their virtues and vices, once laid out for us, neither alter nor undergo compelling trial. Even the positive and
un-English (or superficially English) figures—Klesmer, Mordecai, Mirah, the Meyricks—do not struggle for their virtue; they
are, as it were, habitually admirable. Gwendolen is of course the
central exception; her life is wonderfully open to change. The
point is that, given the moral rigidity of the context I have sketched
out, her life is open to change only in the direction identified in

[3] Meyrick to Deronda: "Mirah takes it [the story of Berenice] as a tragic
parable, and cries to think what the penitent Berenice suffered as she wandered
back to Jerusalem and sat desolate amidst desolation. That was her own phrase.
I couldn't find it in my heart to tell her I invented that part of the story" (515).
Meyrick's delicious awareness of Mirah's penchant for grand-opera phrases is
allowed expression, alas, only this once. For more than one would ever guess to
be implicit in Meyrick's comic mode, see Cynthia Chase, "The Decomposition
of the Elephants: Double-Reading: *Daniel Deronda*."

[4] For further commentary on the increasing rift between Eliot's moral aspirations in the 1870's and her sense of the contemporary English scene, consult
U. C. Knoepflmacher (72-148) and Graham Martin.

Mordecai, the passage through sublime self-transcendence. This is a passage required of no one else in the novel, and perhaps for this reason not persuasively undergone by Gwendolen.

If one compares the richer traffic of moral experience in *Middlemarch*—the nuanced range of moral dilemma and transformation embodied in different ways in Fred and Rosamond Vincy, in Bulstrode and Mrs. Bulstrode, in Casaubon, Lydgate, Ladislaw, and Dorothea—one finds in the earlier novel that moral crisis is enigmatic and ubiquitous.[5] And it issues into an array of human configurations that fall well between the extremes of farce and grand tragedy. Such a generous context of moral travail is absent from *Daniel Deronda*, and Gwendolen must become saint-like on the pattern of Mordecai or stand convicted of a worldly "small life" (876).

ֶ‍ֶ

"IN CREATING Gwendolen," Calvin Bedient writes, "George Eliot's imagination gave birth to a character who both exceeds and resists her novel's predetermined moral content, who stands out against it as a bonfire stands out against moonlight. . . . She is essentially independent of her predestined role, and she comes to us as absorbing, delightful, amusing, rather than ripe for evil" (58-59). Bedient's statement is as saucy as it is welcome, and it succeeds in getting the priorities right. Gwendolen, as Eliot renders her, is essentially charming and vivacious; and the egoism that nourishes this vitality constitutes a flaw for which she will more than adequately pay.

A bit like Hetty rather than Rosamond—but more imaginative and sensitive to the impressions of others than either of them—Gwendolen has her true sister in Maggie Tulliver, Eliot's only other heroine to exhibit a zest for life and an energized capacity for experience that exceed the uses the author knows to make of them. They are her two most brilliantly "unexhausted" creations. Maggie is ridden with self-doubt, whereas Gwendolen

---

[5] Knoepflmacher explores this contrast at some length, though for him it does not tell against *Daniel Deronda* (119-28).

is only tinged with it; Maggie overflows with love, whereas Gwendolen fears herself to be incapable of it. But both share a spellbinding intensity—they are irrepressible, thoroughly embodied figures of energy.

In Maggie that energy elicits confusing responses from Eliot, and I have already suggested the mixture of endorsement and attack in her portrait. Gwendolen comes fifteen years later in Eliot's career, and she is correspondingly freer of her creator's biographical experience, a more distinct and masterly characterization. This being so, the issue I speak of is even more mysterious than the Maggie-issue, for Gwendolen could not so charm us, as Bedient says, if she did not charm Eliot too. We thus have a figure whose "iridescence" strongly suggests other feelings, other responses, other possibilities than the heavily directed course of remorse, anger, and self-confounding paralysis on which Eliot makes her embark.

It is difficult to point to decisive instances of Gwendolen's "iridescence," but one may approach this trait through an explanation which for Eliot herself "may seem to lie quite on the surface:—in her beauty, a certain unusualness about her, a decision of will which made itself felt in her graceful movements and clear unhesitating tones, so that if she came into the room on a rainy day when everyone else was flaccid and the use of things in general was not apparent to them, there seemed to be a sudden, sufficient reason for keeping up the forms of life . . ." (71). Her life matters to her in her moment-by-moment display of it, though, it is true, she has no long-range purpose to live for, and her sense of relationships is radically defective. We watch her continuously express her life-energies. Where she is, there is attention, amusement, displeasure. This immediate deployment of energies is of course what Eliot compellingly renders in every description of Gwendolen, but what she has no intention of admiring. Gwendolen's style is judged as vanity, caprice, self-indulgence, artifice. It is never taken as that aesthetic delight in self-performance which is expressed through spontaneous role-playing. Gwendolen makes scenes, she dramatizes herself. Though this novel proposes—in the expert voice of Klesmer—a low estimate of her theatrical talent, she in fact plays herself with un-failing virtuosity.[6]

In this regard Mirah provides an apt comparison: ". . . and I knew that my acting was not good except when it was not really acting, but the part was one that I could be myself in, and some feeling within me carried me along" (258). Mirah is not by vocation an actress at all. She is openly or covertly her uni-vocal moral self at all times; she has only one tone. Gwendolen, by contrast, is intrinsically histrionic, gesticulative. She acts out—and in so doing makes more of—her occasions. Because this "ge-nius" is ridden with ego and encrusted with conventional ma-neuvers, Klesmer pronounces her to be of slender promise. In his view (a limited one, but wholly endorsed by the author), "genius at first is little more than a great capacity for receiving discipline" (300). To attain excellence, "you must know what you have to strive for, and then you must subdue your mind and body to unbroken discipline" (299). As defined by Klesmer (and implicitly by Eliot), achievement results from self-subdual by hard training to an objective *métier*. Essentially, genius is controlled receptivity. Missing in both definitions—and missing because contaminated by egoism—is inward ardor and capacity, unpre-dictable talent and an energized will to express it. How revealing it is that Mary Ann Evans would have us believe that she became George Eliot by dint of nothing more problematic than disci-pline and self-subdual.[7]

Gwendolen's propensities are assessed at a low level in the professional world of *Daniel Deronda*; in the feminine world they are positively dangerous. Consider the portraits of women in this novel: they are as submissive (and successful) or rebellious (and miserable) a group as Eliot ever assembled.[8] Mrs. Gascoigne and

[6] This paragraph is heavily indebted to Bedient's brilliant commentary on Gwendolen.

[7] For discussion of the internal difficulties that Mary Ann Evans did expe-rience in becoming George Eliot—her protracted hesitancy, as a woman, to as-sume the perquisites of her own authority—see Redinger and Gilbert and Gubar.

[8] The all-important exception is Catherine Arrowpoint. The scene of Kles-mer's proposal and the ensuing family confrontation (Chapter 22) is done with magnificent authority. Catherine, however, never reappears in the novel—she is

Lady Mallinger are repetitively thankful to be their husbands' appendages; neither dares venture an independent sentiment. Mrs. Davilow, nearly wrecked by two bad marriages, is yet sufficiently resigned to advise her daughter, "Marriage is the only happy state for a woman, as I trust you will prove" (58). Along with her sister, she seeks refuge in Gascoigne's masculine wisdom. Anna, we see, is humbly waiting to meet another Rex toward whom she can devote herself unstintingly. As for self-expression, "I am not at all clever, and I never know what to say. It seems so useless to say what everybody knows, and I can think of nothing else, except what papa says" (62). The Meyrick girls divide their devotion between Hans and Deronda, while Mirah divides hers between Mordecai and Deronda. Her professional life appears less as a source of personal fulfillment than as an excurse compelled by hardship and to be happily ended by marriage to Deronda.

Those women who go beyond the cuture's norms to express their own desire—Daniel's mother Alcharisi and Lydia Glasher—appear as sinister pendants to Gwendolen's urge to egoistic (and latently self-destructive) self-realization. The wisdom of the Jewish fathers "is the expression of something stronger, with deeper, farther-spreading roots" (727) than the personal will of Alcharisi to express her own talents. Lydia Glasher, for her part, is Eliot's most vivid example of the desperate aftermath of marital infidelity. Having forsaken her husband, she has lost all grounds of legitimacy. She is so psychically and economically cramped by this action and its consequences that she desires nothing more than marriage with a man who regularly degrades her. Indeed, one of the remarkable elements of *Daniel Deronda*'s plot structure—to which I now turn—is the multiple role played by Lydia Glasher in determining the shape and meaning of Gwendolen's career.

One can begin by examining the previous union between Lydia and Grandcourt. In a startlingly unanticipated passage we learn that "Grandcourt had never disentangled himself from Mrs.

---

at best an absent exemplar—and she is in any case the sole exception, a figure whom Eliot handles admirably but peripherally.

Glasher. His passion for her had been the strongest and most lasting he had ever known; and though it was now as dead as the music of a cracked flute, it had left a certain dull disposedness . . ." (386). Grandcourt is richly drawn, and one grants (though with some surprise) the existence of this earlier passion, but no reader almost four hundred pages into the novel scents in him at present "a certain dull disposedness." This central chapter between the former lovers (chapter 30) certainly indicates no pliancy toward Lydia Glasher. He does not like scenes, and she thus preserves her resolve to deliver the diamonds in her own fashion. But, as Calvin Bedient remarks, nothing in their dramatized relationship and its desiccated history suggests any likelihood of their marriage (63 ff). Why, then, does Eliot repeatedly stress this possibility?

Its immediate effect is to make Grandcourt seem desirable, or—more accurately—to make legitimacy seem desirable. We hear often that Lydia has a prior right to him; we hear nothing of the indisputable inner fact we have already assimilated: that marriage to Grandcourt can only be misery to anyone capable of feeling the effects of his ego. Thus to the reader Lydia appears, in her illicit desperation, as a prominent instance of Eliot's gallery of egoistic women who have foundered in their rebellion against the norms. To Gwendolen she appears as something else, as the stark indictment of Gwendolen's own immorality: "I have thrust out others—I have made my gain out of their loss—tried to make it—tried. And I must go on, I can't alter it" (506).

By stressing Lydia's right to Grandcourt, Eliot emphasizes not what is wrong in Grandcourt himself but what is wrong in Gwendolen's taking him: her immoral egoism and her paralyzing awareness of this wrongdoing. The never-questioned "sinfulness" of Gwendolen's behavior provides the criterion of all of Deronda's counsel: "Take the present suffering as a painful letting in of light. You are conscious of more beyond the round of your own inclinations—you know more of the way in which your life presses on others, and their life on yours. I don't think you could have escaped the painful process in some form or other" (508). Gwendolen tries to object—"But it is a very cruel form"— yet Deronda does not alter his pronouncement a jot. The deeper meaning of Lydia's role in Gwendolen's drama may now emerge. Lydia neutralizes the depravity of Grandcourt. Eliot so structures her plot that the highlighted abuse is between Gwendolen and Lydia ("I have made my gain out of their loss"), the subordinate one between Grandcourt and Gwendolen. Gwendolen has sinned by egoism, and Grandcourt simply gets subsumed with Lydia as "some form or other" through which she must learn that her life impinges on others. In this way an exquisite psychological drama is pre-empted by a stark moral paradigm.[9] We may feel (we do feel) the intolerable weight of Grandcourt's oppression but—because of Lydia—there is no legitimacy in Gwendolen's increasingly desperate response. In the sustained scrutiny that Deronda devotes to Gwendolen's suffering there is, extraordinarily, no admission of Grandcourt's culpability. Instead he tells her: "Turn your fear into a safeguard. Keep your dread fixed on the idea of increasing that remorse which is so bitter to you. . . . It may make consequences passionately present to you" (509).[10] Essentially this means, learn to bear your pain, don't be moved by it recklessly to alter your circumstances.

Gwendolen is drawn toward rebellion, but she remains powerless: "She longed to do it. But she might as well have tried to defy the texture of her nerves and the palpitation of her heart. Her husband had a ghostly army at his back . . ." (503). That "ghostly army" is Lydia Glasher and her children; Gwendolen's usurpation of their rights has removed all justification of outrage: "Search where she would in her consciousness, she found no plea to justify a plaint. Any romantic illusions she had had in marrying this man had turned on her power of using him as she liked. He was using her as he liked" (659). One may grant the strength of this moral equation and yet lament its psychological reduc-

[9] Cf. Carole Robinson: "If the dilemma which George Eliot invented for Gwendolen Harleth is a measure of the magnanimity of her genius, the moral lesson which she insisted upon extracting from this true dilemma falsifies the complexity of her vision" (287).

[10] Deronda is so blinkered by his own sublimity that "the thought that urged itself foremost was—'Confess everything to your husband; leave nothing concealed' " (673). A man who thus counsels Gwendolen at this state of her crisis has failed to understand her dilemma.

tiveness. Their egoism is not of the same kind—his is relentlessly sadistic, hers capricious and thoughtless—and his day-to-day treatment of her is incomparable rougher than hers of him. The fact is that Grandcourt bullies Gwendolen with impunity because Eliot has made illicit any protest against bullying.

The energy that is essentially Gwendolen, under this regimen, alters not in substance but only in form; she sickens with rage and consequent guilt for her rage. Her wrath—now that she has been instructed by Deronda to feel others' pain more, her own less—is deprived of expression and can only increase. Eliot, however, shrouds that wrath even as she insists on it, suggesting within Gwendolen lurid passions, cloaked in the imagery of serpents and demons, colored in Gothic tones. Gwendolen simultaneously imagines murdering—and being murdered by— her husband: ". . . that Grandcourt should die . . . the thought [of] his death was the only possible deliverance for her . . . the thought of his dying would not subsist: it turned as with a dream-change into the terror that she should die with his throttling fingers on her neck avenging that thought" (668-69).[11]

In the moral economy of *Daniel Deronda* there is, awkwardly, no exit from this dilemma but death. Desertion of Grandcourt is considered briefly, but Gwendolen's pride and vanity serve to dissuade her. More dissuasive is "her capability of rectitude [that] told her again and again that she had no right to complain of her contract, or to withdraw from it. And always among the images that drove her back to submission was Deronda" (665). It seems that Eliot's conscience cannot permit Gwendolen to leave Grandcourt, while Eliot's imagination cannot require her to live with him. The solution is a piece of plotting whose clumsiness is as notable as is its necessity. Grandcourt must die; Gwendolen cannot kill him but must feel distraught for having wanted to do so. She is both innocent and guilty, entitled to her modest inheritance but sentenced to remorse. His death is incredible as an accident and inadmissible as a murder; the alternative to death must have struck Eliot as even worse.

[11] The fullest expression of these fears and desires occurs just before the fatal accident. See the end of Chapter 54.

One may surmise that such an alternative would have required, within Eliot, an imaginative capacity to explore anger and acknowledge its occasional legitimacy. Put too baldly, she would have had to recognize the polymorphous identity of the incarnate self's energies, from secular rage to spiritual aspiration. Unable or unwilling to embark on such imaginings, Eliot has Deronda urge Gwendolen to bear up, the repressed anger that won't disappear being described as demonic visitation. The marital scene can neither alter nor be endured: it explodes.

In this "education" of Gwendolen one recognizes something other than comprehensive sympathy. "The truth is," Bedient claims, "that the only certain injury resulting from Gwendolen's marriage is to herself. But this George Eliot ignores; it is of no moral interest to her" (64). Eliot does not quite ignore Gwendolen's suffering. Rather, she sees it as deserved and therefore—unlike that of the Jews—less in need of sympathetic commentary and exploration. Thus Gwendolen's anguish is characteristically perceived from Deronda's vantage point, and Eliot stresses his pain in their encounters rather than hers:

> "And now—will you forsake me?"
> Her hands . . . were now helplessly relaxed and trembling on the arm of her chair. . . . He took one of her hands, and clasped it as if they were going to walk together like two children: it was the only way in which he could answer, "I will not forsake you." And all the while he felt as if he were putting his name to a blank paper which might be filled up terribly. Their attitude, his averted face with its expression of a suffering which he was solemnly resolved to undergo. . . . (755)

Six pages before the end of the novel the same scene recurs:

> "I said I should be forsaken. I have been a cruel woman. And I am forsaken."
> Deronda's anguish was intolerable. He could not help himself. He seized her outstretched hands and held them together and kneeled at her feet. She was the victim of his happiness. (877)

101

Both scenes are moving, but something is awry in their conception. Deronda's grief as helpless witness cannot be equivalent to Gwendolen's as suffering protagonist, yet Eliot insists on Deronda's pain rather than on Gwendolen's. It is as though what he might say to her were more weighty than what she had undergone. Gwendolen is not "the victim of his happiness": the phrase betrays a radical suspicion of happiness itself—a suspicion that no one is entitled to it—rather than a just relation between her state and his. Over eight hundred pages have insisted that Gwendolen is a victim of her own egoism, not of Deronda's aspirations, and Eliot has been at some pains to winnow their relationship of all motives but need and generosity. Indeed, Deronda has all too little to say to Gwendolen, and the narrative begins to suffer from the thinness of their encounters, each striking the same note of plea and counsel. Eliot brings these two characters repeatedly together, but she has not richly related them, just as she has not brought into compelling interpenetration the worlds of Zionist aspiration and English quotidian life.

"The thing for mankind to know is, not what are the motives and influences which the moralist thinks *ought* to act on the labourer or the artisan, but what are the motives and influences which *do* act on him" ("The Natural History of German Life," 271). So Eliot wrote in her essay on Riehl, and the words reveal something about the gap between Gwendolen's problem and Eliot's solution. The moral regime enforced upon the heroine is an inimical physic, opposed to the central "iridescence" of her personality. She is overcome, not cured, by it. Despite repeated assertions that Gwendolen will live, we have no sense of what that life could be.[12] *Daniel Deronda* is not open-ended in the

[12] The irresolution of Gwendolen's future is vacuous rather than rich with implication. In the same way, Deronda's coming voyage to the East suffers from a portentous vagueness made comic (as Henry James realized) by the Mallingers' utterly precise gift of "a complete equipment for Eastern travel" (881). Earlier in the novel Eliot could afford to satirize such vagueness:

Rex: "If you would allow me a small outfit, I should like to go to the colonies and work on the land there." Rex thought the vagueness of the phrase prudential; "the colonies" necessarily embracing more advantages, and being less capable of being rebutted on a single ground than any particular settlement. (119)

Gwendolen: "I would rather emigrate than be a governess." What it precisely was to emigrate, Gwendolen was not called on to explain. (276)

manner of James's *Portrait*, in which the essential elements of Isabel's character are tried but still intact, though her future be unclear. Rather, Gwendolen is herself in pieces, notwithstanding claims for future health. Not just her vanity but her entire psychic economy has been subjected to "a great deal of slow poisoning." One can only wonder what rooted virtues remain in her to bloom.

PART TWO

Late-Victorian: Tragic Encounters

≥• IN THE FICTION of Hardy and Conrad trouble emerges everywhere, and not just (not even mainly) sexual trouble. Tess and Jude, Jim and Nostromo, move through inner and outer landscapes of mounting unpredictability. They know how to read neither themselves nor their careers. Their motives are scripted in a cultural idiom that, they discover under stress, has lost its currency.

The ratio of convention to surprise had shifted massively since the mid-Victorian novels of Dickens and Eliot. There the cultural patterns of identity, aspiration, and career—though threatened—remained reassuringly in place. Truant protagonists maneuvered as best they could to achieve alignment. Here (in Hardy and Conrad) the social arrangements designed to domesticate experience cannot sustain the burdens unexpectedly placed upon them, yet the protagonist is as unable to get clear of these arrangements as he is incapable of making them function. Love and marriage, education and work—these pivotal arenas of societal life have become problematic, unnegotiable spaces. Protagonists in Hardy and Conrad invariably falter; many commit suicide. The purpose of Part Two is to find out in what ways—and why—the life-experiences undergone by the protagonists have become so unlike the life-models sanctioned by society as to lead to despair.[1]

---

[1] "Late-Victorian" is an appellation that many will hesitate to apply to Conrad. I use it, nevertheless, because the skepticism of Conrad's corrosively modern intellect is registered in his work mainly as a negative and unwanted force. The only values he would wish to honor are "Victorian," although his access to them is troublingly Modernist.

Three ❧ Hardy: "Full-Hearted Evensong"

THE SIMPLEST way to orient my commentary on *Tess of the d'Urbervilles* is to juxtapose it against Lionel Johnson's well-known stricture (at the conclusion of his study of Hardy):

> . . . the world was very strong; her conscience was blinded and bewildered; she did some things nobly, and some despairingly: but there is nothing . . . to suggest that she was wholly an irresponsible victim of her own temperament, and of adverse circumstances. . . . Like Maggie Tulliver, Tess might have gone to Thomas à Kempis: one of the very few writers, whom experience does not prove untrue. She went through fire and water, and made no true use of them: she is pitiable, but not admirable. (248-49)

These are cogent and thoughtful remarks, but they seem to me fundamentally amiss. The judgmental bias is strong in them, and that bias is one of immaculateness. "The world" is a place that one is meant to be superior to; Maggie Tulliver succeeded better than Tess at this task, and she is therefore "admirable." By positing Kempis-like self-transcendence as the model of the self, Johnson fails to see that *Tess* is a novel not of failed transcendence but of tragically achieved immersion. Her violated virginity radiates this novel's values, just as Maggie's intact virginity radiates that novel's values. The kindred issue of virginity serves to

108

emphasize the changes in setting, psychology, and plot that we find when we move from Eliot to Hardy. *Tess of the d'Urbervilles* is the story neither of a pure nor of an impure woman: it is the story of an *embodied* woman whose career cuts athwart and exposes transcendental notions of good and evil.

The world outside the self, as Eliot imagines it, resists the transforming moral energies of her protagonists, but it does not ultimately negate them. The wide-awake altruistic decency of figures like Adam Bede, Romola, Felix Holt, Mary Garth, and Daniel Deronda encounters grating setbacks but not defeat. Lydgate's "spots of commonness" are just that—local blemishes rather than cosmic ill—and they are reformable, if not eradicable. Thus one may say of Eliot's world what cannot be said of Hardy's: that the struggle of the moral life is its dominant concern, and that this struggle may in a significant measure succeed, when conducted with humility, sympathy, and a perseverance at once ardent and alert. Maggie and Gwendolen appear in this study because they are suggestive exceptions to the moral norm thus sketched out. What they suggest is that the career of ardent human energy is more wayward, more vulnerable to stresses within and without, than can be conveyed in the set of values through which Eliot chooses to read that career. The embodied behavior of Maggie and Gwendolen, as I have tried to show, means something other and more than Eliot is prepared to say.

In Hardy, by way of contrast, this failure of behavior to square with a paradigm of immaculate values is anything but a novelistic embarrassment: it is the enabling premise of his mature art. He has simply taken some salient characteristics of the nineteenth-century intellectual's view of the natural world—its infinitely gradated causality, its meaningless interpenetration of forces, its play of unsanctioned energy—and found them at work in the human world as well. As J.I.M. Stewart says, "What was felt as potentially subversive in Hardy was not his universe . . . but his predisposition to let his sense of that universe act, however cautiously, upon areas of experience hitherto fenced off because of the explosive material apprehended as buried there" (164). This penetration of the natural into the human results in Hardy's showing us, supremely in *Tess*, "what the woman is—what she

IS—inhumanly, physiologically, materially."[1] More, he shows us this against the human background of what the woman poignantly wills herself to be. The tension within Tess between the "natural" and the "human" is the novel's characteristic note. As Angel tells his mother, with implications he himself is to suffer but never to grasp, "we are all children of the soil" (392). It is a parentage as unsought and uncomfortable as it is inalienable. In Hardy's unsentimental world the soil is simply hostile to the projects of human consciousness. Successful adaptation occurs only at the end, in the consciousless repose of death.[2]

&

REPOSE, the relaxation of a vigilant scrutiny: these are the morally charged terms in which Eliot invites us to evaluate Maggie's lapse with Stephen Guest. Johnson (and a host of critics after him) uses the same framework to judge Tess's lapse with Alec d'Urberville. The two scenes, however, are shaped to different purposes. A metaphoric lapsing in *The Mill on the Floss* is replaced in *Tess of the d'Urbervilles* by literal unconsciousness. Before her intercourse with Alec, Tess sinks into sleep, ringed round and penetrated by the conditions of maculate nature:

> She was silent, and the horse ambled along for a considerable distance, till a faint luminous fog, which had hung in the hollows all the evening, became general and enveloped them. . . . She was inexpressibly weary. . . . By this time the moon had quite gone down, and partly on account of the

[1] The phrase belongs to Lawrence, characterizing his own novelistic goals, in a letter to Edward Garnett (5 June 1914), as quoted in *D. H. Lawrence: Selected Literary Criticism*, 18.

[2] No one has surpassed Dorothy Van Ghent's description of the inhuman, unsymbolic character of the earth in Hardy's fiction:

In *Tess*, of all his novels, the earth is most actual as a dramatic factor—that is, as a factor of causation; and by this we refer simply to the long stretches of earth that have to be trudged in order that a person may get from one place to another, the slowness of the business, the irreducible reality of it (for one has only one's feet), its grimness of soul-wearying fatigue and shelterlessness and doubtful issue at the other end of the journey where nobody may be at home. . . . In *Tess* the earth . . . constantly acts in its own motivating, causational substantiality by being there in the way of human purposes to encounter, to harass them, detour them, seduce them, defeat them. ("On *Tess of the d'Urbervilles*," 201-202)

fog The Chase was wrapped in thick darkness, although morning was not far off. He was obliged to advance with outstretched hands to avoid contact with the boughs, and discovered that to hit the exact spot from which he had started was at first entirely beyond him. . . . "Tess!" said d'Urberville.

There was no answer. The obscurity was now so great that he could see absolutely nothing but a pale nebulousness at his feet, which represented the white muslin figure he had left upon the dead leaves. Everything else was blackness alike. D'Urberville stooped; and heard a gentle regular breathing. He knelt and bent lower, till her breath warmed his face, and in a moment his cheek was in contact with hers. She was sleeping soundly, and upon her eyelashes there lingered tears. (97-101)

Settings in Eliot often seem shaped to symbolize human situations. They exist as passive background, corroborating the potential behavior of the characters in the foreground. (One thinks of scenes like Maggie among the gypsies or her drifting on the water with Stephen, in *The Mill on the Floss*, and of the archery contest at the Arrowpoints' or Deronda rowing on the Thames, in *Daniel Deronda*.) The memorable settings in Hardy (like the one just quoted) rarely function in this way. Rather, the characters, with their relative dispositions, wander into and are penetrated, reshaped, by non-human nature, with its absolute disposition. The dark and foggy Chase minimizes the potency of individual will; the passage of time gradually enervates Tess's powers of resistance. Differences between Tess and Alec are dwarfed by the overarching and quietly penetrative medium that contains them both. Within this setting Tess's self-protective, self-distinguishing consciousness cedes control. Her bodily conditions reassert their primacy.[3]

Prior to Hardy, sleep appears in English fiction mainly as a

[3] Tony Tanner pursues a related argument: "It is in a brilliant continuation of this blurred narcotic atmosphere that Hardy has the rape take place in a dense fog, while Tess is in a deep sleep. Consciousness and perception are alike engulfed and obliterated" (223).

brief interlude between stretches of consciousness. Or it may function poetically as the vehicle of another form of consciousness, that of dreams which prophetically announce future events or reinterpret present ones. In Hardy, and *a fortiori* in Joyce, sleep acquires a measure of its daily weight. It begins to appear not only as the condition in which a rough third of life is passed, but as a revealing sidelight on the phenomenon of consciousness. Hardy's stress on sleep emphasizes the fragile and intermittent hold human beings maintain upon themselves, and it throws into relief those crises attendant upon a relaxation of identity.

The determining scenes in *Tess of the d'Urbervilles* are articulated in terms of sleep; and we can already see, in the one quoted, that the undoing of Tess is something other than simple rape. The softness, stillness, and drowsiness of the setting and its human figures do not permit such a restrictive interpretation of violent resistance (for without resistance there can be no rape). The encounter is best seen as an event poised between consciousness and unconsciousness, between human resistance and natural yielding. As Ian Gregor says, it is "both a seduction *and* a rape," for Alex is simultaneously everything and nothing to her, a man who violated her conscious will and yet retains the most intimate hold upon her in the measure that it was he who "brought to consciousness her own sexuality" (182). Upon scrutiny "her own sexuality" becomes, in Hardy's rendering, a contradiction in terms. Sexuality appears as the incompatible crossing of private and common, human and natural. It is the dimension through which Tess becomes most profoundly her own self and yet nature's plaything; and Hardy's genius, in this decisive scene, is to saturate her identity-bearing encounter in the unindividualized unconsciousness of sleep. We are made to take it as neither her act nor her accident, but instead an event that defines *in nuce* that openness to context which is Tess's authentic mode of response, while yet bearing no part in her conscious identity.[4]

Another passage, this one during Angel's courtship, may shed

---

[4] It is also, of course, an event with a traceable cultural etiology, defined by Tess's and Alec's class orientation. I am less interested here in its societal determinants than in its revealing Tess's involuntary participation in a natural scheme.

more light on the extraordinary perspective Hardy maintains upon his heroine:

> She had not heard him enter, and hardly realized his presence there. She was yawning, and he saw the red interior of her mouth as if it had been a snake's. She had stretched one arm so high above her coiled-up cable of hair that he could see its satin delicacy above the sunburn; her face was flushed with sleep, and her eyelids hung heavy over their pupils. (198)

Need it be said that Eliot does not grasp her people at these moments—before they have "become themselves"? Hardy has an uncanny capacity to render the Tess that exists, incarnate, unthinking, behind "Tess." He gives us here the Tess who is the ground of "Tess." Her bodily gestures are unconscious, massive, lovingly described. The Tess Durbeyfield whom Angel Clare involuntarily falls in love with—though not the one he argues with—is in the main this pre-conscious physical presence. And the Tess Durbeyfield who slays Alec at the end is the same immediate creature; her impact on others and her receipt of their impact are essentially instinctive.[5]

The scene at Stonehenge of her arrest for that act contains Hardy's final description of Tess asleep:

> In a minute or two her breathing became more regular, her clasp of his hand relaxed, and she fell asleep. . . . Presently the night wind died out, and the quivering little pools in the cup-like hollows of the stones lay still. At the same time something seemed to move on the verge of the dip east-

[5] I hope that the reader will not misconstrue this approach to Tess (either Hardy's or mine) as an "excessively male" and narrow-minded focus on her body. It seems to me that Hardy attends to her dual being—as an incarnate woman subjectively known from within and objectively approached from outside—with perfect seriousness and artistic integrity. (By contrast Alec and Angel appear to be more cursory creations, realized by means of broader brush strokes.) In the framework of my own study, I would emphasize that Tess's "physical career" is under scrutiny in the same way that David's and Maggie's were earlier, and that Stephen's and Bloom's and Molly's will be later. The issue is not male/female but immaculate/incarnate.

ward—a mere dot. It was the head of a man approaching them. . . . "It is no use, sir," he said. "There are sixteen of us on the Plain, and the whole country is reared."

"Let her finish her sleep!" he [Angel] implored in a whisper of the men as they gathered round.

When they saw where she lay, which they had not done till then, they showed no objection, and stood watching her, as still as the pillars around. He went to the stone and bent over her, holding one poor little hand; her breathing now was quick and small, like that of a lesser creature than a woman. All waited in the growing light. . . . Soon the light was strong, and a ray shone upon her unconscious form, peering under her eyelids and waking her.

"What is it, Angel?" she said, starting up. "Have they come for me?"

"Yes, dearest," he said. "They have come."

"It is as it should be," she murmured. (417-18)

The scene of seizure is as measured and surprisingly gentle as the earlier one of violation. The law, for this rapt moment, waits upon the breath and pulse of a sleeping woman, taking her natural rhythms as a guide for its own pace: Hardy deliberately lengthens out the process of her awakening. Tess appears for the last time as the creature of sleep, obedient to stresses outside her own consciousness. She entered the concatenation of tragic events by falling asleep in a cart, and she leaves it after a brief respite of self-recomposing slumber atop an oblong slab at Stonehenge. The tension between human and natural will soon be stilled. "I am ready," she says.

を

THIS IMAGE of seventeen men waiting upon the pulse of one woman is more than picturesque; it suggests Hardy's underlying measure for assessing behavior. The clue to human actions lies less in conceptualized principles than in deeply rooted impulses. Moral assessment becomes authentic on condition that it descend to the earth in continuous recognition of the individual creature's incarnate, involuntary pulse beat. For the unsentimental Hardy,

114

impulse may be no model for morality, but no morality that
scorns impulse can be effective. Hortatory and high-minded models
of behavior fail insofar as they ignore the embodied conditions
of the creatures they would elevate.

In an exceedingly ironic passage Hardy has Angel Clare make
just such a discovery:

> He held that education had as yet but little affected the beats
> of emotion and impulse on which domestic happiness de-
> pends. It was probable that . . . improved systems of moral
> and intellectual training would appreciably, perhaps consid-
> erably, elevate the involuntary and even the unconscious in-
> stincts of human nature; but up to the present day culture,
> as far as he could see, might be said to have affected only
> the mental epiderm of those lives which had been brought
> under its influence. (193-94)

The irony is that Angel is more the victim than the master of
this insight. He is moved decisively by "beats of emotion and
impulse" that are foreign to the "improved systems of moral and
intellectual training" that he would call his principles. Beneath
these principles, at a level of emotion and impulse he has no
access to, Angel rages irrationally at Tess, able neither to forgive
her nor to cease loving her. He remains blank to these depths,
however, professing to live on a plane of rational magnanimity
and detachment.

His utterances to Tess are suffused with unacknowledged
resentment:

> "But do not make me reproach you. I have sworn that I will
> not; and I will do everything to avoid it." (258)

> "Don't, Tess; don't argue. Different societies, different man-
> ners. You almost make me say you are an unapprehending
> peasant woman, who have never been initiated into the pro-
> portions of social things." (258)

> "My position—is this. . . . I thought—any man would have
> thought—that by giving up all ambition to win a wife with
> social standing, with fortune, with knowledge of the world,

I should secure rustic innocence as surely as I should secure pink cheeks; but—However, I am no man to reproach you, and I will not." (263-64)

The candor of Tess appears nowhere else in Hardy's fiction, but the duplicity of Angel is writ large in the obscurities of Jude and Sue. Repressing the outrage of his involuntary impulses, denying his anger, Angel passes off his bile—as the gentler Jude will later— under the banner of magnanimity. "You almost make me say" indeed! He can reproach her only by denying that he does so; he can abandon her only by proclaiming that "There is no anger between us" (278).

As sleep indicates the integration of Tess with her natural conditions, so sleep reveals the double truth of Angel's emotional torment:

> Clare came close, and bent over her. "Dead, dead, dead!" he murmured.
>
> After fixedly regarding her for some moments with the same gaze of immeasurable woe he bent lower, enclosed her in his arms, and rolled her in the sheet as in a shroud. Then lifting her from the bed with as much respect as one would show to a dead body, he carried her across the room, murmuring—
>
> "My poor, poor Tess—my dearest, darling Tess! So sweet, so good, so true! . . . My wife—dead, dead!" he said. (272-73)

The conflict between traditional and Freudian readings of this scene is only apparent. It is as true that Clare's principles must be put to sleep before his deeper tenderness for her can emerge, as it is true that at the outraged core of his being he wants her to die. Freud has noted drily in "The Ego and the Id" that "the normal man is not only far more immoral than he believes but also far more moral than he knows" (19:52). Correspondingly, Angle Clare loves and hates Tess Durbeyfield with an intensity of which he is wholly unconscious. Could he find access to this level, he might vent his fury and recover his buried affection. Instead, he proclaims his behavior to be rational and detached:

an affair of the immaculate spirit fulfilling itself in irreproachable conduct. He has yet to learn that life in Hardy, including his own, has no transcendental sanction, but is instead a process of pulsation and interpenetration.

Tess, by contrast with Angel's doubleness, is essentially (often helplessly) attuned to the deeper pulse within and about her. The poetry of this novel consists in Hardy's evocation of the shared pulsebeat connecting the human Tess with her natural matrix:

> She did not know that Clare had followed her round, and that he sat under his cow watching her. The stillness of her head and features was remarkable: she might have been in a trance, her eyes open, yet unseeing. Nothing in the picture moved but Old Pretty's tail and Tess's pink hands, the latter so gently as to be a rhythmic pulsation only, as if they were obeying a reflex stimulus, like a beating heart. (177)

This is the inconceivable motion of process itself, of "earth's diurnal course"; Hardy shares something of Wordsworth's capacity to make perceptible the infinitesimal movement of momentary life. It is idle to read Tess's trance-like state as a regrettable and ominous lapse of attention. Such criticism mistakenly sees her as failing the dictates of a paradigm of immaculateness, rather than fulfilling the conditions of a paradigm of immersion. The terrible beauty of Tess is that she is so unquestionably bodily, penetrable. Hardy never shows her but as, literally, a figure of flesh and blood, colored by what she moves against, with a quicksilver pulse:[6]

> They were breaking up the masses of curd before putting them into the vats . . . and amid the immaculate whiteness of the curds Tess Durbeyfield's hands showed themselves of the pinkness of the rose. Angel, who was filling the vats with his handfuls, suddenly ceased, and laid his hands flat upon hers. Her sleeves were rolled far above the elbow, and bending lower he kissed the inside vein of her soft arm.

[6] Cf. Tanner: "The purest woman contains tides of blood . . . and if the rising of the blood is sexual passion and the spilling of the blood is death, then we can see that the purest woman is sexual and mortal" (226).

Although the early September weather was sultry, her arm, from her dabbling in the curds, was as cold and damp to his mouth as a new-gathered mushroom, and tasted of the whey. But she was such a sheaf of susceptibilities that her pulse was accelerated by the touch, her blood driven to her finger-ends, and the cool arms flushed hot. (205)

The patient physical detail is exquisite; and it shows, among other things, that curds, mushroom, whey, and hands differ in degree only, not in kind. They are all part of the material bounty of nature, a "new gathered" joy for the appetite, to be relished now in their fluid and susceptible ripeness. Such a passage brings home the conviction that in this novel Hardy's imagined world has, as its center, not a disembodied law but a beating heart. There is in *Tess of the d'Urbervilles* plenty (indeed, overmuch) of talk about laws, but deeper than Logos is pulsation. To approach the core of Tess is to move her blood, as Angel does lovingly here. To destroy another is to puncture his heart and stop his pulse: Prince and Alec die through eruption of heart blood. Because pulsation is a rhythm so suffused throughout the novel as to appear its natural law, one accepts as a statement of irresistible process Hardy's words:

In reality, she was drifting into acquiescence. Every see-saw of her breath, every wave of her blood, every pulse singing in her ears, was a voice that joined with nature in revolt against her scrupulousness. (206)

❧

"DRIFTING . . . see-saw . . . wave . . . pulse"—these words convey the gentle sway of nature upon the human. That sway is more darkly described in the language of disfigurement and abrasion. I have already glanced at the crucial instances of penetration—the wounding of Prince, the seduction of Tess, the murder of Alec—and those scenes survive their tincture of melodrama mainly because they are couched upon innumerable humbler instances of the same dynamic. The much-discussed scene in the garden—Tess "gathering cuckoo-spittle on her skirts, cracking snails that were underfoot, staining her hands with thistle-milk and slug-slime" (150)—dramatizes the same process. To move

118

toward Clare is to brush against and become stained by the foul and fecund low-life that fills Hardy's landscape. Margaret Drabble remarks, in an essay on "Hardy and the Natural World," that "oddly enough, the vegetative blemishes [of nature] seem to have upset and preyed on his mind more than the more obvious signs of nature's cruelty" (166). "Upset" is perhaps the wrong verb. Hardy's stance in these descriptions is as often neutral, even celebratory, as it is disturbed. He seems to have visually apprehended in nature less its hostility than its indifference and its inhuman commerce.[7]

The following passage, for example, could be penned by no one else:

> Their gauzy skirts had brushed up from the grass innumerable flies and butterflies which, unable to escape, remained caged in the transparent tissue as in an aviary. (170)

A writer who can see these flies—and elsewhere it is pollen, peat, lichen, algae, scrub plants, caterpillars, and moths—is not likely to take virginity of any sort seriously. The world he imaginatively inhabits is no discarnate vacuum for the transcendental spirit but a material plenitude, teeming with all strata of living creatures, marked by ineradicable stain, humming with cross-pollenization.[8] He who never liked to be touched knows that we are

---

[7] Hardy's natural world, as Tanner and others have noticed, has its emptiness as well as its commerce, perhaps most stunningly rendered in the scene of Tess and Marian in the swede-field at Flintcomb-Ash. More typically, I believe, emptiness is Hardy's *idea* of a nature that knows us not. His actual descriptions are lovingly stocked with instances of its manifold and inhuman vitality.

[8] The supreme description in Hardy of the strange wealth of creatures with whom man shares the scene occurs in *The Return of the Native*:

His daily life was of a curious microscopic sort, his whole world being limited to a circuit of a few feet from his person. His familiars were creeping and winged things, and they seemed to enroll him in their band. Bees hummed around his ears with an intimate air, and tugged at the heath and furze-flowers at his side in such numbers as to weigh them down to the sod. The strange amber-coloured butterflies which Egdon produced . . . quivered in the breath of his lips, alighted upon his bowed back, and sported with the glittering point of his hook as he flourished it up and down. Tribes of emerald-green grasshoppers leaped over his feet, falling awkwardly on their backs, heads, or hips, like unskilful acrobats, as chance might rule; or engaged themselves in noisy flirtations under the fern-fronds with silent ones of homely hue. Huge flies, ignorant of larders and wire-netting, and quite in savage state, buzzed about him without knowing that he was a man. In and out of the fern-dells snakes glided in their most brilliant blue and yellow guise, it being the season immediately following the shedding of their

forced to share the scene: that, in life, human bodies are touched by non-human bodies, and in death devoured by them.

For Tess to be shown in nature means, then, to be shown in an embrace that increasingly erodes her human personality. The embrace is beautiful to the onlooker but eventually abrasive and disfiguring to the subject. Consider her binding the corn:

> Her binding proceeds with clock-like monotony. From the sheaf last finished she draws a handful of ears, patting their tips with her left palm to bring them even. Then stooping low she moves forward, gathering the corn with both hands against her knees, and pushing her left gloved hand under the bundle to meet the right on the other side, holding the corn in an embrace like that of a lover. She brings the ends of the bond together, and kneels on the sheaf while she ties it, beating back her skirts now and then when lifted by the breeze. A bit of her naked arm is visible between the buff leather of the gauntlet and the sleeve of her gown; and as the day wears on its feminine smoothness becomes scarified by the stubble, and bleeds. (117)

The passage is almost beyond commentary. In an eternal present tense (to which Hardy recurs) her way of working, her way of feeling, her sexual bond to the earth (its child, its lover), and the effects of that bond upon her (its victim) are seamlessly fused. Hardy renders both the otherness of the earth—its different substance, detail by detail, from her own substance—and the kinship of the earth—her sustained embrace of its produce. Her movement is so rhythmic and habitual as to be half trance-like. It both exhausts her and defines, in something like the following terms, her commerce with nature: a commerce that is involuntary, bodily, and continuous, that becomes loverly and abrasive as it is prolonged, that leads to bleeding and ultimately (by implication) to death.

---

old skins, when their colours are brightest. Litters of young rabbits came out from their forms to sun themselves upon hillocks, the hot beams blazing through the delicate tissue of each thin-fleshed ear, and firing it to a blood-red transparency in which the veins could be seen. None of them feared him. (262)

Perhaps the richest concentration of this cluster of meanings occurs in the treacle scene with Car Darch:

> "Well—whatever is that a-creeping down thy back, Car Darch?" said one of the group suddenly.
>
> All looked at Car. Her gown was a light cotton print, and from the back of her head a kind of rope could be seen descending to some distance below her waist, like a China-man's queue.
>
> "Tis her hair falling down," said another.
>
> No; it was not her hair: it was a black stream of something oozing from her basket, and it glistened like a slimy snake in the cold still rays of the moon.
>
> "Tis treacle," said an observant matron.
>
> Treacle it was. Car's poor old grandmother had a weakness for the sweet stuff. Honey she had in plenty out of her own hives, but treacle was what her soul desired, and Car had been about to give her a treat of a surprise. Hastily lowering the basket the dark girl found that the vessel containing the syrup had been smashed within.
>
> By this time there had arisen a shout of laughter at the extraordinary appearance of Car's back, which irritated the dark queen into getting rid of the disfigurement by the first sudden means available, and independently of the help of the scoffers. She rushed excitedly into the field they were about to cross, and flinging herself flat on her back upon the grass, began to wipe her gown as well as she could by spinning horizontally on the herbage and dragging herself over it upon her elbows. (94)

The scene is surrounded by others that are just as sexually laden—the "vegeto-human pollen" of the Dionysiac dancers before and the finely penetrating mist of the violation scene after. Here the suggested visual meanings are most portentous, though: like blood or semen, the oozing treacle disfigures the female whom it stains, descending down her back "to some distance below her waist," glistening "like a slimy snake." If the serpent simile conveys the evil of sexuality, yet the treacle is intrinsically delicious and life-sustaining. Its connection with honey and hives brings

121

Tess's ill-fated trip with Prince to mind; and here, as there, the image powerfully coalesces richness and violation: "the vessel containing the syrup had been smashed within." It takes violation to release richness, and the life-stuff—blood, semen, treacle—flows out, staining and deforming what it touches, bringing ecstasy or violence as its consequences. Car Darch, trying to rid herself of the treacle, writhes on the grass as though in the throes of sexual frenzy. In a moment she will seek to punish Tess physically for having stolen her lover, and will thus catapult her into Alec's arms. With its tumult and its ritual beauty, its drunkenness and prolific waste of sweetness, its disregard for individual preferences, such a scene conveys, in lyrical epitome, the Schopenhauerian ordeal that Hardy envisaged as the plight of human beings, caught up in the unsought stresses of inhuman nature.

愛

WHAT is the effect of such a world upon the human beings who suffer it? Can the human assimilate the natural and remain human? Before assessing Tess's final stance, one needs to note that the pantheistic solution of amoral merging with natural forces is possible only for Hardy's coarser characters, those with a less individualized consciousness. Tess's parents may drift into a drunken haze of painlessness, Car Darch and her friends may see "themselves and surrounding nature [as] forming an organism of which all the parts harmoniously and joyously interpenetrated each other" (93). But Tess is condemned—like all of Hardy's reflective people—to absorb the impress of nature's inhuman otherness. Not harmonious merging but sustained abrasion is her portion: "She lay in a state of percipience without volition, and the rustle of the straw and the cutting of the [corn] ears by the others had the weight of bodily touches" (316).

The final effect of accumulating experience upon the human organism is something like an overwhelming. Despite his awareness of the circulating blood and its restorative flow, Hardy permits his protagonists little psychological capacity for assimilation: they are unable to *get done* with anything. They forget nothing, nor do those who can make them suffer ever disappear. The cycle of fermenting nature around and within them is silhouetted against the echoing stasis of Hardy's gaunt, unchanging geography and cast of characters. Because nature is cyclical and memoryless, Tess physically blooms again, but it is only nature in her that is fully recovered and blooming. Humanly, as opposed to naturally, she is moving in an irreversible linear direction. What appears to her in its early stages as "a liberal education" (127) will eventually, inevitably, be perceived as an absurd "sport."

This tension in Tess between nature that meaninglessly renews itself and humanity that ages and darkens wisely is held, until the end, in precarious balance. Tess is, as it were, "layered" in time, speaking both dialect and standard English, containing still "her twelfth year in her cheeks . . . her ninth sparkling from her eyes, and even her fifth" now and then in "the curves of her mouth" (40), emerging as a composite of Christian and pagan, Victorian and Jacobean, Durbeyfield and d'Urberville. Her time-enriched, culturally crossed identity contains a mixture of elements whose range neither she nor Angel can grasp—she wanting to believe that she is unchanged, he that she is all changed. Both refer to a partial entity named "Tess," whereas Hardy shows us the wholeness of an embodied Tess—what the woman is, as well as what she feels—a wholeness that alters in time and yet remains (to us, not—finally—to her) recognizably one. For the worst breach that Tess suffers is the severance of Tess from "Tess": the inability, after her last experience with Alec, to keep her moral idea of herself and her felt awareness of her own body any longer together: "But he had a vague consciousness of one thing, though it was not clear to him till later; that his original Tess had spiritually ceased to recognize the body before him as hers—allowing it to drift, like a corpse upon the current, in a direction dissociated from its living will" (401).

In a novel that is unfailingly sagacious, this insight is perhaps supreme. The fate of being embodied, of being a child of the soil, has so violated Tess's transcendental image of herself as immaculate and unchanged, as still Angel's, that her mind, in a paroxysm of guilt, has snapped away from its container of estranging dross. In the mid-twentieth century R. D. Laing writes cogently about "the divided self," but Hardy's contemporary reviewers could have done little with this perception. Andrew Lang protests: "She does not die, like Clarissa . . . but she goes back to the atrocious cad who betrayed her, and wears—not caring what she wears—the parasol of pomp and the pretty slippers of iniquity" (385). Annoyed by Tess's flashy clothes, Lang is asking her to recover from her moral lapse at least to the extent of feeling and expressing guilt. He does not see that Hardy is dramatizing, in Tess's torpor, not a deficiency but an excess of guilt: indeed, a kind of temporary insanity that transpires when the spiritual insistence on immaculate self-definition abrades once too often against the indifferent moral facts of embodied life. The identity of "Tess" can no longer sustain the incarnate career of Tess. Humanity and nature are irreconcilable in the same human being: the outraged soul disowns the body, ceding it and its apparel to Alec.

If you are small enough, in Hardy's world, you can retain civil relations between soul and body, and this unaspiring civility marks the charm of Hardy's rustics. His Prometheans, however, those who make demands on life, regularly collapse upon themselves, their human project exploded by the forces of nature within and without. As J. Hillis Miller says, Hardy responds to this collapse less by questioning the human project that has collapsed than by quarreling with the immovable natural obstacle. Hardy bemoans the inevitability of failure, rather than asking what change in human values might permit success. "Like so many of his countrymen, like Dickens for example," Miller writes, "he fears the guilt involved in becoming the value-giving center of his world" (21). If one grants the menacing contours of Hardy's natural world, then this fear simply guarantees the miscarriage of human aspiration. Penetrated through and through with nature, we are what we are; Hardy knows this, and he knows that this is not what we would be. He cannot rise to Nietzsche's audacious counsel to redefine therefore what we would be: "You shall become who you are."[9]

As a result there are few moments of crisis overcome in

[9] Friedrich Nietzsche, *The Gay Science*, Book Three, Section 270, as quoted in Walter Kaufmann, 159.

Hardy's novels—moments when the natural, having invaded the human, finds itself assimilated and humanized. Two such moments, though, can be found in *Tess of the d'Urbervilles*. The first in Tess's burial of her child Sorrow. Rising into godlike authority, generating the terms of good and evil out of her own bodily travail, Tess baptizes her child and buries it "in that shabby corner of God's allotment where he lets the nettles grow, and where all unbaptized infants, notorious drunkards, suicides, and others of the conjecturally damned are laid" (125). The second moment of serenity is the "fulfilment" of Phase the Seventh, Tess reunited with Angel. Beyond expectation, she is finally beyond pain; relinquishment of the future permits the past to subside. Having taken in Alec to the full, she now has seven indescribable days with Angel. "This happiness could not have lasted," she rightly says, for duration and fulfillment are conflicting notions in Hardy's world.

Rather than fulfillment, then, let us call it penetration, absolute yielding. This is a novel about living richness, about the release, despoliation, and exhaustion of human resource. Tess is ready to die because she has given and taken as much as a human being can give and take. Like those prime milchers whose excess of liquid "oozed forth and fell in drops" (134), Tess is recurrently described with "drops upon her hair, like seed pearls" (158). Living things exist here to be penetrated and to pass on their very last drop of sweetness to other living things. "Songs were often resorted to in dairies hereabout as an enticement to the cows when they showed signs of withholding their usual yield" (137). The song is *Tess*.

"THE SPIRIT UNAPPEASED AND PEREGRINE": *JUDE THE OBSCURE*

"It is a city of light," he said to himself.

"The tree of knowledge grows there," he added a few steps further on.

"It is a place that teachers of men spring from and go to."

"It is what you may call a castle, manned by scholarship and religion."

After this figure he was silent a long while, till he added: "It would just suit me." (49-50)

Alone and in a setting which fails wholly to corroborate his utterance, Jude sounds a characteristic note of the novel. He would be where he is not, and he has only words to express this desire. More than Hardy's other novels, *Jude the Obscure* stresses the importance and the impotence of words, the huge arena between actuality and ideality which they fill. Jude's Christminster is a place less visualized than conceptualized, a mirage of words— "the tree of knowledge . . . what you may call a castle manned by scholarship and religion." He imagines it as existing spatially "out there" while Hardy reveals it, through Jude's words, as a fabric of "figures," woven from "in here." When Jude resolves, in one transcendent apotheosis, to house his spirit in its ideal home, he ignores the extensive gap between actual and ideal, the instrumental steps necessary if one would try to journey from the one realm to the other. On a scale unique in Hardy's work, this novel insists on the hopelessness of making that journey, and on the fraudulence of its imagined end. The novel spreads before its hero, not the transcendental home of the spirit, but innumerable halfway houses that betray the spirit even as they promise it material abode.

"There was no law of transmutation" (55), Jude learns in his painstaking study of the classical languages.[1] No key exists that will magically ease his transformation from artisan to savant, transposing the languages of learning to the grammar of his native discourse. Between Jude and knowledge there lie the certainty of years of study, the risk of faulty pedagogic methods, the obstacle of immovable class prejudice. Jude remains childlike in his approach to these barriers. Seeking unconditional union with the ideal itself, he hardly hesitates over the means for this achievement:

[1] Ian Gregor comments suggestively on this phrase in his excellent study of Hardy (210).

What was most required by citizens? Food, clothing, and shelter. An income from any work in preparing the first would be too meagre; for making the second he felt a distaste; the preparation of the third requisite he inclined to. They built in a city; therefore he would learn to build. (59)

In his mind's eye he is already there. His clichés as to a profession have no specific reference. The actual conditions of his approach, like the actual conditions of Christminster, are scarcely considered. Jude moves absentmindedly through the material of his life—its contingent days and places—enamored of the immaterial absolute, bruising himself on the fleshed-out conditional. He seeks, outside himself, a perfect receptacle for his immaculate spirit. He finds, outside himself, no such receptacle but instead a bewildering array of strictly human approximations: not pure but adulterate, not ideal but embodied, not transcendentally given but mediated and ambiguous. The landscape of *Jude the Obscure*, unlike that of *Tess of the d'Urbervilles*, is overwhelmingly cultural. The landmarks within it comprise the range of human institutions and conventions by which the journeying spirit finds itself stymied rather than fulfilled: a landscape of signifiers emptied of those meanings they promise. If the basic unit of *Tess* is the blood, the basic unit of *Jude* is the word. (In *Jude* wounds are expressed through talk, not blood.) If the world of *Tess* is mainly the horizontal one of natural immersion, the world of *Jude* is the vertical one of cultural aspiration, counterfeit, and failure.

≥●

JUDE is Hardy's most insistent seeker—his characteristic posture is dedication—and he inhabits a novel crammed with advertisement, with signifying artifacts that promise to fulfill the seeker's desire, to connect him with his goal. At the simplest level of false advertisement there are Arabella's dimple and false hair, Vilbert's quack medicine, the adulterated beer whose impurities Arabella (but not Jude) detects. At the next level, not deceptive in themselves but slippery in their relation to the seeker, are the icons of Greek and Biblical culture—the statues of Venus and Apollo, the

Latin cross and the Ten Commandments—which misleadingly propose a realizable harmony between acolyte and symbolized values.[2] More diffuse are the secular institutions of education and profession, of marriage and divorce. Designed to bestow communal structure and purpose upon inchoate human desire, these institutions remain oblique to the movement of Jude's and Sue's actual lives. In their role as the culture's licensed forms for individual thought and feeling, they act as false beacons, beyond following, beyond ignoring. As Robert Heilman suggests, they are inextricably woven into the fabric of the characters' consciousness.[3]

Misleading connectives, promising to deliver the spirit of its burden or connect it with its goal, punctuate the novel. Jude and Sue tirelessly write each other letters, seeking to express their deep selves and to make contact with the other. The letters are more eloquent than speech. By ignoring the disconcerting presence of an interlocutor, they succeed, if not in telling the truth, at least in making a narrative of their lives.

The fundamental category of a misleading mediator, a connective that fails to make good on its promise, is language itself. *Jude the Obscure* uses discourse in a thoroughly modern way, unique in Hardy's novels; the words a character uses appear less as the transparent bearer of private spirit than as the opaque, already motivated property of a public culture: the words have already been coopted.[4] (Words as the property of an alien culture engage Conrad and Joyce massively, and I return to this theme in my discussion of these later writers.) What may be most ob-

---

[2] The most pathetic instances of icons that express the gap, rather than connection, between worshipper and sacred image are the models—first of wood and then of cake—that Jude constructs of Christminster.

[3] Heilman's astute analysis considers convention in the novel only indirectly, insofar as Sue's failure to transcend the clichés of her period reveals the extent to which personal identity itself is socially composed.

[4] Janet Burstein shows persuasively that in *Jude*, unlike many of the earlier novels, there is no mythic return. The past in all its facets is inaccessible, not least because its language is no longer applicable to the conditions of modern life: "Instead of nurturing human relationships by illuminating personal insights that may be generally valid, language in a postmythic world seems chiefly to reflect the disparity between individual and general or conventional perceptions" (505).

scure about Jude Fawley and Sue Bridehead is that, at the center of their being, they are mute. The language they have access to—and it pours out of them helplessly, it is the blood of their spirit—is often an incoherent amalgam of the commonplaces of their culture, more faithful to the psychic stresses of a Swinburne or Newman, a J. S. Mill or Matthew Arnold (whom they are echoing) than to their own inarticulable need.

A. Alvarez is right when he claims that "the essential subject of the novel is not Oxford, or marriage, or even frustration. It is loneliness" (421). Jude and Sue's abundant speech only accentuates their separateness. Alvarez (and J.I.M. Stewart makes the same point) notes that "no character ever properly seems to connect with another in talk" (420), but this aspect of the novel—which is endemic in Hardy's art—seems to me not a flaw in *Jude the Obscure*. For once Hardy has constructed a novel which accommodates the awkward silence at the core of his vision. The characters are there, given in their completeness, before they are empowered with speech. Speech is, as it were, a late accomplishment of the species, more capable of releasing chorus-like platitudes than of articulating individual need. The spoken words proliferate in *Jude the Obscure* like cartoon utterances, cascading like soap-bubbles from the already finished figures who remain mute beside their utterance.

Whether such effects of verbal alienation are intentional or not, the novel certainly renders the conditional thinness, the ardent abstractedness of Jude's dedication to western culture. He has its words, but they never sound quite like his own. J.I.M. Stewart writes:

> We are nowhere made to *feel* what brought him his Greek and Latin; he is seen in virtually no concrete situation relevant to it. . . . Again, the extended passage in which Jude is represented as wandering about Christminster and hearing the ghostly *ipsissima verba* of departed Oxford men . . . is a poor and even embarrassing substitute for something not really created in the book. (189)[5]

[5] Critics like Stewart, Alvarez, Irving Howe, and Ian Gregor have helped me most in my reading of *Jude the Obscure*, because they confront directly the

"No concrete situation . . . something not really created": that is less the novel's problem than its elusive achievement. Indeed, it is not surprising that this facet of Hardy's art should be more pronounced in *Jude the Obscure* than in his other novels. Only here is the protagonists' discourse insistently intellectual; elsewhere they do not proclaim their insertion within this or that larger cultural tradition. Insofar as the insertion is itself suspect— revealing the protagonists' isolation rather than their belonging— then the abstractness of the urged positions, the precarious purchase of the speaker upon his own utterance, is itself germane.[6] Jude's relation to his sought-after culture *is* ghostly and abstract rather than fleshed-out and instrumental; it is right that he should enter the city at night, hearing its medley of disembodied voices. Jude's great moments at Christminster are equally verbal—his two orations rehearsing "the Articles of his Belief, in the Latin tongue" (141) and grappling with the "difficult question" (335) of his intellectual career—and on these occasions Hardy stresses the only facet of Christminster available to Jude: its words.

Jude is so enamored of these words that he tends to speak them as a substitute for his own, and even the "autobiographical" sketch he gives of himself in that last oration is ringed round with ironies. It is a speech "from the heart" delivered to a coarse and unreceptive audience rather than to the university hearers he craves, and it is not the truth of Jude but the "story" of Jude, the fiction he must shape to deliver himself at all:

> It takes two or three generations to do what I tried to do in one; and my impulses—affections—vices perhaps they

---

novel's recurrent linguistic awkwardness. None of them argues that the dislocation of discourse is part of Hardy's purpose. Nevertheless, in their uneasiness they take the reader further into the novel than those critics who speak of Jude as an unproblematic, Promethean, or Job-like hero.

[6] John Bayley makes a similar point in his fascinating *Essay on Hardy*, which I came upon while completing my own study: "His [Hardy's] autodidacticism, his acquired learning, helped to disorientate him, as it helps to give that characteristic instability to his prose. There is a sharp contrast in it between the physical perceptions, which are always his own, and the opinions and ideas which seldom are: it is indeed a part of his honesty to advertise their coming from somewhere else" (17).

should be called—were too strong not to hamper a man without advantages. . . . I was, perhaps, after all, a paltry victim to the spirit of mental and social restlessness, that makes so many unhappy in these days! . . . And what I appear, a sick and poor man, is not the worst of me. I am in a chaos of principles—groping in the dark—acting by instinct and not after example. . . . (336)

In each of its twists (the speech begins on a cheerful note but turns bitter and self-indicting as it goes on), Jude's oration exaggerates and distorts his nature. Successively presenting himself as too impatient, too impulsive, too passionate, too restless, in "a chaos of principles," Jude's words miss the naive sweetness and hesitancy, the gently yearning idealism, the desire to respond coupled with the baffled resentment of failure, that most deeply characterize his way of encountering experience.[7] Jude is no Prometheus, no peer of Huxley or Spencer; nor is he an impulsive man, raging in the dark. Rather, he is a mild and civil man, confused by the words and promises of others and by the flux of possibilities within himself, a man who really seeks, in Lawrence's fine phrase, "not a store of learning, nor the vanity of education . . . [but] to find conscious expression for that which he held in his blood" ("The Study of Thomas Hardy," 210). Had he discovered that the richness he yearned for lay inchoate in his own blood, he might have succeeded in forging an authentic voice.

[7] Some such rationale is needed to place a passage like the following: "You know what a weak fellow I am. My two Arch Enemies you know—my weakness for womankind and my impulse to strong liquor. Don't abandon me to them, Sue, to save your own soul only! They have been kept entirely at a distance since you became my guardian-angel!" (361)

This is plausibly how Jude would characterize himself but certainly not—in its capitalized simplicities—an accurate portrait. Eliot's Sweeney says, "I gotta use words when I talk to you," and Jude's words are likewise condemned to come from a cultural stockpile and therefore to remain at a distance from the private dilemma they would describe. Though he pursues a different argument, Jerome H. Buckley also notes the inaccuracy of Jude's self-portrait: "Jude is neither the drunkard nor the amorist; he is betrayed by ordinary appetites and feelings, by his own temperament, and perhaps most of all by the disparity between flesh and spirit in the world itself, the distance between the real and the ideal" (175).

As it is, both Jude and Sue rely upon one external voice after another to make sense of their confusing experience. At their nadir, Father Time's murder of himself and the two younger children, they engage in a desperate game of quotations, seeking to alleviate their misery by finding a previously articulated ground for what would otherwise seem unbearably groundless:

"No," said Jude. "It was in his nature to do it. The doctor says there are such boys springing up amongst us. . . ."

She sobbed again. "O, O my babies! They had done no harm! Why should they have been taken away, and not I!"

There was another stillness—broken at last by two persons in conversation somewhere without.

"They are talking about us, no doubt!" moaned Sue. " 'We are made a spectacle unto the world, and to angels, and to men!' . . . There is something external to us which says, 'You shan't!' First it said, 'You shan't learn!' Then it said, 'You shan't labour!' Now it says, 'You shan't love!' . . . I talked to the child as one should only talk to people of mature age. I said the world was against us, that it was better to be out of life than in it at this price; and he took it literally. . . . We went about loving each other too much—indulging ourselves to utter selfishness with each other! We said—do you remember?—that we would make a virtue of joy. I said it was Nature's intention . . . It is best, perhaps, that they should be gone. . . ."

"Yes," replied Jude. "Some say that the elders should rejoice when their children die in infancy."

"But they don't know! . . . I am driven out of my mind by things! What ought to be done!" She stared at Jude, and tightly held his hand.

"Nothing can be done," he replied. "Things are as they are, and will be brought to their destined issue."

She paused. "Yes! Who said that?" she asked heavily.

"It comes in the chorus of the *Agamemnon*. It has been in my mind continually since this happened." (346-48)

These three pages allude to a veritable chorus of voices. Jude and Sue inhabit a world of verbal echoes; they automatically refer the inexplicable events of their lives to the swarm of formulae cluttering their heads. Sue's consciousness is like a larder stocked with nothing but phrases. She has so persuaded herself that the key to the children's disaster lies in something she said or failed to say that she (and Jude with her) misses one of the primary causes silently visible to every reader: the paucity of wordless physical affection has scarred Father Time as deeply as any utterance. It is typical of Sue and Jude to overlook such an incarnate cause, as they despairingly cast about among their treasury of remembered sayings for an intellectual formulation that will fit the case. None does fit the case, and at a certain point the accumulation of allusions takes on a tinge of absurdity. The event is so overexplained as to become unexplained. The pointed weight of allusive wisdom suddenly turns arbitrary and weightless—a bandying of words.[8]

IT TAKES the insight of someone like Nietzsche (a thinker whom Hardy cursorily repudiated) to identify the verbal malaise here.[9] Jude and Sue have not impressed upon their discourse the form of their own embodied spirit. They have not mastered the words they utter, making them their own, for Jude and Sue remain trapped within a linguistic world-view which holds that truth is external, universally applicable, and has already been uttered. The purpose of education in such a world-view—and this is the ed-

[8] In its exploration of the space between formless actuality and substanceless allusion, *Jude the Obscure* is, surprisingly, a precursor of *Ulysses*. Few writers prior to Joyce reveal better than Hardy does (even if unwittingly) the potential arbitrariness of allusive reference, the failure of external verbal contexts to provide alignment for internal embodied dilemmas. I return to this point later in my discussion of Joyce.

[9] Hardy's few references to Nietzsche are dismissive: "To model our conduct on Nature's apparent conduct, as Nietzsche would have taught, can only bring disaster to humanity": so wrote Hardy to *The Academy and Literature* in 1902 (quoted in Florence E. Hardy, 315). In 1914 he mentioned Nietzsche again, writing to the *Manchester Guardian* that "[Nietzsche] used to seem to me (I have not looked into him for years) an incoherent rhapsodist who jumps from Macchiavelli to Isaiah as the mood seizes him, whom it is impossible to take seriously as a mentor" (quoted in William R. Rutland, 48).

ucation that Jude seeks—is to acquaint the student with this already articulated body of truths. Nietzsche knows, by contrast, that what passes for a culture's truths are its willed assertions, its claims rather than its discoveries:

> Whatever exists, having somehow come into being, is again and again reinterpreted to new ends, taken over, transformed and redirected by some power superior to it; all events in the organic world are a subduing, a *becoming master*, and all subduing and becoming master involves a fresh interpretation, an adaptation through which any previous "meaning" and "purpose" are necessarily obscured or even obliterated. (*On the Genealogy of Morals*, 513)

It may now be possible to identify one of the peculiar tensions in *Jude the Obscure*. It is the tension between the morally elusive facts of embodied life, as Hardy presents them, and the static assumptions of discourse, as Sue and Jude reveal them. On the one hand—in the realm of behavior—we find the ever-changing, morally opaque play of power and penetration; and on the other—in the realm of discourse—we find the naive expectation of a fully appropriate moral paradigm, one that accounts for all contingencies, as promised by the formulae of the Greek and Judeo-Christian traditions. This tension exists in one form or another throughout Hardy's novels, for his vision of behavior is far more sophisticated than his or his protagonists' assumptions about the ways in which their culture's discourse organizes and evaluates experience.

Another way of putting it is to say that Hardy sees the dynamics of behavior with a moral flexibility approaching Nietzschean candor, but that—unlike Nietzsche—he has not extended his perception of life as an interplay of powers into a perception of language as an interplay of powers as well. He stops short of Nietzsche's claim that discourse is not the transparent reflection of a pre-existent and static reality waiting to be named by the words, but rather the mediated expression of a thrusting will to make sense of experience. Discourse is actually as non-transcendental, as unsanctioned and contingent, as the experience that it is meant to organize: a dilemma that Hardy seems more to reveal than to acknowledge. Put most simply,

since all discourse is inflected by will, Jude and Sue will either
inflect their terms so as to express their own experience or parrot
the terms that express someone else's experience. Thus, to return
to Nietzsche's verb, Jude and Sue do not *master* the meaning of
Father Time's act because they do not personally will that knowledge into consciousness and language with sufficient intensity.
Borrowers rather than makers of discourse, they do not generate,
from their own anguish, the native phrasing that will put them
in touch with their own inchoate experience. Their dependence
on prefabricated formulae marks their evasion of (to paraphrase
Lawrence) that which they hold unseeing in their own blood.
Through borrowed discourse they remain obscure to their own
necessities, looking passively without for explanations that lie un-
formulated within. As Howells remarked in 1895, "All the characters, indeed, have the appealing quality of human beings really
doing what they must while seeming to do what they will" (379).

❧

"WHAT they must" do is dramatized by Hardy, if not conceptualized by Jude and Sue. Arabella's effect upon Jude rarely extends as far upward as his consciousness. He receives "a dumb
announcement of affinity *in posse*," and he responds instinctively,
"in commonplace obedience to conjunctive orders from head-
quarters, unconsciously received" (63). "In short, as if materially,
a compelling arm of extraordinary muscular power seized hold
of him—something which had nothing in common with the spirits and influences that had moved him hitherto" (67-68). This
"muscular power" of Arabella is as unquestionable as it is unexplained, and Hardy shows us how her unwelcome suasion affects
Jude's speech even as it bypasses his consciousness. He is not the
man openly to air resentment against her (or against anyone), so
it must emerge in the disowned duplicity of his language:

> "Of course I never dreamt six months ago, or even three, of
> marrying. It is a complete smashing up of my plans—I mean
> my plans before I knew you, my dear. But what are they,
> after all! Dreams about books, and degrees, and impossible
> fellowships, and all that. Certainly we'll marry: we must!"
> (80)

"Do be quiet, Arabella, and have a little pity on the creature!"

"Hold up the pail to catch the blood, and don't talk" . . .

"It is a hateful business!" said he.

"Pigs must be killed." . . .

"Thank God!" Jude said. "He's dead."

"What's God got to do with such a messy job as a pig-killing, I should like to know!" she said scornfully. "Poor folks must live."

"I know, I know," said he. "I don't scold you." (88)[10]

There is something amiss—literally, something missing—in these speeches, as though Jude's consciousness could not tolerate

---

[10] It is worth juxtaposing the notorious pig-killing scene in *Jude the Obscure* against a vastly different treatment of the same material in *A Pair of Blue Eyes*:

Robert Lickpan, the pig-killer, here seemed called upon to enter the lists of conversation.

"Yes, they've got their particular naturs good-now," he remarked initially. "Many's the rum-tempered pig I've knowed."

"I don't doubt it, Master Lickpan." Martin's answer expressed that his convictions, no less than good manners, demanded the reply.

"Yes," continued the pig-killer, as one accustomed to be heard. "One that I knowed was deaf and dumb, and we couldn't make out what was the matter wi' the pig. 'A would eat well enough when 'a seed the trough, but when his back was turned, you might a-rattled the bucket all day, the poor soul never heard 'ee. Ye could play tricks upon him behind his back, and 'a wouldn't find it out no quicker than poor deaf Grammer Bates. But 'a fatted well, and I never seed a pig open better when 'a was killed, and 'a was very tender eating, very; as pretty a bit of meat as ever you see; you could suck that meat through a quill.

"And another I knowed," resumed the killer, after quickly letting a pint of ale run down his throat of its own accord, and setting down the cup with mathematical exactness upon the spot from which he had raised it—"another went out of his mind."

"How very mournful!" murmured Mrs. Worm.

"Ay, poor thing, 'a did! As clean out of his mind as the cleverest Christian could go. In early life 'a was very melancholy, and never seemed a hopeful pig by no means. 'Twas Andrew Stainer's pig—that's whose pig 'twas."

"I can mind the pig well enough," attested John Smith.

"And a pretty little porker 'a was. And you all know Farmer Buckle's sort? Every jack o' em suffer from the rheumatism to this day, owing to a damp sty they lived in when they were striplings, as 'twere." . . . (236-37)

The passage is of course whimsical and bucolic, but its legendary porkers are artistically superior to their sentimental counterpart in *Jude*, if only because the latter's "eloquently keen reproach of a creature recognizing at last the treachery of those who had seemed his only friends" (54) is incredible. The pigs in *A Pair of Blue Eyes* are also incredible, but they are not drawn so as to require belief: their interest is openly humorous rather than unpersuasively realistic.

the tension in his feelings. "I mean my plans before I knew you, my dear" is a feeble lie to Arabella and to himself, and "I don't scold you" is the age-old formulation used to avoid acknowledgment of scolding. Jude is avoiding his own emotional confusions; his language achieves clarity at the expense of candor. Nietzsche refers to this behavior as a particular species of lying: "wishing *not* to see something that one does see; wishing not to see something *as* one sees it. . . . The most common lie is that with which one lies to oneself" (*Twilight of the Idols*, 640).[11]

Jude's discourse with Sue displays as well these pockets of disingenuousness:

> "Of course I may have exaggerated your happiness— one never knows," he continued blandly.
>
> "Don't think that, Jude, for a moment, even though you may have have said it to sting me! . . . If you think I am not happy because he's too old for me, you are wrong."
>
> "I don't think anything against him—to you, dear." (207)

When he takes her hand a little later, she draws it away. He then retorts that his gesture is innocent and cousinly, whereupon she repents but insists on apprising Phillotson that he has held it:

> "O—of course, if you think it necessary. But as it means nothing it may be bothering him needlessly."
>
> "Well—are you sure you mean it only as my cousin?"
>
> "Absolutely sure. I have no feelings of love left in me."
>
> "That's news. How has it come to be?"
>
> "I've seen Arabella."
>
> She winced at the hit; then said curiously, "When did you see her?"
>
> "When I was at Christminster."
>
> "So she's come back; and you never told me! I suppose you will live with her now?"
>
> "Of course—just as you live with your husband." (228-29)

---

[11] See also Richard Benvenuto's argument that Jude's human dignity resides in his capacity to tell such lies to himself and thus continue to value objects that he knows to be tarnished: Arabella, Sue, Christminster.

She winced at the hit: Hardy underlines the strategic skirmishing within their intimacy. The point is not that Jude is sinister but that he maintains his obscurity; he will not acknowledge the cutting edge of his own voice. These two lovers like to speak of their love as something too sublime for earth, but there is considerable malice lurking in their discourse, and the scene in which he coerces her to marry him by using the threat of a return to Arabella can only be called extortion. Jude's behavior (like David's for Agnes, discussed above) is steeped in the exigencies of his embodied feelings, but his language reflects those exigencies only on condition that it need not acknowledge them. If this be true of Jude, so much the more does it apply to Sue.

I shall say little about Sue since she has already received exhaustive critical commentary. She bears on my argument, however, because it is through her portrayal that Hardy most asserts and then undermines the reader's confidence in a common standard of values capable of articulation. "The 'freedom' she has been at such pains to assert," Ian Gregor notes, "and which . . . would seem to have provided an unequivocal point of vantage . . . [begins to be] seen as something much more ambivalent, a nervous self-enclosure, the swift conceptualizing, safeguarding the self against the invasions of experience. Sue's scrutiny is keen, but it is judiciously angled" (215). Sue's verbal assertions are gradually revealed as fully vulnerable to the contortions of her instinctual life. She is uncontrollably capricious, addicted to a coquetry that (in Robert Heilman's words) "is, in the end, the external drama of inner divisions, of divergent impulses each of which is strong enough to determine action at any time, but not at all times or even with any regularity" (313). She is incurably at war with her own body, and her final behavior amply bears out Freud's contention that the sting of conscience is fueled by aggression turned inward.[12]

---

[12] Freud's fullest discussion of conscience (in *Civilisation and its Discontents*) provides an unimprovable gloss on Sue Bridehead:

His [the individual's] aggressiveness is introjected, internalized; it is, in point of fact, sent back to where it came from—that is, it is directed towards his own ego. There it is taken over by a portion of the ego, which sets itself over against the rest of the ego as super-ego, and which now, in the form of "conscience," is ready to put into action against the ego the same harsh aggressiveness that the

Hardy reveals in Sue perhaps his most audacious perceptions about the human aspiration for clarity of purpose and a life devoted to realizing the spirit within. Hardy shows not only that her asserted values have no transcendental basis (they are stained and mediated by the very fact of her being embodied), he shows her bodily grounding to be—itself as well—something opaque and indeterminate, a source of further confusion rather than clarifying authority. She confesses to Jude that "I am called Mrs Richard Phillotson, living a calm wedded life with my counterpart of that name. But I am not really Mrs Richard Phillotson, but a woman tossed about, all alone, with aberrant passions, and unaccountable antipathies" (223). Not really Mrs Richard Phillotson, and not in any clarifying way a woman at all. Jude's great-aunt's friend notes the elusiveness of Sue's natural identity: "She was not exactly a tomboy, you know; but she could do things that only boys do, as a rule" (133).

By way of contrast with such elusiveness, the profound solidity of *Tess of the d'Urbervilles* derives from its hold on sexual identity as something absolute. Sexual identity appears there as an ultimate ground of amoral meaning, lying beneath the relative and collapsible ones of moral assertion. The world of *Jude the Obscure* has become unmoored from this natural certitude. In the portrait of Sue Bridehead Hardy suggests that, to the unappeased spirit in search of articulate paradigms, nothing—not even the body's native stresses—can be reliably categorized. Life is a something foreign to the classificatory demands made by the spirit. In its utterances, its values, and even its bodily grounding, life is a phenomenon of stain, illogic, and obscurity.

Within this context Arabella and Father Time come into focus as the polar opposites of the novel. Arabella lives in the contingent. She is as canny about daily survival and as ignorant of ultimate purposes as Jude is learned in cosmic platitudes and

---

ego would have liked to satisfy upon other, extraneous individuals. The tension between the harsh super-ego and the ego that is subjected to it, is called by us the sense of guilt; it expresses itself as a need for punishment. . . . As long as things go well with a man, his conscience is lenient and lets the ego do all sorts of things; but when misfortune befalls him, he searches his soul, acknowledges his sinfulness, heightens the demands of his conscience, imposes abstinences on himself and punishes himself with penances." (21:123-26)

inept in local procedures. She has no goal but knows unerringly the way. She measures accurately the appropriate method for killing a pig just as, during Jude's final illness, she "critically gauge[s] his ebbing life" (407). The stains and deformations of time are unthinkingly accepted by Arabella. Pious and pagan utterances flow forth from her, with equal appositeness, either genuinely attuned to her desire or asserted with conscious hypocrisy. She is true to herself because she recognizes no standard beyond her embodied nature that she could betray. In her very fickleness she places and measures the obscure deceits of others, their attempt to square their incarnate existence with those immaculate values to which it is alien. She is exactly as well adjusted to the meaningless conditions of life as Father Time is incapable of coping with them.

That solemn child is the ultimate doomed Platonist in Hardy's world. Absorbing somewhere in his consciousness the full ravage wrought by time upon value, he has frozen his perception of the world into a posture of unforgivable stasis. He lives in a perpetuated, last-judgment landscape, all things appearing to him in their form of final exhaustion. Accepting time's ravage, he repudiates utterly the mercy and promise of its moment-by-moment process. On the train he passively regards "his companions as if he saw their whole rounded lives rather than their immediate figures" (290). Unlike his mother, whose rough humanity resides in her openness toward process rather than meaning, Father Time has fixed upon an absurd meaning at the expense of process. He "seemed to have begun with the generals of life, and never to have concerned himself with the particulars" (291). His optic can only envisage life as a gathered and complete insult inflicted on himself and others. He is an extreme instance of that mentality that Nietzsche calls "Socratism":

> Wherever Socratism turns its searching eyes it sees lack of insight and the power of illusion; and from this lack it infers the essential perversity and reprehensibility of what exists. Basing himself on this point, Socrates conceives it to be his duty to correct existence. (*The Birth of Tragedy*, 87)

Father Time corrects existence too. He cancels his role within it.

ॐ

I BEGAN by noting Jude's characteristic desire to be where he is not, a desire that reflects, according to J. Hillis Miller, "the experience of an 'emotional void' within, a distance of oneself from oneself" (xii). Miller claims that this absence in Hardy's characters is at last recognized as inalterable, and that they end by seeking the only release conceivable, that of death. More important to my reading of Hardy is the impact of an "emotional void" upon behavior itself: the pockets of dream-like passivity, of mental absence, that lie submerged within his protagonists' most earnest aspirations, waiting to wreck them. Jude and Clym are only the most reflective instances of a range of characters— Troy, Wildeve, Fitzpiers, Henchard among them—whose project, whatever energetic flourish it may begin with, contains a debilitating emptiness within. Their projects fail because all projects, once embarked on, either fail to meet the conditions of daily life or—meeting them—produce ennui and then disabling fatigue. These characters have sufficient energy to scorn the available, not to create alternatives; and this is so, one finally gathers, because their imagination is stocked with nothing but unrealities. The desirable is keyed to a mental vocabulary that simply negates whatever in Hardy's world can be actually experienced. Thus Hardy dramatizes characters whose consciousness of what they want and why they want it remains continuously out of phase with the vagaries of their incarnate behavior. They have no terms for finding out what they are actually doing, and no way of actually doing what they want. Indeed, they seem, in some central part of their being, to be spirits stunned to find themselves placed on earth and embodied in flesh. This gap between the consciousness of essential being and the opacity of contingent existence they express through a lurking and inexpungeable passivity. At critical moments they blank out.

Jude, for example, first slides back into his married routine with Arabella with an eery complicity. She tells him she can get a day off; he finds the notion "particularly uncongenial," yet says, "Of course, if you'd like to, you can." She tells him the train they can take, and he responds, "As you like." She gathers her luggage, "and they went on to the railway, and made the half-hour's journey to Aldbrickham, where they entered a third-rate inn near the station in time for a late supper" (200-201). They pass the night together. Where, one wants to know, is Jude during this transaction? Bodily, of course, with Arabella, and the effortless complicity of his physical behavior seems dependent on a corresponding mental absence. Jude's spirit has, for the moment, slipped out. Hardy provides no notation of a conflicted state of mind.

Such "absences" mark Jude's spiritual career as well. His campaign displays such a blundering and absentminded sense of purpose that no reader can be surprised by its failure. When, for instance, a casual acquaintance at Marygreen avers that "Such places [as Christminster] be not for such as you," Jude's long-sustained undertaking immediately falters:

> It was decidedly necessary to consider facts a little more closely than he had done of late. . . . "I ought to have thought of this before," he said, as he journeyed back. "It would have been better never to have embarked in the scheme at all than to do it without seeing clearly where I am going, or what I am aiming at." (135)[13]

Again, one wonders, where has his consciousness been during these previous years of "preparation"? Why is he so unaware of himself as a conditional creature? When under stress he is incapable of looking about him and charting the most intelligent course; instead he leaps into the transcendent and allusive ideal. Consider his behavior when being pressed to remarry Arabella:

> "I don't remember it," said Jude doggedly. "There's only one woman—but I won't mention her in this Capharnaum!"
> Arabella looked towards her father. "Now, Mr. Fawley, be honourable," said Donn. "You and my daughter have

[13] Hardy's use of plot is at moments like this so overtly clumsy that one wonders if he is not verging upon intentional absurdity—an intentional repudiation of the salient lines of a strong plot. For instance, when Jude attempts to commit suicide and the ice ignobly refuses to permit his romantic gesture, we are not far from Beckett's impotent Molloy, helplessly setting about, when he has a spare moment, to open his veins, and never succeeding.

been living here together these three or four days, quite on the understanding that you were going to marry her. . . . As a point of honour you must do it now."

"Don't say anything against my honour!" enjoined Jude hotly, standing up. "I'd marry the W— of Babylon rather than do anything dishonourable! No reflection on you, my dear. It is a mere rhetorical figure—what they call in the books, hyperbole."

"Keep your fingers for your debts to friends who shelter you," said Donn.

"If I am bound in honour to marry her—as I suppose I am—though how I came to be here with her I know no more than a dead man—marry her I will, so help me God! I have never behaved dishonourably to a woman or to any living thing. I am not a man who wants to save himself at the expense of the weaker among us!"

"There—never mind him, deary," said she, putting her cheek against Jude's. "Come up and wash your face, and just put yourself tidy, and off we'll go. Make it up with father." (387)

The scene is remarkable, and Hardy has no other novel in which one can imagine it. We see strikingly how Jude's allusive words create his "absence" from his coming fate. His mind rises into the empyrean, with Capharnaum, the Whore of Babylon, rhetorical figures, the theme of honor; it will not register the meaning of the specific act he is about to commit. Indeed, he *would* marry the Whore of Babylon because, somehow, his sense of himself remains idealized—permanently astray from, immune to, the sordid physical situations in which he finds himself. One hears a sense of verbally engendered immunity in his bland twaddle about "mere rhetorical figures," and Hardy nicely places Jude's tone of smug caprice, by having Donn retort: "Keep your figures for your debts. . . ." Donn and his daughter are content to humor Jude's proliferation of weightless abstract identities ("I have never . . . I am not . . ."). The more he breezily defines his unfettered spirit, the more easily they exploit his befuddled and conditional body.

What we see in such behavior is absence, and absence increasingly marks Jude's career.[14] He defines himself at first by what he will do, at last by what he has not done. He cherishes at first expectations of what is to be, at last memories of what has not happened. His return to Christminster indicates a final surrender of his attempt—at best half-hearted—to realize himself, to make an authentic home for his unsponsored and unreleased spirit. Thereafter he is given over to the "Remembrance Games." He lives wholly, now, in the schizoid space between failed expectation and ignored actuality, his mind focused on poignant scenarios (more fictive than true) with Sue and Christminster, his body abandoned to approaching death. His last gesture is characteristically verbal—he dies in words—and as usual he is quoting someone else. I think it is crucial to see that he is not Job; he is not an innocent and successful man, massively undone by an unholy pact between God and the devil. Rather, he is obscurely complicit in his own downfall, though it be his peculiar fate never to identify that complicity, never to find the words that will tell him who he is in all his incarnate perplexity. His death scene only gains poignance through its verbal indeterminacy, and it is the apex of Hardy's art that, four pages later, he can create a dialogue between Arabella and the Widow Edlin that matches Jude's death speech in resonance:

> "Die he forgive her!"
> "Not as I know."
> "Well—poor little thing, 'tis to be believed she's found forgiveness somewhere! She said she had found peace!"
> "She may swear that on her knees to the holy cross upon her necklace till she's hoarse, but it won't be true!" said Arabella. "She's never found peace since she left his arms, and never will again till she's as he is now!" (413)

Words at their best reveal the inadequacy of other words, and Hardy puts this last speech with unchallengeable authority

[14] The treatment of Jude and Sue's children, unnamed and of no importance while alive, obsessively and injuriously mourned when dead, reveals the same theme of absence.

144

in the mouth of Arabella. Rooted in the earth and stained in every way by it, strengthened as much as stained, Arabella places Sue's verbal and emotional evasions before us. Beyond this, though, Arabella's words bear the mark of subjective limitation that is the fate of words in this novel. Behind the verbalized truth that "she's never found peace since she left his arms," there lies, in the silence created by her speech, a truth that is darker yet: that, condemned to a body whose stresses she could neither disown nor make her own, Sue Bridehead found no peace in Jude's arms either. She found no peace anywhere. In this most unsettling of Hardy's novels the obscure spirit is compelled to move, in Eliot's words, "unappeased and peregrine,"[15] able to achieve nowhere—not in thought or feeling, not in the discourse of culture or the ground of nature—a form for its embodiment.

[15] The relevant lines are from "Little Gidding," II:
But as the passage now presents no hindrance
To the spirit unappeased and peregrine
Between two worlds become much like each other,
So I find words I never thought to speak
In streets I never thought I should revisit
When I left my body on a distant shore.

Four 🐌 Conrad: Against Nature

THE COLLAPSE of human structures, when subjected to un-remitting natural forces, troubles Conrad's imagination more than it does Hardy's. Despite the bleakness of Hardy's outlook—his view of life as an inherently unsanctioned process, an empty sequence of happenstances—he retained an enabling attachment (however complicated) to his native Dorset countryside. He absorbed its legends, its history, its customs, its landscape; and these absorptions may account for the modulated tone of even his darkest utterances. He is not surprised, his tone keeps repeating, because what is human history if not the immemorial story of expectation drained dry by time's passage?

> Black is night's cope;
> But death will not appal
> One who, past doubtings all,
> Waits in unhope. (From "In Tenebris")

Conrad also "waits in unhope," but he waits in greater isolation. His work can less easily afford the melancholy yet sustaining acknowledgment that collapse is our common fate. He seems to have discovered the bad news on his own, and he creates a fictional world in which that news, while everywhere insinuated, is not easily broadcast. Hardy's pessimistic peasants are as quick to foregather in gossip over enterprises that have miscarried as their counterparts in Conrad are ready to enjoin enterprises that (so they think) might prosper. Even Marlow, who is Conrad's supreme figure of circumspection, works in behalf of others' undertakings (some of them quite dubious); and Conrad's most

146

knowing pessimists, men like Decoud and Heyst, eventually become embroiled in fantastic schemes.

The point is clear. Campaigns are launched in Hardy against the ubiquitous choral awareness that they will fail as they have always failed, that it is saner to stay at home and sit still. In Conrad these enterprises are conducted in an atmosphere equally inhospitable to success, but in which, oddly, other options are hardly thinkable. There is never in his work a home to stay at, and his people are usually placed in quandaries that equate sitting still with drowning. For reasons I shall explore in this chapter, Conrad attends to his characters in the measure that they have chosen, or strayed into, situations of maximum risk.

Why they are likely to fail is susceptible to many explanations. One of the most acute is suggested by Edward Said in his distinction between experience-as-it-is-lived and experience-as-it-is-retrospectively-shaped:

> The first mode is to experience reality as an unfolding process, as action-being-made, as always "becoming." To experience all of this is to feel oneself in the midst of reality. The second mode is to feel reality as a hard quantity, very much "there" and definable. To experience this is to view reality retrospectively, since only in looking back upon what has already occurred can one master the unceasing movement of action-being-made. In other words, the first mode is that of the actor, the second that of the author. (106)

One may say that the actor's enterprise fails insofar as he has attempted to transpose the perfected conditions of author-ity to the fluid realm of ongoing action. His instigating dream of himself—self-authored yet composed from cultural models, hard, definable, and complete—is submitted to the public arena of moment-by-moment "becoming," and there it founders. Hardy and Conrad both expose the fiction that a life might be actually experienced according to authoritative patterns mastered and assembled in retrospect. In their work this discrepancy occasions a variety of tragic encounters, whereas Lawrence and Joyce will turn the same discrepancy into a point of creative departure.

"NOTHING CAN TOUCH ME": *LORD JIM*

A ship firing into a continent—this is one of Conrad's most striking images for the relationship between self and world that this chapter will explore. As the image suggests, it is an uneasy, antagonistic, and potentially absurd relationship, based on incomprehension and issuing often in violence, necessitated by some project of the self that may range from mercenary greed to high-minded idealism. What motives actuate the firing subject? What qualities characterize the receiving object? What are the effects of the one upon the other? These questions guide the following sketch of Conrad's phenomenal world: the ways in which he characteristically apprehends his people, their commerce with each other, and their relation to their settings.

Despite Conrad's vexation at being considered a writer of sea tales, the relations between the exigent subject and the world he inhabits—the deeper lines of stress in his fiction—indicate the traces of a "maritime" orientation. A basic *donnée* of his imagination is the assertion of human will against a shapeless and unaccommodating natural backdrop. His typical story is of a willed invasion, a precarious attempt to make a foreign medium support a private desire.[1] The humanly willed vs. the naturally given is of course a tension in, as well as a constitutive condition of, all fiction. No art naively engages its object, simply giving voice to nature, free of all convention. What distinguishes Conrad's work from that of his Victorian predecessors in this regard, however, is his uneasiness, his problematic and even debilitating awareness of the artifice in his art. Fictions lie, and he must continually find ways of "tilting" his fictive world, to make it reveal its artifice and thus suggest its unconventional truth. Hence the complexity, not to say perversity, of his approach to his materials, for though the materials are what he must deliver, the conventional forms into which they most readily fall are embarrassingly inappropriate: a betrayal as much as a clarification. The

---

[1] Peter J. Glassman makes a kindred point about the fixed landscape of the Conradian narrative: "As in each of his previous novels, Conrad in *Lord Jim* again imagines a geography of presented serenity which conceals enormously threatening and undivinable dangers . . ." (254).

abrupt transitions and extended deviations of his narrative stance serve to keep the materials "undomesticated" by rendering his events and characters opaque in themselves, enigmatic in the view of others (including the reader), and unplaced within any larger unifying setting. Harmony, order, interrelationship—these emerge in Conrad's world (its structure as well as its plots) as willed achievements crafted against an incessant pressure toward entropy and discontinuity. Whether its subject be the mastery of the sea (as in all the sea narratives) or the pacification of the land (as in "Heart of Darkness," *Nostromo*, and to a lesser extent *The Secret Agent* and *Under Western Eyes*), the Conrad narrative emphasizes the strain and unlikelihood, the unnaturalness of such a willed enterprise, as set within the overwhelming inertia of an inhuman medium.

Characters at home in their setting or at ease with their calling rarely interest Conrad. In "Heart of Darkness" and *Nostromo*, for instance, he focuses less on the passive natives (who are at home, even if invaded) than on the enterprising and disoriented foreigners—Kurtz, Marlow, Charles Gould, Decoud, Viola, Nostromo—men who have no home to fall back on, whose identity and survival depend on the maintenance of a willed private project or an ideal self-image. The people Conrad chooses to explore in both his land and his sea novels have ventured away from a sustaining turf. No longer able to take anything for granted, their self-image no longer supported and held in check by the paternal authority of native customs (Conrad's fiction has no native customs, only foreign ones), they are already immersed in the "destructive element." Like Charles Gould, they are in too deep to withdraw; there is no going back.

The "maritime" model extends further. As on a ship, Conrad's people appear typically grouped together in a common endeavor, yet actually isolated each within his own inexpressible concerns.[2] Their unity is the public and voluntary bond of a

---

[2] Ian Watt makes the same point with reverse emphasis. "The characters are intensely individual, but their consciousness is very largely determined by what they do in the world of work, and both their internal conflicts and their relationships with others are deeply and continually subject to the external and internal conditions imposed by collective human activities" (*Conrad in the Nine-*

commercial contract or moral code, not (as often in Dickens and George Eliot) the deeper and irrational bond of family kin. If the Dickens orphan ends by discovering his hidden brotherhood, the Conrad brother ends by discovering his hidden orphanhood. Jim in the boat with the rest of the crew, Nostromo and Decoud in the lighter, Verloc and Stevie walking together toward Greenwich, Haldin and Razumov in the same bedroom—these are images of radical isolation underlying surface unity. (Conrad has his doubles, to be sure, and more than one orphan discovers his ghostly brother; but these devastating likelinesses are rarely a source of familial comfort or strength to the aghast solitary.)[3]

Conrad's best work awakens within his reader a state of disorientation akin to that which he portrays in his characters. The world one enters in his pages is murky, evasive, and incongruent. Perspective shifts unexpectedly from character to character, from scene to scene, from time frame to time frame. On a given two pages in Chapter 5 (23-25) of *Lord Jim* Marlow's narrative moves impressionistically from Jim to the German captain to DeJongh to Archie Ruthvel to a Portuguese half-caste to Captain Elliott and his three daughters' matrimonial problems.[4] These figures loom into and then vanish out of the reader's uncomprehending

---

teenth Century, 336-37). Watt's shrewd, informed, and sympathetic study appeared after I had thought through and drafted my own chapter. My argument coincides with his in acknowledging the range of pressures that determine human enterprises, but he would reject my contention that Jim's heroic position is fundamentally suspect.

[3] The important exception is of course the double-relationship in "The Secret Sharer." I agree with Bruce Johnson, however, that the Captain's commerce with Leggatt is unrepresentatively fruitful and optimistic. Indeed, the widespread anthologizing of this story conveys to the casual student a misleading image of Conrad's fiction: an image of psychic flexibility, of successful trafficking with those illicit energies of character and behavior that have been repudiated by the authorized code. Conrad is considerably more troubled and less modernist than this image suggests.

[4] Albert Guerard's magisterial study of Conrad includes a useful "slow-motion" synopsis of these pages, paragraph by paragraph. Only by slowing down one's critical pace does one register the subversiveness of Conrad's narrative structure in the first half of *Lord Jim*. See Guerard, *Conrad the Novelist* (134-40). Ian Watt also devotes some twenty-five pages to Conrad's extremely flexible deployment of time in *Lord Jim* (286-310).

view. They are present before they have been explained and absent before the explaining is over. Conrad's fiction contains scores of such peripheral floating figures, and they contribute unobtrusively to its effect upon us. They make us take this fictional world as a scene of fleeting, opaque objects, glimpsed in passing rather than prepared for, made transparent, fixed. Thus the impressionistic Conrad narrative may be said to be most "maritime" in its proliferation of peripatetic figures against a background as uncaring and unfocused as the Pacific Ocean. This metaphoric sense of "maritime" applies also to the Congo of "Heart of Darkness," the Costaguana of *Nostromo*, and the cityscapes of London, St. Petersburg, and Geneva in *The Secret Agent* and *Under Western Eyes*: sprawling inhuman places that contain but do not nourish the human pursuits within their midst. The urban setting in Dickens is equally unfriendly, but the Dickens protagonist is provided with pockets of familial security, from which he emerges to do battle and to which he returns for reassurance and ratification.

Few characters appear so fleetingly in the novels of Dickens, Eliot, or Hardy; and by the end of those novels almost everyone has settled into focus, been assigned his appropriate meaning and setting. The landscape in Dickens, Eliot, and Hardy eventually illuminates the human figure; the landscape in Conrad only silhouettes his mystery. If Dickens, Eliot, and Hardy end by placing their protagonists in the most charged and embracive setting—Lady Dedlock at Tom-all-Alone's, Maggie in the flooded river, Tess at Stonehenge—Conrad by contrast shows his tragic figures to be conventionally placed but inwardly adrift. Jim, Decoud, Nostromo, Razumov—these men are each depicted, at their moments of catastrophe, in psychic isolation from the physical setting that strikes them down. They are exposed, so to say, as foreigners, role-players, counterfeiters. In some central part of themselves they have all along been vacant, focused somewhere else.

Related by their conscious will to their settings, moved by private desire if not obsession, the characters of *Lord Jim* are typically roamers, not natives. Chester, Robinson, Brown, the French lieutenant, and Stein wander across the Marlovian nar-

rative, likely to emerge from nowhere and to be heading anywhere. Many ports know them; no port defines them. My point
is that narrative plot and structure reinforce each other here. These
men move through their lives, uprooted, enigmatic, acknowledging no native context, simultaneously isolated and activated by
their imperious will, precisely as Conrad moves them through
his narrative: self-enclosed objects that surge into view and then
vanish into the mist.

&

A GALLERY of willful figures, brought by Marlow's narrative
suddenly into and then out of focus, enigmatic to the reader,
unclear to other characters and often to themselves as well, moving with their private projects within a medium that bonds them
intensely without impairing their solitude—such is a rough summary of the phenomenal world of *Lord Jim*. The keynote of its
composition, though, is seen less in its shape than heard in its
utterance. Rather than condense its speech into the unified and
recollected voice of an authoritative narrator, Conrad quotes it.
His genius is to make us hear the disjointed multiplicity of its
polyglot speakers.

Everyone talks in *Lord Jim*; few achieve verbal coherence.
Conrad is extraordinarily alert to the strangeness of speech, the
ways in which it wells out of one human subject, reaches stam-
meringly toward an attendant second subject, then subsides in
failure. "The blight of futility that lies in wait for men's speeches
had fallen upon our conversation, and made it a thing of empty
sound" (90). This writer for whom only Polish was native, all
other languages being learned—achievements of the will, against
the grain—renders sensitively the gap between a feeling and an
utterance, a speaker and a listener. Each speaker characteristically
deforms the medium of language as he exploits it. The words
uttered reflect the speaker but rarely the object he is attempting
to describe. "Look at dese cattle" (10) says the German captain,
" 'She was full of reptiles' " (32) says the Chief Engineer. " 'Impossible de comprendre—vous concevez' " (84) says the French
lieutenant. " 'One thing alone can us from being ourselves cure!' "
(129) says Stein. " 'Jove! Get out of this. Jove! This is luck at

152

last. . . . You wait. I'll . . .' " (144) says Jim about to try his chance at Patusan. " 'An awful thing has happened . . . I must now at once . . .' " (207)[5] writes Jim at the end, brokenly, obscurely, making his last futile attempt to explain the impact of Brown upon his destiny.

In each instance the utterance is shaped, if not skewed, by the subjective inflections of the speaker. Even where the language is common, ten men in sufficient distress will speak ten different dialects. At moments of deep need the Conradian psyche verges on inarticulateness, issuing cryptic words about reptiles, stammering broken phrases. Conrad is a master of fragmented utterance. He had doubtless suffered—at any rate he makes us hear—the incapacity of the soul to deliver itself in language. What he portrays is not the transparency of communication but the opacity of frustrated men talking, each in his own idiom and syntax, circling vainly for "that full utterance which through all our stammerings is of course our only and abiding intention" (137).

Utterance in *Lord Jim* is embodied, inflected, opaque. Again and again we wait expectantly with Marlow as a privileged commentator—Brierly, Chester, the French lieutenant, Stein, Cornelius, Brown—draws close and begins to speak. Always the speech reaches toward Jim, fleetingly silhouettes him, then retires extinguished to its subjective point of origin. Speech in Conrad is either teasingly inadequate or radically inadequate. The Pilgrims on the Patna understanding nothing of their coming betrayal, the Malay helmsmen hearing the white crew's words but convinced of "secret reasons" for their behavior, Jewel pressing Marlow to explain the enigma of Jim—each of these instances expresses the parochialism of words, their status as simultaneously conveyer and concealer of meaning. There are only words available, and the words are often no better than noises. Discourse is strictly conventional, by way of translation and interpretation.

[5] The first of Jim's passages is excerpted, but both are quoted without abridgement. The unfinished utterance is typical of Jim. (In order to simplify the morass of quotes within quotes in *Lord Jim*, I shall stylize my citations as follows: Marlow's commentary will be placed in double quotes, all commentary cited by Marlow will be placed in single quotes within double quotes.)

The deep reality remains inaccessible, mute, and would doubtless be unbearable if confronted directly. As Marlow says in "Heart of Darkness," "The inner truth is hidden—luckily, luckily" (34). Against such a world of flickering and isolated figures, each burdened with obscure dreams of self-ratification, speaking each in his own inflected tongue—against, precisely, the murk and slipperiness of this phenomenal world we need to assess the rigid and simplistic perfection of Conrad's moral code. His people speak many tongues, but his code is a universal grammar.

"One of us"—the group, not the individual, is the source of value, and it is urgent to know quickly if one belongs to it or not. Membership is indicated by a symbolism of shared uniforms, shared skills, shared vocabulary. These surface signs attest to belief in "a few very simple ideas . . . notably . . . the idea of Fidelity" (*A Personal Record*, xix). For Fidelity, read rigorous self-restraint in the pursuit of a common goal. The crisis-model implicit in Conrad's moral formulation is a fragile ship in a destructive element. It will *naturally* founder should its crew relax their hold upon themselves. A successful voyage is a kind of miracle, a continuous repression of the anarchic possibilities of self-release. Neither spoken (and thus subjectively inflected, stammering, ambiguous) nor written, the requirements of the seaman's code are universally symbolized in the form of a certificate. It is a document as briskly impersonal as the uniforms its followers wear.

Uniforms in Conrad are no picturesque decoration. Their aim is to make uniform, to maintain the conviction of uniformity, to hold in the narcissistic urges of ego-release. "I have a horror of losing even for one moving moment that full possession of myself which is the first condition of good service," Conrad writes in his Preface to *A Personal Record* (xvii). There can be no doubt that the stress is on possession, not self.[6] The hidden impulses of the self represent not a resource to be exploited but a menace to be controlled, kept in uniform ("The inner truth

[6] Centering his study on Conrad on this passage and another similar one in *A Personal Record*, H. M. Daleski reads the entire Conrad *oeuvre*—rather too programmatically, I think—in the light of the tension between self-possession and self-surrender.

is hidden—luckily, luckily"). Clothing—Jim's, Nostromo's—is almost as eloquent a phenomenon in Conrad's world as the body beneath it is in Lawrence's.

Indeed, when approached close up, Conrad's characters often reveal grotesque bodies. Brown, Robinson, and Cornelius are drawn in broad, aggressively offensive strokes that radiate their author's disgust. But the crowning portrait of physical repulsion is the German captain:

> "The skipper gazed in an inanimate way between his feet: he seemed to be swollen to an unnatural size by some awful disease. . . . His thick, purplish lips came together without a sound, he went off in a resolute waddle to the gharry and began to jerk at the door-handle with such a blind brutality of impatience that I expected to see the whole concern over-turned on its side, pony and all. The driver . . . displayed at once all the signs of intense terror . . . looking around from his box at this vast carcass forcing its way into his convey-ance. The little machine shook and rocked tumultuously, and the crimson nape of that lowered neck, the size of those straining thighs, the immense heaving of that dingy, striped green-and-orange back, the whole burrowing effort of that gaudy and sordid mass troubled one's sense of probability with a droll and fearsome effect, like one of those grotesque and distinct visions that scare and fascinate one in a fever. He disappeared." (29)

It is, in several senses, the scene of a misfit. The clothes are not fitting in themselves, and the body neither fits into them nor into the gharry. More deeply, spirit cannot conceivably fit into such a body. Conrad suggests the disease of pure uncontrolled matter. Free to roam about the vast Pacific, uncoerced by "your verfluchte certificate" (26), the German captain has "swollen" cancerously along the lines of his worst susceptibilities. Like all of Conrad's grotesques—and some of Conrad's protagonists—he has abandoned his native culture, been exposed to a foreign set-ting, lost his sustaining bond with a shaping code, and simply collapsed into himself. His monstrous figure suggests the poten-tial of unbridled self-release. His body has no internal order. Unharnessed by any sanction outside itself, it swells into the sordid overripeness of a "vast carcass." *Mutatis mutandis*, his physical enormity is a figure for Kurtz's spiritual monstrosity. In the German captain—as in Verloc, Nikita, and others—Conrad fuses physical obesity with moral deformity with vocational vagrancy: men faithful only to their internal propensity lapse into vile bodies.

Such figures suggest the liabilities to which, in Conrad's imagination, undisciplined flesh is heir. There already exist several studies of the perverse implications that insinuate themselves into the prose whenever Conrad dilates on a woman's physical charms. Suffice it to say here that the erotic body beneath the clothes is explosive material for Conrad. The complex of feelings—desire and dread, awe and disgust—to which its depiction gives rise are never artistically mastered.[7]

But with uniforms, with chosen, crafted signs that promise to control the impulses and vicissitudes of flesh even if they do not guarantee it—with these he excels. An expression of the conscious will, they bear the hallmark of Conradian value: they have been painstakingly created. They represent less a virtue that is indigenous to the human animal than one he has willed upon himself.[8] And of course it is the encounter between these Procrustean values and the ambiguous phenomena they fail to con-

[7] Guerard is brief but acute on this cause (among others) for the recurrent failures in Conrad's art. Thomas Moser's *Joseph Conrad: Achievement and Decline* is the classic book-length study of Conrad's fiction from a Freudian perspective. Bernard Meyer's *Joseph Conrad: A Psychoanalytic Biography* frankly exploits the work as a quarry harboring the psyche of its author, but even so it contains some arresting perceptions for the literary critic. See especially Chapters 3-4, 6, 13-15, and the very suggestive Conrad drawings reproduced and interpreted on 326-32.

[8] The conscious will is of course also "indigenous," but my point is that it is a will opposed to the spontaneous inclinations of the subject, and of secondary rather than primary importance as a key, so to speak, for interpreting Conrad's imagination. For a cogent opposed view of these two strains in Conrad's work, see Ian Watt, "Joseph Conrad: Alienation and Commitment." Watt argues that the nihilistic strain is to be seen as part of Conrad's late-Victorian intellectual inheritance, "the findings of the alienated intellect" (269), whereas the positive strain of commitment is a product of his immediate experiences as a seaman.

trol that generates Conrad's tragic novels. I turn now to the crises of identity that beset the protagonist once his uniform has slipped.

ॐ

FREUD WRITES in *The Interpretation of Dreams*: "Very rarely does the complexity of human character, driven hither and thither by dynamic forces, submit to a choice between simple alternatives, as our antiquated morality would have us believe" (5:621). The ambivalence of Conrad comes into focus when one sees that he illogically endorses both sides of Freud's polar statement. He knows that character is polymorphous and unpredictable, often disobedient to the trained will. Yet the only schema of assessment that he can accept is the seaman's code based on "our antiquated morality."[9]

As much as Dickens or George Eliot, Conrad relies on the habitual self; as much as Lawrence or Gide, he disbelieves in its efficacy. " 'But habit—habit—necessity—do you see?—the eye of others—*voilà*' " (90), affirms the French lieutenant. Like work itself, habit narcotizes the anxious imagination; it is king in the realm dominated by learned gesture and conscious will. However, Conrad so arranges his fictions that the habits generated by conscious training are insufficient. A surface garment, like protective coloration, habit loses its mediating efficacy the moment the landscape essentially alters; and Conrad's plots insist on such an alteration. Kurtz in the Congo, Jim on a ship about to founder, Decoud on the Great Isabel, Razumov confronted by Haldin— these shattering encounters break through the willed defenses of habit. A propensity deep within the menaced self—deeper than anything learned—is awakened, and against the crisis caused by this intrusive impulse Conrad knows no governing remedy.

In an interesting recent study, Bruce Johnson approaches

[9] To complicate the paradox further, Conrad retains as well an aristocratic scorn for those whose careers are effortlessly congruent with the code, those who (as he puts it in the famous passage in *Typhoon*) ". . . go skimming over the years of existence to sink gently into a placid grave, ignorant of life to the last, without ever having been made to see all it may contain of perfidy, of violence, and of terror. There are on sea and land such men thus fortunate—or thus disdained by destiny or by the sea" (208).

these crises of identity in the spirit of Sartrean existentialism, claiming as "Conradian assumptions . . . first, that identity, sense of self, must be created continuously by will; second, that the realm of will is also that of morality. Identity does not exist as a given natural fact. . . . If identity were part of established natural certainties, man would indeed be godlike" (17). As the French lieutenant says, " 'it would be too easy otherwise' " (90). Johnson goes on to set up a brilliant contrast between Jim and Stein. Jim believes in

> a predetermined self which, though experience may temporarily frustrate its appearance, will ultimately shine forth. Stein—who, we are told, is instinctively heroic—ironically believes in the contingent self; Jim, who is contingently cowardly or heroic believes in the ordained self. . . . What Stein's advice suggests . . . is that the man who recognizes his contingency, his moment-to-moment formlessness, pursues the ideal as an expression of his humanity. To be human is . . . to be unlike the butterfly, not the precise and peaceful balance of cosmic forces, but the magnificent imbalance of a lust for perfection in a creature aware of his imperfection. To pursue the ideal as one's already innate essence is not to *pursue* it at all. (60)

This commentary is so illuminating that one quarrels with it in a spirit of indebtedness. Still, Johnson's Sartrean model is misleading. It proposes more flexibility, more choice in this matter of identity (and more smugness in Jim's quest), than Conrad dramatizes. A Schopenhauerian lens is the appropriate one here, for while Conrad does show identity to be inscribed in the will, this will is not Sartre's instrument, obedient to the dictates of consciousness. Schopenhauer writes:

> According to my fundamental point of view . . . will is first and original; knowledge is merely added to it as an instrument belonging to the phenomenon of will. Therefore every man is what he is through his will. . . . Through the knowledge which is added to it he comes to know in the course of experience *what he is*, i.e., he learns his character. Thus

158

he *knows* himself in consequence of and in accordance with the nature of his will, instead of *willing* in consequence of and in accordance with his knowing. According to the latter view, he would only require to consider how he would like best to be, and he would be it. . . . I, on the contrary, say that . . . he cannot resolve to be this or that, nor can he become other than he is; but he *is* once for all, and he knows in the course of experience *what* he is. (212)[10]

This somber notion of identity is a shade—but only a shade—more deterministic than Conrad's in his major fiction. Essentially, if not entirely, we harbor what we are within us, and catastrophe releases it: "A clean slate, did he say? As if the initial word of each our destiny were not graven in imperishable characters upon the face of a rock!" (113)[11] *Lord Jim* is a haunting as much as it is a soaring, and if one sees in it, according to Johnson, "the power of human ego . . . to confer value upon abstractions and to idealize its own desires" (65), one sees as well Jim's sustained and hopeless attempt to erase that "initial word" inscribed in his unconscious will and revealed in his jump. As Dorothy Van Ghent lucidly puts it, ". . . at no time does he consciously acknowledge that it *was* himself who jumped from the *Patna*—it was only his body that had jumped; and his career thenceforth is an attempt to prove before men that the gross fact of the jump belied his identity" (233-34). (We are back to the Maggie Tulliver-Stephen Guest enigma. Is identity the transcendental construct ratified by habit and betrayed by momentary passion, or is it a contingent construct, conditioned by the body and revealed by a moment of passion? The difference between Eliot and Conrad relevant to my argument is that Eliot cannot take up this question whereas Conrad cannot put it down.)

Given his isolation, his exposure, and his idealized self-im-

[10] Johnson himself speculates as to whether Conrad's model of mind is better described in Schopenhauerian or Sartrean terms (126-30).

[11] Watt maintains a similar view of the inalterable givens within Conradian identity: "In general Conrad's novels suggest that he thought character was impervious to full comprehension; it was also nearly as intractable as circumstance, and equally unlikely to be transformed in accordance with our wishes" (*Conrad in the Nineteenth Century*, 340).

age, the Conradian protagonist rarely learns from his crises and almost never absorbs what he learns. Nietzsche's advice, "Become who you are," is intolerable to him, for what he has glimpsed in himself is usually his worst possibilities.[12] The willful invader has been involuntarily invaded. Something inside has slipped through the uniform of chosen identity, and he moves not to accommodate the despised intruder but to stiffen trebly his resolve. His nature a door he wants to keep closed, his native culture a past he has abandoned, his isolation now intensifies and he either collapses (like Kurtz and Decoud), sinks deeper into his ego-dream (like Gould and Jim), or engages in a species of conscious role-playing that soon becomes desperate and untenable (like Nostromo and Razumov). In every instance the setting he inhabits freezes into the shape of the crisis scene: Jim and his jump are as inseparable as Nostromo and his hidden silver, Razumov and his betrayed Haldin.

Men so brittle as Conrad's protagonists cannot accommodate stress; they can only resist it or be shattered by it. This I take to be the implication of Conrad's proliferating doubles, invasive figures who express in caricature propensities that the immaculate protagonist cannot afford to acknowledge in himself. Jim's effect on Brierly is duplicated by Brown's effect on Jim. An unbearably besmirching resemblance *in posse* is glimpsed, and *posse*, of course, is the enemy. In Jim's case, Brown intensified a sullying that began with the jump from the Patna, for Brown reactivates George:

> "Eight hundred living people, and they were yelling after the one dead man to come down and be saved! 'Jump, George! Jump! Oh, jump!' . . . With the first hiss of rain, and the first gust of wind, they screamed, 'Jump, George! We'll catch you! Jump!' . . . I heard as if I had been on the top of a tower another wild screech, 'Geo-o-o-orge! Oh, jump!' She was going down, down, head first under me . . . I had jumped . . . it seems. . . ." (68)

[12] Again the significant exception is the Captain in "The Secret Sharer." See above, footnote 3.

Jim's account unintentionally but insistently associates himself with George. He jumps into the place reserved for George; more darkly, he jumps into George, at a stroke taking on George's moral obliquity. He carries George within him—a secret sharer—and George is dead. The implication, borne out in a number of ways, is that Jim is dead too. He has ceased to live after the Patna disgrace; or, to put it another way, he has fallen outside the aegis of his transcendental identity. His life has lost its unfolding promise, has become (essentially) a suspension. Rooted mentally to the time and place of one traumatic scene, he lives to prove that he will know how to die next time.[13]

The reiterated refrain of "Nothing can touch me" (this phrase or a slight variant of it occurs at least eight times)[14] points to this death-like immunity in Jim. His heroism on Patusan is founded on a continual risking of his life. He once a month drinks the Rajah's possibly poisoned coffee, and his willingness to die suggests that, in a psychic sense, he has already conceded his life. " 'Nothing is lost,' " he tells Jewel minutes before Doramin fires. Everything he could lose has already been lost. Invaded by the impulse released in the Patna disaster, his identity underwent an unsurvivable humiliation: he became not-himself. Having psychically suffered death already, he is on easy terms with his coming physical dissolution, and he swells with pleasure at the first death he can exact in obscure recompense for his own:

> He told me he was experiencing a feeling of unutterable relief, of vengeful elation. He held his shot, he says, deliberately. . . . He held it for the pleasure of saying to himself, That's a dead man! . . . The explosion in that confined space was stunning. . . . He saw the man jerk his head up, fling his arms forward, and drop his kriss. . . . With the impetus of his rush the man drove straight on, his face suddenly gaping disfigured, with his hands open before him gropingly, as though blinded. . . . Jim says he didn't lose the

[13] As though completing a single action that began with his jump from the Patna, Jim says at the moment of crisis to Tamb' Itam (and even more to himself): " 'Time to finish this' " (250).

[14] See 16, 109, 147, 151, 178, 198, 203, 251.

smallest detail of all this. He found himself calm, appeased, without rancour, without uneasiness, as if the death of that man had atoned for everything. (183)

Jim relishes this death scene too intensely for it not to relate massively to his own.[15] His prolonged savoring of this moment in which a dangerous man is about to be annihilated by his own greater power reverses satisfyingly his earlier nightmare of impotence. "Relief . . . vengeful elation . . . appeased . . . atoned"— this is the language of a man with a death inside him, and he is ready to inflict it on others, as he is "heroically" ready to inflict it on himself. Other people, other places hold no promise for intimacy but serve only as the setting for this unchanging offer of his death. Marlow says that on Patusan "all these things that made him master had made him a captive, too . . . it was they that possessed him and made him their own to the innermost thought, to the slightest stir of blood, to his last breath" (152). Jim pledges them his death; he cannot bring them into his life.[16] In his psychic drama only one figure holds the stage. Even with Jewel the bond is as limited as it is intense:

> "I—I love her dearly. More than I can tell. Of course one cannot tell. You take a different view of your actions when you come to understand, when you are *made* to understand every day that your existence is necessary—you see, absolutely necessary—to another person." (185)

He loves her for loving him, trusting him, requiring his daily existence. He speaks not of his need of her existence, for he is past needing anyone's existence; all he requires is their immaculate belief.[17] Marlow closes the narrative of Jim's life with a scene

[15] Guerard makes a related point in terms of Jim's "compulsion to make others reenact his sudden jump from the *Patna*" (*Conrad the Novelist*, 145-46).

[16] J.I.M. Stewart notes, but does not attempt to explain, the resultant dramatic thinness of Jim's relationships on Patusan: "If Jim is not quite so real to us in Patusan as he has been on board the Patna or before his judges, it is partly because of this uncertainty of relation and implication with his final background" (118-19).

[17] The Novalis epigraph to *Lord Jim* ("It is certain my conviction gains infinitely, the moment another soul will believe in it") contains *in nuce* this entire

that silhouettes vividly his spotless immunity against the tribe's vulnerable humanity. We are shown Doramin, unwieldy, barely able to move, leaning upon "the neck of a bowed youth," a figure of total penetrability: bereft father, betrayed chief, decrepit man, ravaged by his emotions. And we see Jim, finally fixing on them all the "proud and unflinching glance" (253) he has been unable to summon until now. It is the face of a hero—"as unflinching as a hero in a book" (5), the face Jim dreamed of when a boy—[18] and he can summon it now because he has finally paid its price: he carries a bullet through the heart. For an exquisite instant he is perfect, knowing himself to be, securely, and without possibility of change, at one with his own ideal. His death, outrageously withheld by the leap from the Patna, heroically offered thereafter, is finally accepted. He dies "with his hand over his lips" (253), as though to still any sound of pain or protest that might sully this immaculate payment.

&

"NOTHING can touch me." Encased in his dream of himself, Jim could be shattered but not touched. His perfection is as inflexible as that of the code he had betrayed. Against both these perfections—Jim's and the code's—we may finally set the frailer values that remain: the communities that are not Community, the truths that are not Truth. These values are implicit in the voice and structure of the novel.

The narrative voice of *Lord Jim* is as tentative and polyvalent as the moral code it refers to is crisp and absolute. Further, the contextual presence of others—their look, talk, and behavior—is as insistently borne in on the reader as it is kept at bay from the hero's idealizing and isolating consciousness. "The infernal joke was being crammed devilishly down his throat," says Marlow,

---

point, for it expresses the need of a beleaguered ego, not the hope for a common bond. The belief of "another soul" is indispensable because it corroborates "my conviction." The language of "souls" and "convictions" suggests the often disembodied thinness of Conradian community: a dependence of the fragile subjective self upon a comprehending objective other, not a mutual intimacy between two incarnate subjects.

[18] I owe this connection to David Thorburn (55).

"but—look you—he was not going to admit of any sort of swallowing motion in his gullet" (67). While Jim proudly says No, however, his body does Yes, does Yes continuously and involuntarily. Whatever he may *say*, he swallows.

Community—not the ideal one of his private dream but the actual ones of his embodied life—is always in force, its transactions are continuous.[19] It is not a matter of choice; there is nothing but community. It can be honored or betrayed but not banished. Conrad's figures are helplessly social; they exist together in (to use Melville's words) "a mutual joint-stock company." Whatever contracts the hero acknowledges or ignores, he is contracted up to his neck, and he calls upon these contracts incessantly, unwittingly, to keep himself afloat. The support of others—to be believed by them—is as stringently required as intimacy with them is denied. Surrounding the Conradian roamer—ostensibly alone with his dream—is the unemphasized, often unsought, but ever-present medium (supportive or destructive) of other people. And it is his relation to this medium that determines, at the moment of maximum stress, whether he survives or is shattered.

"We exist only in so far as we hang together" (136), Marlow tells his listeners. " 'Nobody is good enough' " (194), he hurls at Jewel. " 'The example of others who are no better than yourself, and yet make good countenance . . .' " (90), the French lieutenant affirms. Each has his private point of collapse; each borrows from the collective strength of others, even as he lends from his own strength. All human projects require collaboration; and this commerce of continuous, involuntary, even unconscious acts of dependency and support makes up the actual Conradian community. Such a community may be obscured by the hero's grandiose visions, but it is implicit wherever men foregather. Jim therefore starts with alarm when, on board the Patna, his gorgeous dreams of achievement are interrupted by the appearance of the German captain:

[19] Commenting on Marlow's friend's distinction between fighting either in the ranks or elsewhere, J.I.M. Stewart remarks: "In fact, we cannot fight anywhere else. There are only the ranks" (109).

164

Red of face, only half awake, the left eye partly closed, the
right staring stupid and glassy. . . . There was something
obscene in the sight of his naked flesh . . . the odious and
fleshly figure, as though seen for the first time in a revealing
moment, fixed itself in his memory for ever as the incarna-
tion of everything vile and base that lurks in the world we
love: in our own hearts we trust for our salvation in the
men that surround us, in the sights that fill our eyes, in the
sounds that fill our ears, and in the air that fills our lungs.
(14)

So much of the novel is here: the allure of immaculate dreams
that satisfy the idealizing will, the vileness of mere motley flesh,
the reality of community as something ineluctable—the sound in
our ears and the air in our lungs. Jim has unknowingly entrusted
himself where he knowingly despises; inundated by bad air and
bad sounds, he goes under. Thus betrayed, he turns (unaware)
betrayer, for one way of assessing his career is to see it as a
recurrent betrayal of real though (for him) subordinate communities—the Pilgrims on the Patna, Denver, Egstrom and Blake,
Dain Waris, Doramin, Jewel—while in pursuit of an ideal one,
glimpsed in a dream, lost in a nightmare. Dedicated to this pursuit, all subsequent situations perceived as ghostly simulacra of
his collapse-that-must-be-redeemed, Jim is absolute and un-
touchable. The figure of flexibility and survival and presence is
not Jim but Marlow.

Marlow's moving voice generates the image of community
in *Lord Jim*. Digressive, quizzical, judgmental, compassionate,
Marlow's talk bodies forth the shape of Conrad's phenomenal
world. On the periphery of that talk we find the unchosen presence of others—Chester, Denver, the French lieutenant, Stein,
Brown—there for support or damage, but in any case there. And
at the center of that talk is Jim—probed, judged, sympathized
with, abetted, and yet never fully fathomed.[20] "It is as if loneli-

[20] Ian Watt cautions against a nihilistic reading of *Lord Jim* by reminding
us that the bond between Marlow and Jim, despite its gaps, is the novel's central
achievement: "Among Conrad's novels, [*Lord Jim*] is unique in having at its
center so rewarding and touching a personal relationship; and this undertone of

ness were a hard and absolute condition of existence; the envelope of flesh and blood on which our eyes are fixed melts before the outstretched hand, and there remains only the capricious, inconsolable, and elusive spirit that no eye can follow, no hand can grasp" (109). In *Lord Jim*'s world of flickering objects and impenetrable motives, of stresses that no solitary can withstand and communities that implicate the self without fathoming its secrets or consulting its will, the connective element is Marlow's voice. Scrupulously unsimplistic, sympathetic and judgmental, his voice insists on supplying both darkness and light, both confusion and clarity; and it thus acknowledges "that doubt which is the inseparable part of our knowledge" (135).

Shortly after finishing *Lord Jim*, Conrad wrote: ". . . In the sphere of an art dealing with a subject matter whose origin and end are alike unknown there is no possible conclusion. The only indisputable truth of life is our ignorance. Besides this there is nothing evident, nothing absolute, nothing uncontradicted. . . ."[21] These words resonate with the grave and unconsoling spirit of *Lord Jim*. Notwithstanding the poignance of Jim's heroic quest, they make explicit the illusion of a transcendental code, and they at least imply the genius of a novel that, unable to reach the authority of a transparent center, expends its energies in opaque approaches, seeking tentatively to touch what it cannot state.

FICTIONS OF DISCOURSE, PURPOSE, AND IDENTITY IN *NOSTROMO*

"The air of the New World seems favorable to the art of declamation" (80), Charles Gould avers to his wife. "I am a public character, sir" (289), Captain Mitchell fumes at Dr. Monygham. *Nostromo* is Conrad's most declamatory novel, and also the one that distinguishes most trenchantly between the assertions of public language and the confusions of private reality. It is as filled as *Lord Jim* with the insistence of words, but whereas in *Lord Jim* that insistence is groping and poignant in its inade-

---

emotional warmth goes far to qualify the sadness of Jim's life and the gloom of Marlow's meditations" (*Conrad in the Nineteenth Century*, 337).

[21] Letter of 1901 to the New York *Times*, quoted in Lawrence Graver, 44.

quacy, in *Nostromo* the insistence tends to be callous and vain. *Nostromo* is Conrad's most unsettling novel in the sense that the language mainly available for evaluating people and events is a public rhetoric, and that rhetoric is false.

Words serve to foment confusion and hatred. "But why was it that nobody was looking at him? he [General Montero] wondered to himself angrily. He was able to spell out the print of newspapers, and knew that he had performed the 'greatest military exploit of modern times' " (109). Montero learns this "fact" about himself by reading it, just as Mitchell assumes his worth because others seem to express a conviction of it. Resolutely ignorant of the inward state of things, the eye looks outward to the public arena for all endorsements of value. In order to explore the causes and consequences of this external focus, my commentary begins with Mitchell's public space, the world defined by elaborate epithet.

Everything in *Nostromo* is labeled; the description and the price on the label are usually inflated. Pedrito Montero's demeanor, his repertory of gesture and motives—these are parodistic imitations of someone else's label. He is no one unless he can pass himself off on the model of others. Fantasizing a court to be based on that of the Duc de Morny, attempting to assume "the tone of an enlightened man of the world . . . speaking with closed teeth slightly through his nose, with what he imagined to be the manner of a *grand seigneur*" (334-35), Pedrito is hopelessly enmeshed in the reified signs and trappings of other men's success. He can imagine enlisting the support of Charles Gould only through the appeal of a public title:

> A man singled out by his fellow-citizens for the honourable nickname of El Rey de Sulaco could not but receive a full recognition from an imperial democracy as a great captain of industry and a person of weighty counsel, whose popular designation would be soon replaced by a more solid title. "Eh, Don Carlos? No! What do you say? Conde de Sulaco—Eh?—or marquis . . . ?" (335)

Worth is visible, audible, congealed into titles; motives and energies not advertised are not acknowledged to exist. The prose of *Nostromo* (and not just that which reflects a Montero style of mind) is laden with display, both in its grosser phrases like "El Rey de Sulaco" and in the less gaudy phrases of its routine construction: "imperial democracy . . . captain of industry . . . person of weighty counsel." The novel's fundamental syntactic unit for its "art of declamation" is the appositive phrase, the verbal "guarantor" of the entity it embellishes. Thus, to cite only a few, Ribiera is "Excellentissimo, the hope of honest men" (107), Barrios is "the Tiger-killer" (143), Viola is the Garibaldino, Hirsch is Señor Hirsch, the well-known merchant from Esmeralda, Nostromo is the magnificent Capataz de Cargadores. Well known, well respected, well dressed, *we-all-agree-on-this-assessment*: such is the justificatory mantle asserted by the appositive phrase.[1]

The effects on the reader of this unremitting rhetoric are to draw attention to what lies behind the swollen words and to encourage speculation about the obsession in *Nostromo* with *naming*. The novel comes into focus as a narrative whose communal beliefs and values are rhetorical alone (as frail as they are shrill), a novel whose protagonists are determined to make the names and titles of public enterprise serve as the locus of release for their indwelling desire. They are intent upon tapping (to use one of the novel's recurrent metaphors) their innermost treasure; and they can do this, strangely enough, only by translating its value into the currency of public rhetoric. The public world must ratify (by reifying, by reflecting in its mirror) their identity and their value; its language for doing so—as we have seen—is bloated and degraded. The common idiom is mere propaganda.[2] Political language expands cancerously out of proportion to the phenomena it purports to describe, claiming impossible powers, out-

[1] Edward Said, identifying "Conrad's excessive use of appositional phrases," makes a related point: "A source of constant ironic shocks, excessive in its jocularity and courtesy, the technique is Dickensian. Phrases of this sort used repeatedly cannot be developed; hence they serve to remind us of the character's beginning authority, of his initial desire to be a public institution or monument or record" (127).

[2] Guerard makes the point concisely: "There is first of all a total distrust of political discourse, spoken or written. All governments however corrupt seek the 'peace,' 'progress,' and 'security' of Sulaco; all journalism and all propaganda is deceitful" (*Conrad the Novelist*, 194).

rageous merits.[3] Indeed, this gap between non-verbal reality and the linguistic claims "epithetically" made for it is what many of *Nostromo*'s audacious formal experiments seem designed to emphasize.

Reiterated justificatory epithets serve as the clothes the public figures in *Nostromo* wear, and the reader is repeatedly shown the puniness of the body behind the regalia. Ribiera ceremoniously escorted by Captain Mitchell onto the Juno, attired royally and in the company of the great, there to give an official sanction to the National Central Railway's enterprise in Costaguana—this man may be acceptably addressed as "the Excellentissimo Señor don Vincente Ribiera, the Dictator of Costaguana" (41). But the phrase seems comically excessive for the same man eighteen months later, fleeing for his life over the mountains on a lame mule, desperately shuttled by Mitchell aboard the Minerva. *Nostromo* is so constructed as to present the collapse scene before the celebration scene, and salient parallel elements—similar cast, setting, and action—make us glimpse the collapse implicit within the celebration. What we behold, the moment the parallel comes into focus, is not Mitchell's "public history" but Conrad's absurd theater, not the unfolding of political reality, but the ritual of political declamation. The asserted history collapses in upon itself, amorphous and betraying. Only the empty words are left, making their familiar claims.

As several critics have noted, nothing builds in *Nostromo*. Ribiera is deposed, so to speak, before he is crowned.[4] Ribiera himself may remain the same, but when the uniform, the title, and the precarious though propagandized support of others are subtracted, there is almost nothing left. Intrinsic private identity in the imaginative world of *Nostromo* is minimal; the accoutrements are the actors. Others lack even Ribiera's modest integrity. They play many parts, and the parts are all contingent, cast in

[3] Perhaps the most colorful instance of verbal excess is Señor Gamacho's oration, in which he urges "that war should be declared at once against France, England, Germany, and the United States . . ." (325).

[4] More gruesomely, Decoud is memorialized before we see him die, and Hirsch is hanged and resurrected several times. I return to this structural device later in the essay.

motley. Unlike *Lord Jim, Nostromo* does not permit that intimate and ennobling connection between a man's desires and the role he plays that makes for a sense of destiny. Rather, the career of the man who was "ruling" Sulaco when Charles Gould returned suggests the typical case: sub-collector in a Customs House, cafe waiter in Madrid, now—for the moment—his Excellency (and carefully so called by the prudent Charles Gould) (85).

Events in *Nostromo* sabotage the dignity of a subject with a continuous moral identity. Unitary entities, sufficiently exposed to pressure, deconstruct. At the tragic level there is the transformation of Dr. Monygham, exacted under torture. Less somberly, there is Don Juste Lopez, with half his beard singed off during the Sulaco riot. Decoud writes: "And as he [Don Juste] turned his head from side to side it was exactly as if there had been two men inside his frock-coat, one nobly whiskered and solemn, the other untidy and scared" (199). And so there are. Pressure literally deforms men in *Nostromo*, alters Monygham's gait, undermines the tone of Nostromo's speech, finds out the frightened Don Juste hiding in the noble one. Throughout his vicissitudes Don Juste will continue to declaim, but it will be words alone. A rhetoric that can identify Montero (last week's "gran' bestia") as this week's "distinguished man" can do anything, is severed from reality and exposed as a plastic and worthless medium.[5] Typically, the resultant defectiveness is denied by the words, but glimpsed behind them. The price exacted by Don Juste's survival is inscribed in the shaved beard: "Don Juste, astonishingly changed by having shaved off altogether his damaged beard, had lost with it nine-tenths of his outward dignity" (304).

There are other ways in which Conrad exposes the gap between phenomena and the justificatory names bestowed upon them. Decoud's newspaper the *Porvenir*, for example, carries in its name the complacent promise that the meaning of the future can be tidily perceived by its writers and verbally delivered in its columns. The enterprise is as propagandistic, as solipsistic, as

[5] The plasticity of words, so devastating in Conrad's world of brittle values, will become a comic device in Joyce's world of flexible values. See the discussion of *Ulysses* below.

Kurtz's phrase "My Intended": the imposition of a smug subjective scenario upon a bewildering array of uncoopted facts. Something of the anarchy of real events is conveyed by the perversity of *Nostromo*'s entire structure—so resistant to recuperation—and it is telescoped as well into single passages, like the one describing the location of Decoud's newspaper:

> It was next to Anzani's great emporium of boots, silks, iron-ware, muslins, wooden toys, tiny silver arms, legs, heads, hearts (for ex-voto offerings), rosaries, champagne, women's hats, patent medicines, even a few dusty books in paper covers and mostly in the French language. The big black letters formed the words, "Offices of the *Porvenir*." (140)

Against these fragments testifying to polymorphous consumerism, one glimpses the fatuousness of the *Porvenir*'s promise of unitary meaning.

Despite Don Jose Avellanos' nobler intent, one may see a similar irony leveled against his magnum opus, *Fifty Years of Misrule*. Written (so far as one can tell) with a periodic eloquence unsuited to the illogic of its subject, the book is destined to be useless, its very title conveying a hope—that the epoch of misrule has finally come to an end—which the narrative reveals to be groundless.[6] Rather than rarefied discourse generated by one spirit and sent out to elevate other spirits, *Fifty Years of Misrule* last appears, during the riots, as one more instance of dishonored and fragmented matter, "littering the Plaza, floating in the gutters, fired out as wads for trabucos loaded with handfuls of type, blown in the wind, trampled in the mud" (200). The word cannot bless; here it has literally become an instrument of violence.

The word is out of relation to its referent in the novel's inflated epithets. Its claims upon non-verbal reality are exaggerted in both Sulacan journalism and Don Jose's scholarly study. Further, the two definitive phenomena in the Costaguanan land-

---

[6] Indeed, *Nostromo* shows that nothing comes to an end. Charles Gould takes up the silver mine to redeem its appalling history, and he fails. More broadly, the history of Costaguana, from the legendary gringos up to and beyond Holroyd, is always—despite idealistic disclaimers—a narrative centering upon the plunder of treasure.

scape—the Golfo Placido and Mount Higuerota—refuse to take the impress of the projective human spirit altogether. They are recalcitrant to scenarios. Invasions of the Gulf eventually become becalmed, collapsing inwardly upon their own latent confusion of motive. Attempts to "civilize" this Latin American country inevitably bow before the unmeaning otherness of Higuerota. The mountain stands, somewhat like the Garibaldino, as an impressively mute and alien witness to the sordid turmoil in its midst. One of Conrad's finest paragraphs joins the mountain and the man:

> On this memorable day of the riot his arms were not folded on his chest. His hand grasped the barrel of the gun grounded on the threshold; he did not look up once at the white dome of Higuerota, whose cool purity seemed to hold itself aloof from a hot earth. His eyes examined the plain curiously. Tall trails of dust subsided here and there. In a speckless sky the sun hung clear and blinding. Knots of men ran headlong; others made a stand; and the irregular rattle of firearms came rippling to his ears in the fiery, still air. Single figures on foot raced desperately. Horsemen galloped towards each other, wheeled round together, separated at speed. Giorgio saw one fall, rider and horse disappearing as if they had galloped into a chasm, and the movements of the animated scene were like the passages of a violent game played upon the plain by dwarfs mounted and on foot, yelling with tiny throats, under the mountain that seemed a colossal embodiment of silence. (35)

One is tempted to say that the "Higuerota perspective" of this passage is Conrad's own. Certainly it is close to Decoud's perspective in its refusal to associate full emotional reality with these furious antics, and Decoud pays with his life for such detachment. The passage expresses the musing, as it were, of a deaf man; despite its staccato sentences full of rabid and uncohering gestures, the passage evokes a quiet scene. Viewed from far enough away, normal-sized throats become "tiny" and their death-cries faint. The physical activity depicted here, wholly ungraced by spirit, verges upon the absurd.

A humbler instance of a physical entity resisting the projection of human significance is the naming of Viola's house: the Albergo d'Italia Una. Conrad saturates this sanctifying gesture in the "intentional" rituals of human dignity. He shows Mrs. Gould asserting her generous will to obtain a promise from Sir John that the Viola house not be interfered with, and Sir John exercising his benevolence by granting the wish. She then informs the Garibaldino:

> "And is it for ever, *signora?*" he asked.
> "For as long as you like."
> "*Bene.* Then the place must be named. It was not worth while before." . . .
> "And what is it going to be, Giorgio?"
> "Albergo d'Italia Una," said the old Garibaldino. . . .
> (113)

The ironies are touching. Mrs. Gould cannot make good on what Sir John does not control. The fictions of ownership, permanence, and security—indeed, of promise itself—accompany the authoritative investment of spirit that is a naming. Conrad ensures that we see in the transaction not only Viola's subjective yearning—his desire for unity just underscoring Italy's actual fragmentation—but also a piece of unreal theater: this is the very house under siege four chapters earlier. Chronological dislocation thus begets a retrospective irony—how shortlived this verbalized sanction has proved to be—and it points ahead to more intricate betrayals, not fully appreciated until the novel's end. For this house contains no united Italians either. Straining within the surface form of domestic unification are latent anarchic impulses. The house of Viola—like the houses of Costaguana and Italy—is suffering a civil war. Eventually its two parents and three children (Nostromo as the third child) will have destroyed each other, all moving within an inextricable tangle of undeclared passions and misidentifications.

Finally there is the ranker deceptiveness of military rhetoric: the "Army of Pacification" which has little to do with peace, the "interrogatories" that have little to do with questions. Describing Guzman Bento's practices, the narrator writes: "Always an army chaplain—some unshaven, dirty man, girt with a sword and with a tiny cross embroidered in white cotton on the left breast of a lieutenant's uniform—would follow, cigarette in the corner of the mouth, wooden stool in hand, to hear the confession and give absolution" (123). The symbol of spirit—the "tiny cross"—appears makeshift, minuscule, almost an afterthought in this overmastering clutter of material details. Yet it is no afterthought, but the justificatory sign under which the sadistic impulses of incarnate men—their desire to inflict pain on other men's bodies—can be released with minimum damage to the conscience of the torturers.[7] Guzman Bento's proclamations, Conrad informs us, issue forth "spluttering and indistinct" (124) from a mouth of broken teeth. The gap between the lofty claim of the words and the brutishness of their embodied source is as emphasized here as it will be in the later portrait, etched into the deeper recesses of Dr. Monygham's consciousness, of "Father Beron."

THE FLURRY of words in *Nostromo* expresses only the propaganda of communal claims. Untouched by epithet, phenomena themselves betray a sickening lack of inherent structure, tending toward the amorphousness of pulp, even as the formulae for apprehending them harden into the petrifaction of stone. It is as though, for a character or an event to retain its uniformity long enough to achieve public identity, all complicating and disturbing counter-meanings must be suppressed. The establishment of public significance is simultaneously the reification of public purpose, and thus Charles Gould is repeatedly compared to stonework—the equestrian statue of Charles IV and the cracked marble urn that catches the eye in his proposal scene (63). Gould and Viola both become identified with undeviating projects. The rigor of this identification contrasts handsomely with the flaccid opportunism of a Sotillo or a Montero, but it necessarily engen-

---

[7] The erotic desire to cause pain to other bodies is a pronounced motif in *Nostromo*, present in Father Beron's "dull, surfeited look" (309) after he has tortured a prisoner, in Sotillo's "ardent desire to beat" (276) Captain Mitchell, and in the prolonged torture of Hirsch, whose screams of agony "started some of the officers in the hall babbling excitedly, with shining eyes" (368).

ders its own blindness. Pressing against their declaration of allegiance to self-transcending communal projects is the whisper (unheard by them) of private confusions and betrayals. Gould has abandoned his wife and doesn't know it. Viola has lost a son and daughter but doesn't know it:

> The Garibaldino—big, erect, with his snow-white hair and beard—had a monumental repose in his immobility, leaning upon a rifle. She [Linda] put her hand upon his arm lightly. He never stirred.
>
> "What have you done?" she asked, in her ordinary voice.
>
> "I have shot Ramirez—*infame!*" he answered. . . . "Like a thief he came, and like a thief he fell. The child had to be protected."
>
> He did not offer to move an inch, to advance a single step. He stood there, rugged and unstirring, like a statue of an old man guarding the honour of his house. (452-53)

Save the children, defend the honor of the Albergo d'Italia Una, the dying Teresa had implored. But ambiguities of desire, morally anarchic, lurk within the noble statuary of these manifest allegiances. Viola's irreproachable wife Teresa was also "in a way, don't you see? in love with him—the Capataz" (267). Only Monygham would dare to perceive this connection, but the reader assents to his description of a counter-meaning that crosses and complicates the overt one of conjugal devotion. In like manner the high-minded Linda, momentarily beside herself, reveals a fund of sensual passion at odds with her declared identity, as she sinks her teeth into the base of her sister's "whitest neck in Sulaco" (449). Most strikingly, Nostromo relinquishes his hold on himself, relapsing into the moral vagrancy of Ramirez, as he treacherously conducts his illicit courtship of Giselle. These private counter-meanings coursing through the same phenomenon, these emotional betrayals hidden within publicly established allegiances, are fluid complications beyond the ken of a rock-like idealist like Viola. Formed once and for all, he can be "uprooted by a treacherous gust of wind" (462) but not made adaptable. A man of crystalline allegiances, he insists that men retain their proclaimed identity. Thus he dies, having heard what he cannot fathom: "He cried out in son Gian' Battista's voice" (460).

The history that Viola goes to his death believing resembles, in its form if not its themes, the public history that Captain Mitchell spouts to distinguished and unwary strangers visiting Sulaco many years after the tumult has ended. Of all Conrad's structural experiments in *Nostromo*, the shift in mid-sentence (on 389) from the narrator's present murkiness to Mitchell's retrospective "clarity" is perhaps the most brilliant. It reveals, as powerfully as Sartre was to reveal some thirty years later in *La Nausée*, how men narrate the events of their lives by continuously fictionalizing them. Mitchell has recuperated everything at the price of understanding none of it.

Conducting a guided tour through Sulaco, he provides history as Madame Tussaud provides it. Antonia, Don Juste, Mr. and Mrs. Gould, Hernandez, Father Corbelan—these figures walk through Mitchell's narrative in a waxy and unreal present tense, each appearing on the stage as though to take his final bow before Mitchell's appreciative and coopting applause. Emptied of the ambiguities of private motive and temporal process, the history he proposes is a retrospective gathering of reified blocks of material, each complacently labeled with a phrase from the Mitchell repository of fixed meanings: all so much memorial portraiture and monumental statuary that makes for the march of material progress. The few elements of genuine history in his recital—like Nostromo's recovery of the lighter and inquiry into Decoud's death—are narrated without being understood.

Perhaps, therefore, the most remarkable aspect of this novel's form is the way its petrified heroes—smugly domesticated by Mitchell's breezy epithets—proceed unexpectedly back into the motions of life, their complexities of feeling and motive again intact. The narrative boldly moves from Mitchell's reified version to Nostromo's actual behavior, and even more boldly from the piety of Decoud's marble medallion—a memorial to the "young and gifted Costaguaneran's" "glorious success" (402)—to the stark despair of his suicide. His ironic words— "Do you hear, Capataz? Use the words glorious and successful when you speak to the *señorita*" (251-52)—have been heard in a radically unironic tone and white-washed by Antonia's tears. But in Decoud's last withering scene Conrad shows how little, when deprived of the corroborating language and bolstering presence of others, a man really is.

The corroborating language is condemned to inaccuracy, and the bolstering presence does not dispel the farce of misapprehended motive, but no one in Conrad's fiction survives alone. As in *Lord Jim*, the ratification of identity is inherently social, done with mirrors. The impress of others upon identity and behavior is a given, whereas liking or disliking comes later. Decoud's last words to Nostromo, involuntarily rushing out of his mouth to forestall the coming isolation, are "What do you think has become of Hirsch?" (252) Decoud's last thought before suicide is likewise social: "I wonder how that Capataz died" (411). Unable to live unaided on his own terms or to put up with the inflation and inauthenticity of others' terms, Decoud withdraws, then disintegrates.[8]

The bleakness of that disintegration is accentuated by the bright marble medallion that precedes it. The structure of *Nostromo* makes Decoud's death doubly appalling, by "resurrecting" him, as it were, after the societal commemoration of his death, and then making him die again, this time in bodily isolation and nihilistic despair. Conrad's most malignantly manipulated figure, though—the man whose terrified body, now dead, now alive, is dragged through 150 pages—is not Decoud but Hirsch.

ॐ

IN THE IMAGE of Hirsch's destruction we perceive an operative and chilling psychological pattern in *Nostromo*. "Nature, who had

---

[8] There is nothing finer in Conrad than the manipulation of point of view in Decoud's death scene:

His eyes looked at it [the "dark, thin string" of silence] while, without haste, he shifted his seat from the thwart to the gunwale. They looked at it fixedly, while his hand, feeling about his waist, unbuttoned the flap of the leather case, drew the revolver, cocked it, brought it forward pointing at his breast, pulled the trigger, and, with convulsive force, sent the still-smoking weapon hurtling through the air. His eyes looked at it while he fell forward and hung with his breast on the gunwale and the fingers of his right hand hooked under the thwart. They looked— (411).

The prose no longer assigns "his" actions to the authority of a unitary self named Decoud, but instead refers drily to the behavior of his sundry physical parts. His identity as a centered subject has disappeared, and his fragmented body puts an end to its fragmented existence.

made him what he was, seemed to have calculated cruelly how much he could bear in the way of atrocious anguish without actually expiring" (230). In the world of *Nostromo*, a man's mental and physical being will have to absorb the maximum number of shocks it can absorb. Men with strong egos like Gould, Viola, and Mitchell retain their shape; they can be destroyed but not invaded. They simply have no imagination of "the whole scheme of things of which [they] form a helpless part" (409). For them, the not-self can be molded to reflect the aspirations of their strong-willed self or they will die trying.

Hirsch, by contrast, suffers from an "undue development" (282) of imagination. He sees and foresees the utter unsuitedness of the world around him to the needs of his own existence. In a word, as opposed to the petrification of Mitchell-like formulae of self-assertion, Hirsch's project collapses, his bodily panic overtakes him, and he assumes the pulpy shapelessness of mere human matter and its jangling nerves. In him Conrad expresses the fate of a man overtaken by his own contingent body, undone by his inability to will its appalling openness into the closure of purposive form. That fate is grotesque, and Conrad expresses its grotesquerie with tireless reiteration in the cat-and-mouse game of Hirsch's torture and death.

It is a dying so protracted as to cast its absurd shadow over the last half of the novel. The heroic potential of Nostromo and Decoud's adventure on the lighter is sabotaged by Hirsch's ghostly sobbing. Decoud worries: "What if Hirsch coughed or sneezed? To feel himself at the mercy of such an idiotic contingency was too exasperating to be looked upon with irony" (238). Hirsch brings the stain of "idiotic contingency" to every scene he enters, robbing it by his very *bodiness* of any claim to noble or tragic necessity. Playing dead near the Custom House, discovered "limp—lifeless" (227) in the lighter, his shadow glimpsed later in the Custom House by the returned Nostromo ("He was doing apparently nothing . . . as though he were meditating—or, perhaps, reading a paper" [349]), then approached and seen to be hanged and shot, then "revived" and tortured by Sotillo (in a prose as detachedly comic as it is painful), thereafter focused on sadistically as a silent and presiding witness to the decisive transactions between Nostromo and Monygham: Hirsch oscillates crazily between death and life, terrified while alive of dying, prodded and stared at once dead. Conrad's prose addresses Hirsch's cadaver in epithets of scrupulous and insulting politeness. He is always "the late Señor Hirsch," and in the ten subsequent descriptions of his hanging body he is alternately coming "to a rest" (371), "swinging rigidly" (371), "waiting attentive, in impartial silence" (372), in "persistent immobility" (374), "seem[ing] to have come nearer" (375), and "preserv[ing] the immobility of a disregarded man" (377). What does Conrad mean by this perverse insistence?[9]

I propose that the image cast by Hirsch's grotesque life and death reveals Conrad's most sinister perception of an embodied life exposed to the menace of an indifferent medium, without answering subjective fictions of its own. He finally appears as a shapeless, projectless, tortured body. Every reiteration of "Señor" underlines his absurd pretence to titles of dignity, to epithetical considerations. No longer anything in himself but sentient and woundable nerves, he is the man deprived of all "sustaining illusion[s]" (409), the man become all body and on whose body all indignities are heaped. The shape of his career obliterated, formal distinctions dissolved between purpose and accident, subject and object, Hirsch hangs interminably over the last half of *Nostromo*. He has died but the structure of the novel refused to grant him the repose of death. In this he exemplified most precisely and spectacularly old Viola's plaint, "Life lasts too long sometimes" (388).

Life lasts too long sometimes. Like those gringos fatally condemned to live with their success; like those survivors of Guzman Bento's tortures who wander into further life, physically intact but spiritually betrayed—their old immaculate identities in pieces; like Nostromo whose muttered refrain, "I am not dead yet" (341,

---

[9] Both Guerard and Stewart note the unpleasant fixation upon Hirsch's cadaver: "Conrad's imaginative concern with the death of Hirsch is obsessive, even sadistic" (Guerard, 207). "The dead body of the tortured Hirsch so remains—we never hear of its being cut down—and serves as a kind of dreadful punctuation mark in the long colloquy between Nostromo and Dr. Monygham" (Stewart, 158-59).

357, 386), hints at his inner knowledge that he is dead, his public identity as Nostromo gone—like all these figures Viola suffers
(but does not probe) the gap on which the tragedy of this novel
centers: the gap between the confusion or collapse of inner purpose and the continued display of mere outer coherence.[10] "Je
me survis," says Annie in Sartre's *La Nausée*. The projects meant
to ratify human identity fail in the measure that they are brought
to public and material enactment. "There was something inherent in the necessities of successful action which carried with it
the moral degradation of the idea" (427). Why need this be so?

ﻪ

THE ELEMENTS that compose a Conradian character's ideal
identity—the lineaments he seeks to make his own—are incompatible with all that is involuntary and confused in the transactions of communal life. Further, they are incompatible with the
just-glimpsed obscurities of his own nature. In Conrad's imaginative universe, the drive for unconditioned self-realization is
doomed to defeat on both inward and outward grounds.

Let us begin with the outward grounds. Conrad's world,
though peopled with solitaries, is constitutively plural. Its plu-
rality is the all-containing and usually hostile medium within which
his solitaries pursue their way. However subjectively conceived,
their projects are objectively enacted. They are group projects,
requiring group support, and they become inevitably intertwined
with the group projects (also subjectively conceived) of others.
Insofar as his figures seek self-actualization, they are all Nostro-

---

[10] Bernard Meyer's biography of Conrad is especially illuminating in its
portrait of Conrad as a doubt-ridden man in frustrated search of a crystalline,
invulnerable identity:

Like Heyst, departing from his dead father, and like Captain Anthony, escaping
from his living one, Conrad quitted his father's Poland carrying within his sailor's
kit those very attributes which he hoped to shake off—a ready susceptibility to
physical ailment, a disposition to recurring melancholy, a nervous distrust of
human closeness, and a vague and fluctuating conception of who or what he
really was. Burdened by this underlying frail and uncertain sense of self, Conrad's
search for a new identity was doomed to failure. Instead, in the course of his
wandering and in his restless changes of vocation, he acquired but a succession
of facades, each accompanied by the language and the attitudes appropriate to
the particular role he was enacting: adventurous French sailor, British Master
Mariner, Belgian Congo river captain, English man of letters. (287)

mos, our men, public characters exposed to the contaminating or corroborating touch of other public characters, other projects.

Immersed in private dreams of immaculate self-sufficiency, Conrad's solitaries abhor the contact of others. And with good reason: the air which men share is foul, their common language is declamatory and spurious, their communal values are inauthentic. But air, language, and value exist only as commodities in common. Whatever its drawbacks, community remains necessary in the measure that it at least may support life, whereas unshaped nature is a medium to drown in, undisciplined body a medium to suffer in. To conceive and enact an identity at all, one moves through the conventions of community, the medium—simultaneously enabling and destructive—of cross-purposes.

The inward grounds for the collapse of self-actualizing projects are even more compelling. The self the hero is attempting to ratify is itself an artifice, a work, a selective portrait culled from the rhetoric provided by his culture. He is therefore a figure on the stretch, his will always engaged to make him coincide with that stylized, artful image he has not yet attained. Nature is anathema to him; its givens—both within and without—loom as an inchoate menace to his project of himself. Nothing he wants is conceived in natural terms. His unchanging enterprise is to rise from the amorphousness of uncurried nature to the disciplined form proposed and ratified by community. To be anything at all is a willed achievement of self-focussing, for the natural state (which beckons, to which he is tempted) is either void or monstrous. All threats (as Decoud eloquently reveals) reduce to one: self-dissolution. The opposite of the Nietzschean hero, he seeks to become, not what he latently and intrinsically is, but what—through the corroboration of others—he is not yet.[11]

---

[11] Such a willed and artful identity closely resembles what Lawrence calls "the *ideal* self: this is personality. The self that is begotten and born from the idea . . . a spurious, detestable product. . . . This is the self-conscious ego, the entity of fixed ideas and ideals, prancing and displaying itself like an actor" ("Democracy," 711). Lawrence's enterprise, as my next chapter argues at length, may be defined as the attempt to free the incarnate self from this imprisoning construct of the ideal self.

181

Self-actualizing is—for Nostromo, Gould, and Viola—self-transcending, self-public-making. These men come together because their self-actualizing purposes require collaboration, but betrayal remains the deepest motive in Conrad: it is the natural sequence of events. A man pressed hard enough may reveal his nature; his nature is the faithless, formless animal in him and therefore his doom. Moral coherence involves a ceaseless struggle for community and against nature, and the gravity of the struggle lies in this: the motives and discourse of the community so-called common are an artifice when not a lie, and the nature so resisted is, under the right stress, irresistible.

To the degree that he dares to be introspective, the Conradian protagonist recognizes this artifice, this lie. Conrad's distinction as a novelist is that, through his unwanted but ineluctable inwardness, he exposes in his best work the inaccessibility of his most cherished values, without ceasing to cherish them.[12] The treasure (literal and figurative) on which this novel focuses cannot be enjoyed because (as in Hardy) nothing a man's public rhetoric defines as treasure can materialize, and nothing he has access to can be long seen as worth treasuring. The Conradian protagonist defines wealth only in the currency of public enterprise, and there is no bridge between this inflated currency and the confused but authentic idiom of his actual seeking.

Here, finally, is the tragic waste of *Nostromo*. The treasure its protagonists seek—Don Jose and Antonia, Charles Gould, Nostromo, Viola—never coincides with the interior wealth (the reservoir of moral aspiration and amoral desire) which they have been continuously and unconsciously spending. These resource-

---

[12] George Levine pursues a different argument but arrives at a kindred, if slightly more consoling, conclusion: "Conrad's fiction creates its tensions from an invincible conviction of solidarity . . . a conviction held against the evidence of the universe. Trapped within his own sensations, each individual shares the loneliness of the self and responds to his awareness of that loneliness in another. That the community of mankind is built on the unreal constructions of consciousness is for Conrad inevitable. . . . What gives dignity to mankind is not withdrawal and detachment from the illusions of consciousness, but engagement in them" (289).

ful subjects all break their hearts on the unobtainable image they have been pursuing in the public mirror.[13] What they have actually invested and forfeited—what their projects have really dramatized—amounts to more than an outpouring of vanity. It is their spontaneous life-energies, their desire to actualize themselves, to make good on their natural birthright as incarnate men and women. This potential may be small or great, but in *Nostromo* it cannot achieve recognition. The licensed idiom of value is reifying and strictly public: an idiom that, by bypassing the abysmal confusions of the embodied subject, is as false in its high-minded claims as it is—for Conrad—irreplaceable. He cannot risk an appeal to the natural self; the treasure remains untouched.

One concludes that he who would tap the treasure would have to track it back to its origins and risk the abyss of nature, the plunge into subjective desire "where all the ladders start." Such a writer would have to imagine the realm of natural impulse as a promise as well as a threat—a promise and a threat so great that they require a revaluation of values. And he would seek to forge a new idiom of value and purpose, of self-knowing

---

[13] The exceptions to my argument are of course Emilia Gould and Dr. Monygham, the novel's potentially tragic figures. Tragic because they alone know that the true idiom of wealth flows from the heart (is the gift of self), and that it is continuously wasted (never recognized) in *Nostromo*. Mrs. Gould patiently endures her husband's adolescent dream, paying for its gorgeous aridity with the barrenness and estrangement of her marriage. Monygham is luckier. He neither deceives himself about his motives nor misassesses the treasure he seeks: the companionship of Mrs. Gould as the object of his anguished love (a love described "not as the most splendid of illusions, but like an enlightening and priceless misfortune" [420-21]). He knows that heartbreak, the unreciprocated (but in his case recognized) outpouring of devotional energies, is the true locus of wealth, the "priceless misfortune" through which, with whatever pain, he is achieving self-fulfillment. Conrad darkens this heroic portrait both by insisting on the crippling experiences Monygham has undergone en route to his authentic devotion, and by emphasizing the recklessness implicit in *any* devotion. Enthralled by the idealized image he cherishes of Mrs. Gould (355), "extremely dangerous to himself and to others, all his scruples vanishing . . ." (356), Monygham emerges less as an exemplar of virtue than a figure of imposing (and potentially tragic) passion.

and self-ratifying. His idiom would proceed openly from the givens of an incarnate self rather than (generated by cultural abstractions) rebounding in fear and disgust upon those givens. Conrad, for the most compelling reasons, cannot afford this risk. The writer who knows that "Whatever flames upon the night/ Man's own resinous heart has fed," is Lawrence.

PART THREE

Modernist: Beginning the Revaluation

LATE-VICTORIAN tragic encounters: the subject stymied or annihilated by the incompatible mix of nature and culture within his own identity. In Hardy and Conrad, "become who you are" is a calamitous and unwanted pronouncement. What these protagonists want is immaculate self-fulfillment, achieved in the idiom of their culture's prescriptions. Tess would be pure, Jude would be learned, Jim would be a hero, Nostromo would be admired. They are unfree exactly in the measure that their incarnate propensities—the fears and desires that they carry into every activity—are anathema to the models of behavior and achievement they propose for themselves: the models of identity licensed by their culture. Laboring under such sanctions, stung by who they are, these protagonists move in a circular trap; they cannot escape their alienation.

Lawrence and Joyce attempt to break out. In their lives they found it necessary (and possible) to quit their native culture; once outside, they return (refreshed) in their work, subjecting the assumptions of that culture to an extraordinary scrutiny. Each writer seeks to identify the bedrock of nature underlying the conventions of culture, and to affirm what he has identified. Both could say with Nietzsche: "I want to learn more and more to see as beautiful what is necessary in things; then I shall be one of those who make things beautiful. *Amor fati*: let that be my love hence-forth!" (*The Gay Science*, 223)

Amor fati: a love of life in its essential terrestrial conditions, a desire to move beyond the superficial and more deeply into the necessary. I examine the Lawrence world in three ways: first, as a body of fictions geared to a life that seeks, always, to come upon and release its unknown energies. Lawrence's fiction is optative, invested in the future, genuinely interested (as Hardy's and Conrad's fiction is not) in what unpredicted liberations may take place on the other side of societal prohibitions. Next, *Women in Love* is discussed as Lawrence's perplexing masterpiece of exploration: a novel that weaves into a single narrative one range of perfectly mastered experiences, another that is deftly suggested, and a third that is latently incoherent. The chapter on Lawence concludes by comparing the three pubished versions of *Lady Chatterley's Lover* as stages in Lawrence's fretful attempt to free the native quick of his material from its dead cultural wrappings. All three discussions attend to the problematic character of Lawrence's art, its blend of the achieved and the inchoate. (It should go without saying that the Modernist attempt to get clear of cultural obstacles is not the same as getting clear; their creation of novels based on a different model of identity ensures different novels, not better ones: not a fiction free of problems, but a fiction interested in other problems.)

The chapter on Joyce is frankly a meditation (gathering for over a decade) on *Ulysses* as a Modernist novel. I take *Ulysses* to be the supreme narrative of our century, and every claim this book has made about Modernism can be accommodated within its spacious confines. There is much that I ignore (in both senses) in *Ulysses*. Even so, it permits me to conclude the considerations—about being in bodies, having desires, achieving a career, living in the moment, and exposing the artifice of cultural scripts—that have been pursued throughout this study. Self and society, mind and body, fidelity and betrayal, freedom and conditionality, success and failure: *Ulysses* shows how these binary oppositions appear, on scrutiny, as over-simplifying lenses upon a world of immeasurable affiliations.

Five 🍂 "Become Who You Are": The Optative World of D. H. Lawrence

"GOD IS THE flame-life in all the universe; multifarious, multifarious flames. . . . Whichever flame flames in your manhood, that is you, for the time being" ("The Novel," 426). Lawrence seeks to center identity on flame-life (he even sees the surrounding world of matter, the sun and the moon, as derived from flame-life),[1] and the goal of the Lawrentian protagonist is as simple as it is elusive: to achieve the mobile flame-life of pure being. In each of his novels, in the course of his life, the struggle to center takes different forms, but it remains recognizably the same: to get free of the culturally sanctioned obstacles that prevent access to the flame. This access liberates one's uniqueness; simultaneously it permits, "for the time being," a perfect relationship with the other elements—human and natural—in one's world. "And a man, if he win to a sheer fusion in himself of all the manifold creation, a pure relation, a sheer gleam of oneness out of manyness, then this man is God created where before God was uncreated" ("The Crown," 412). The exaltation of Lawrence's language betrays his awareness of how rarely anyone "wins to" a fused expression of his inchoate energies. Yet a faith in its possibility is the hallmark of Lawrence's career. "I am rather great on faith just now," he writes Murry in 1914; "one ought to have

[1] See *Psychoanalysis and the Unconscious and Fantasia of the Unconscious*: "It was the living individual soul which, dying, flung into space the two wings of the infinite, the two poles of the sun and the moon. . . . Matter, all matter, is the Lifeborn. . . . So from the earth our radiance is flung to the sun, our marsh-fire to the moon, when we die" (188-89).

189

faith in what one ultimately is, then one can bear at last the host of unpleasant things which one is en route" (*Letters*, 2:160-61).[2]

Lawrence was, as the letters and reminiscences testify, a host of unpleasant things en route, and his writings reveal the same large admixture of the incoherent with the achieved. Few great writers require the critical sympathy that Lawrence does. He is more easily savaged by selective quotation than any other novelist of comparable status.[3] His greatness is inseparable from his vulnerability; he insisted on speaking his spontaneous mind and making (in his life and his art) his moment-by-moment mistakes. He was beautifully willing to be all kinds of unpleasant things en route because he maintained "faith in what one ultimately is." Authentic being always beckoned in the future, and it was not to be arrived at without a passage of unadulterated candor and therefore turmoil in the present. Lawrence does not truck, rarely looks before and after. Denis Donoghue quotes his response to Mabel Dodge Luhan's angry letter—"As for reviling you, when I am angry, I say what I feel. I hope you do the same"—and who can fault this integrity? (200) "Don't mind me," he writes Edward Marsh in 1913, "I find it frightfully easy to theorise and. say all the things I don't mean, and frightfully difficult to find out, even for myself what I do mean" (*Letters*, 2:105).

"Become who you are" points to a wayward journey in Lawrence's life and work; the self to be released cannot be known in advance.[4] "I am what I am, not merely what I think I am," he writes in "Pornography and Obscenity" (35). "What I am" is for Lawrence an unconscious core unlike Freud's unconscious core of incest desires. "By the unconscious we wish to indicate that essential unique nature of every individual creature, which is, by

[2] Note how Lawrence's formulation relates the temporal and the timeless: one discovers, in the course of time, that which one has always potentially been. There is no question here of wish-fulfillment transformations.

[3] The variety of attacks upon Lawrence is wide. A representative selection of texts that range from ambivalent praise to heated abuse would include Murry's *Son of Woman*, Vivas' *The Failure and Triumph of Art*, and Millett's *Sexual Politics*. Of the six novelists in my study Lawrence is the one critics most enjoy correcting.

[4] Alan Friedman remarks that if you deny the existence of "any 'other' self, the experience of reading Lawrence must be uniquely unpleasant, like drifting accidentally into somebody else's bad dream" (241).

its very nature, unanalysable, undefinable, inconceivable. . . . As a matter of fact, *soul* would be a better word. . . . But the word *soul* has been vitiated by the idealistic use, until nowadays it means only that which a man conceives himself to be" (*Fantasia*, 15). Access to that center beyond self-conception is fraught with difficulties, since the conscious will—molded, like Freud's superego, by the culture's assumptions—must be forsworn as a guide for the journey.

The kinship with Nietzsche's concept of unconscious identity is close. Like Lawrence, Nietzsche takes the given social postulates (what Stephen Dedalus will call the imperatives of "home, fatherland, and church") as so many distractions from the deeper body of desires that make up one's unconscious identity. Nietzsche writes in *Ecce Homo*:

> To become what one is, one must not have the faintest notion *what* one is. . . . The whole surface of consciousness—consciousness *is* a surface—must be kept clear of all great imperatives. . . . Meanwhile, the organizing "idea" that is destined to rule keeps growing deep down—it begins to command; slowly it leads us *back* from side roads and wrong roads; it prepares *single* qualities and fitnesses that will one day prove to be indispensable as a means toward a whole—one by one, it trains all *subservient* capacities before giving any hint of the dominant task, "goal," "aim," or "meaning." (710)

In an equally pertinent passage Nietzsche writes: "But at the bottom of us, really 'deep down,' there is, of course, something unteachable, some granite of spiritual *fatum*. . . . Whenever a cardinal problem is at stake, there speaks an unchangeable 'this is I' . . ." (*Beyond Good and Evil*, 352).

Lawrence's relation to Hardy and Conrad, in the matter of unconscious identity, emerges by way of these formulations of Nietzsche. What is elemental in Tess, what is obscure in Jude—that stratum of "unchangeable 'this is I' " located "deeper down" than any surface ideal modeled on the altruistic teachings of Newman or Arnold—this is the stratum upon which Lawrence seeks to center identity. Tess and Jude go to their deaths unaware of the fusion of amoral nature and high-minded culture that informs their true identity. In Conrad's work the gap between the givens of nature and the admonitions of culture has widened further. The impulses seeded by nature are abhorrent; the goals proclaimed by culture are fictions as precious as they are, under stress, beyond sustaining. The Conradian tragic narrative, as Joyce Carol Oates claims, regularly holds in suspension these "blatantly self-contradictory beliefs . . . until the concluding pages . . . when chaos rushes in, is in fact welcomed in . . . [and the drama is] ended if not resolved" (6). Nature and culture are, in the Victorian imagination, intrinsically opposed; and the tragic world of late-nineteenth-century literature can be most simply defined as the failure (within the protagonist's identity and behavior) of a set of debilitated cultural paradigms to account for the stresses of an amoral and empowered nature.

Lawrence reconceives the relation of nature to culture within human identity. He removes their necessary hostility and thereby rejects the inevitability of tragic impasse. "Tragedy is lack of experience," he writes in "Sun," and the statement reverberates. For the great nineteenth-century idealists, for Tolstoy or Dostoevsky, Hardy or Conrad, our most cherished culture-derived images of ourselves are liable to be rebuffed by the sordid realities of social life and the amoral impulses seeded in our natural bodies. In these writers tragedy is an overdose of experience, the result, as for Anna Karenina, of an exposure of one's moral self-image to both the unbearable restraints of an indifferent society and the flame-like exigencies of an indifferent nature. "Human kind / Cannot bear very much reality," T. S. Eliot writes: tragedy occurs when we relax our hold upon our culturally posited identity and allow ourselves—as Anna and Raskolnikov, as Tess and Jim do—to release what we naturally harbor: to become who we are. Lawrence, unlike Dickens and Eliot, Hardy and Conrad, anticipates this prospect of release with joy. The exposure of the artifice of culture to the flame of nature is the only means of cultural renewal.

The deeper stratum of nature beneath culture which his narratives seek to locate is what he called, in the famous letter to Garnett, carbon: "Like as diamond and coal are the same pure single element of carbon. The ordinary novel would trace the history of the diamond—but I say, 'Diamond, what! This is carbon!' And my diamond might be coal or soot, and my theme is carbon" (*Letters*, 2:183). Focus on the unchanged radical element means not that Lawrence rejects the rendering of surface detail which is the bread and butter of novelistic narrative, but that he reads the surface for signs of the play or repression of the impersonal carbon beneath.[5] At the core of the known and possessed self burns an unknown and unpossessable flame. "Character is a curious thing. It is the flame of a man, which burns brighter or dimmer, bluer or yellower or redder, rising or sinking or flaring according to the draughts of circumstance and the changing air of life" ("The Novel," 423). These general remarks will serve to orient the differences between Lawrence's characteristic fictional form and that of his predecessors.

THE OPTATIVE world: Lawrence's novels typically move forward, through confrontations and crises, into new arenas. He liked to speak of man as a "thought-adventurer," and the adventure deals in new feelings as much as in new thoughts. Unlike Eliot, Hardy, and Conrad—who focus most compellingly on the present as a product of the past—Lawrence's focus on the present acts mainly as an intimation of the future. His narrative voice eschews omniscience. He rarely projects a space of superior knowledge between himself and his characters, tending instead to imagine their present maneuvers as pregnant with an unforeclosed future.[6] (This may be a reason why he typically rewrites his narratives *de novo*. His creative access to his characters is by way of imagining what the carbon in them might lead them to

---

[5] Keith Sagar quotes Lawrence's response to Edwin Muir's complaint that we would not recognize Lawrence's characters if we met them on the street: "Alas, that I should recognize people in the street by their noses, bonnets, or beauty. I don't care about their noses, bonnets, or beauty. Does nothing exist beyond that which is recognizable in the street?—How does my cat recognize me in the dark?" (*Phoenix*, 802; quoted in Sagar, I)

[6] The striking exception to this tendency is Gerald Crich. I return later to the dilemma he poses.

do; he rarely forces them to do what he had already projected. In a kindred way, as Frank Kermode has noted, he will interweave his most recent personal experiences into narratives already under development [11-12]. The wonder is not that this procedure fails on occasion but that it does not fail more often. It does not because his eye is attuned to the present "quickness" of his materials, the possibilities that they might house. A writer more anxious about the final shape of his design could less easily afford such intrusions.)

By contrast to this sense of unpredictable movement, Dickens' later novels reveal a deepening sense of nemesis. The opening pages present a character, a landscape, an activity that, so to speak, haunt what follows; and the novels achieve resolution by returning to the opening malaise. Dombey engulfing his newborn son; London in fog and mire; "Now, what I want is, Facts"; the sun blazing on Marseilles and the prison there; a small boy in the marsh country, shivering and lonely; two figures rowing in the Thames, looking for bodies; a man eerily awakening from an opium trance: all these beginnings set forth the problem with which the subsequent narrative must wrestle. *The Mill on the Floss* opens with a description of the river, *Daniel Deronda* with Deronda watching Gwendolen gamble and lose. Eliot has her eye, like Dickens, on the restricting element, on the gesture or setting that threatens the protagonist's unfolding. The "slow poisoning" of Gwendolen's vanity is a good phrase for the chastening form of the Eliot narrative: they are plots to humble the ego's pride, to reveal the forces—societal, natural—that constrain and delimit the self.

With Hardy and Conrad the sense of nemesis has increased. The description of Egdon Heath, Henchard's sale of his wife, Jack Durbeyfield's discovery of his ancestry, the schoolmaster leaving Marygreen: these openings present radical obstacles; the plot never gets past them. Indeed, the notions of departure and return are revealed to be illusions of free movement in Hardy's world. Clym does not "return," once we discover (as that opening chapter should inform us) the sense in which he can never have left. The Paris of *The Return of the Native* is a Utopia, a fantasy other place that never for a moment dislodges the stranglehold of the Heath upon the narrative. Anyone who can do damage to the protagonist appears early in a Hardy novel and does not disappear until the damage has been done. The fermity woman reappears to give evidence, the farmer Angel once punched had known Tess earlier at Trantridge and will abuse her later at Flintcomb Ash. Phillotson not only doesn't depart; he outlasts Jude and remains, for the reader, posted forever in his bedroom, participating wearily in Sue's ritual of sexual torment. All is foreclosed. Although the desire to break away is irrepressible, deeper laws in Hardy's imagination condemn these figures to repeat their customary and unwanted gestures of entrapment. What they painfully, repetitively, *are* is opposed, precisely, to what in their fantasies they would become.

In Conrad the role of the immovable looms larger yet. Almayer startled "from his dream of splendid future into the unpleasant realities of the present hour"; Mr. Baker's question, "Are the hands aboard, Knowles?" leading to the emergence of "Wait!" some ten pages later; "he was an inch, perhaps two, under six feet"; the all-becalming Golfo Placido and the legend of the stranded gringos; Mr. Verloc leaving his house for "business," his wife "in charge of" the boy; Razumov finding Haldin in his room, unbid: these openings announce not just obstacles but a scene of potential disorientation that will amount to paralysis: the foundering of all projects. Almayer is doomed; Wait is beyond accommodation; Jim cannot be a six-foot hero; the Golfo Placido is uninvadable; Verloc has misconceived beyond recovery his business, his wife, and his brother-in-law; the entrance of Haldin into Razumov's life can never be assimilated. In its form, the Conrad narrative tortuously advances and recoils, distancing its materials behind presentational screens and actively discouraging, in the reader, any sense of working through and past the obstacles. Conrad's narrative voice characteristically breaks free from the immediate pace of his plots (their forward movement in time), delimiting in advance their possibilities, so as to apprehend more fully their hidden liabilities. Conrad's major work reveals an imagination of disaster, enlivened most by the myriad hidden reasons why the enterprises men must embark on cannot be sustained.

The Lawrentian plot enacts by contrast a testing and un-folding of possibilities. No fiction he wrote, with the revealing exception of *The Trespasser*, undercuts its own movement toward relatedness and release. Only in *The Trespasser* does Lawrence, by a retrospective opening chapter, fall into what he himself would diagnose as the sentimentality of a foreclosed plot. "The Conrad, after months of Europe, makes me furious . . . why this giving in before you start, that pervades all Conrad and such folks—the Writers among the Ruins. I can't forgive Conrad for being so sad and for giving in" (*Letters*, 1:465).[7] For the writer to know in advance how it all must come out is to lock himself into a sterile form and to encourage posturing and toying with his ma-terial. The material becomes statuary, already seen around, op-eratic but inert.

The later narratives seek more arduously their appropriate form. Lawrence's terse reply to Arnold Bennett's strictures is un-answerable: "Tell Arnold Bennett that all rules of construction hold good only for novels which are copies of other novels. A book which is not a copy of other books has its own construc-tion, and what he calls faults, he being an old imitator, I call characteristics" (*Letters*, 2:479). *Sons and Lovers* moves through stage after stage, and Lawrence stoutly defended the final ver-sion. "I tell you it has got form—*form*: haven't I made it pa-tiently, out of sweat as well as blood" (*Letters*, 1:476). With *The Rainbow* he is even more patiently committed to the realization of his materials' possibilities: "I have begun my novel again—for about the seventh time," he writes A. W. McLeod. "I hope you are sympathising with me. I had nearly finished it. It was full of beautiful things, but it missed—I knew that it just missed being itself" (*Letters*, 2:146).

It just missed being itself: become who you are. In his fiction, as in his poetry, ". . . if the mood is out of joint, the rhythm often is. I have always tried to get an emotion out in its own course, without altering it" (*Letters*, 2:61). *Women in Love* I shall save

[7] "After months of Europe" is not an irrelevant phrase. Lawrence wrote this letter to Garnett in October 1912, six months after his elopement with Frieda and in the midst of his personal discovery that "plots" need not be fore-closed.

for later discussion, but all the novels benefit—and suffer—from Lawrence's enabling aesthetic premise: keep the materials moving until both their unique "whatness" and their unpredictable interrelatedness have found expression.[8] Sometimes, as in *Aaron's Rod* and *Kangaroo*, he abandons his material before he finds its focus, but he does not package it into Arnold Bennett plots. The novels are wander narratives. Paul, Ursula, Aaron, Somers, Kate, and Connie move through a landscape, seeking half-consciously some set of human and natural relationships that will release their potential energies. "And here lies the vast importance of the novel, properly handled. It can inform and lead into new places the flow of our sympathetic consciousness, and it can lead our sympathy away in recoil from things gone dead" (*Lady Chatterley's Lover*, 106). If Eliot, Hardy, and Conrad are imaginatively attuned to those pressures within and without that spell disaster, to the "things gone dead" that block fulfillment, Lawrence is interested in breaking away and coming upon the "new places," the possibilities, despite all, for greater life.

ða

To get to the new places requires "recoil from things gone dead," and Lawrence is pitiless when he scents carrion. Dickensian carrion is recognized as such by societal mores. The slums and law courts of *Bleak House*, the prisons and governmental bureaucracy of *Little Dorrit*, give off a stench that all right-thinking characters and readers agree in condemning. But Lawrence finds the smell of decay within the precincts of Dickensian domesticity, in the midst of love. "A new relation, a new relatedness hurts somewhat in the attaining; and will always hurt. So life will always hurt. Because real voluptuousness lies in re-acting old relationships, and at the best, getting an alcoholic sort of pleasure out of it, slightly depraving" ("Morality and the Novel," 112).

Such commentary makes me wish that Lawrence had probed Dickens and George Eliot as acutely as he probed Hardy and Dostoevsky. He would have scented the differences in their work

---

[8] Roger Sale discusses perceptively Lawrence's capacity to render Mr. and Mrs. Morel always in *relation* to each other. See *Modern Heroism*, 26-52.

between the quick and the dead. Annie and Dr. Strong, David and Agnes, Peggotty and Little Emily, Clennam and Amy Dorrit—these relationships (as I argued above) reveal the play of energies quite incompatible with the moral assessment asserted by the narrative voice. Especially in the parent-child relationship Lawrence is alert—in his own life and work, in that of others—to the "alcoholic" repetition of earlier, lover-to-lover feelings. The dissatisfied parent, under the guise of offering selfless protection, engulfs the child with despotic tenderness, makes up for the failure of his or her adult erotic life. As keenly as Nietzsche or Freud, Lawrence discerns the release of illicit desire in licit forms. The vexed erotic relations between Paul Morel and his parents; the anguished blend of tenderness and bullying in Will Brangwen's intimacy with Ursula; the inwardly poisoned marriage of Mr. and Mrs. Crich, radiating outward in the psyches of Gerald and Winifred: these richly troubled domestic/erotic bonds may have their counterpart in the family dramas of Victorian fiction, but their conventional facade is rarely probed before the advent of Freud.

By the time of *Sons and Lovers* Lawrence had fully absorbed the potential craziness of family relationships. Critics like to fault *Sons and Lovers* for inadequate mastery of its materials, but Kermode is right in claiming that the "overdetermined" text invites criticism as well as justification of Paul Morel. Lawrence did not need to wait until years later to discover that the violation done him by the mother would damage his capacity for subsequent relationships. He writes Rachel Annand Taylor on 12/3/1910:

> This has been a kind of bond between me and my mother. We have loved each other, almost with a husband and wife love, as well as filial and maternal. We knew each other by instinct. . . . We have been like one, so sensitive to each other that we never needed words. It has been rather terrible, and has made me, in some respects, abnormal. (*Letters*, 1:190)

Sons and Lovers spells out in art-language what can be terrible in a mother's love. When, a decade later, Lawrence approaches these materials again, in *Fantasia of the Unconscious*, he does not so much discover the damage parents can inflict as finally conceptualize it. There he identifies the move in parents to rouse their children before the children are ready. Beneath the bizarre terminology of solar and lumbar plexuses, thoracic and cardiac ganglia, one finds an emergent paradigm. Wives unsatisfied by husbands (who have failed to make good on their own unconscious potential) turn to their sons for the male "quickness" they need. The sons, prematurely roused, become damagingly self-conscious and idealistic about their own sexual identity, develop "sex in the head," and rarely find a wife who can dislodge the prized internal image of the mother. "And the fatal round of introversion and 'complex' starts once more" (*Fantasia*, 157). In this paradigm Lawrence has sought to understand his father's failure, his mother's response, his own resultant dislocation; and he has approached these through the prism of his own mature need to satisfy Frieda so that she, in her restlessness, will not take her recompense in her own children. The insight is considerable. It cuts through, in its focus on carbon, any number of protective conventional formulations.

Lawrence continues throughout his career to identify impediments to self-liberation. On his own pulse he discovers, as discussion of the family has already suggested, the range of conventional forms that his culture imposes on feeling. His 1912 letters from Germany—during his first months with Frieda—breathe the air of escape from these cultural assumptions. He has found out that "the world is wonderful and beautiful and good beyond one's wildest imagination. Never, never, never could one conceive what love is, beforehand, never. Life *can* be great—quite godlike. It *can* be so" (*Letters*, 1:414). He has moved from sickness to health, lapsed out into a sexual ecstasy through which he feels reborn. From 1912 on he will struggle to maintain his awareness that the miracle of life consists in just this phoenix-like capacity for death and self-renewal, for possibilities on the other side of annihilation. Later in 1912 he writes Garnett: "I should like to bludgeon [the English] into realising their own selves. Curse you, my countrymen, you have put the halters round your necks, and pull tighter and tighter, from day to day. You are strangling yourselves, you blasted fools. Oh my countrymen!" (*Letters*, 1:424) This imagery of boxes and nooses, of suf-focating conventions and prohibitions, permanently characterizes Lawrence's utterance. "We roam in the belly of our era," he writes in "The Crown," and there will have to be many a death before there can be rebirth. Our era confines us; "the walls of the old body are inflexible and insensible, the unborn does not know that there can be any travelling forth" (367, 390). By the end of the war Lawrence could no longer hope to awaken his country-men. Unlike the mix of apologia and critique that characterize Dickens' and Eliot's, Hardy's and Conrad's, approach to English conventions of thought and feeling, Lawrence took the full measure of his country's antipathy to quickness: and he left.[9]

The culture's more insidious prohibitions are so deeply seated as to be involuntarily shared. Lawrence can write magisterially, almost disinterestedly, of this malaise in "A Propos of *Lady Chat-terley's Lover*." In an earlier piece on "The Good Man," however, he discusses the culture's bind on feeling in terms that touch his own life and art more nearly: "We can only feel things in con-ventional feeling-patterns. Because when these feelings-patterns become inadequate, when they will no longer body forth the workings of the yeasty soul, then we are in torture. It is like a deaf-mute trying to speak. Something is inadequate in the expression-apparatus, and we hear strange howlings" (258).

"Strange howlings" betoken an unresolved conflict in the speaker, a balked attempt to break free of cultural convention and rise into the clear utterance of one's desire. We hear them often in Lawrence, most poignantly in the baffled rendering of homosexual attraction, an attraction Lawrence could neither dis-own nor acknowledge.[10] His Puritan culture had primed him to endorse strictly heterosexual love, his first years of passionate union

---

[9] For a full account of Lawrence's doomed attempt to alter the course of his country, see Paul Delany, *D. H. Lawrence's Nightmare: The Writer and his Circle in the Years of the Great War*.

[10] The issue of Lawrence's latent homosexuality has received considerable attention. The *locus classicus* of homosexual desire in Lawrence is the suppressed Prologue to *Women in Love* (see *Phoenix II*, 92-108). One of the best recent studies of Lawrence's work as a sustained evasion of its own homosexual impetus is David Cavitch's *D. H. Lawrence and the New World*.

with Frieda had ratified the endorsement, and his 1915 exposure to casually epicene Cambridge reinforced his abhorrence of homosexuality. The resultant interplay between unsought and unprofessed carnal desire for a male, on the one hand, and a variety of high-minded, portentous, and vague schemes of male confraternity or leadership, on the other, is never fully mastered into utterance. The salient instance of this confusion is of course the Gerald-Birkin relationship in *Women in Love*, and I shall return to it when discussing that novel.

Moving to the widest arena of Lawrence's societal critique, one arrives at that core of moral and religious values which empower the culture's specific arrangements and which Nietzsche calls its "idols." Many of these derive from a kindred version of the attenuated Christianity that Nietzsche attacked. "Today the long light of Christianity is guttering to go out and we have to get at new resources in ourselves," Lawrence writes ("On Human Destiny," 628). His fictions confront the sickness of a debilitated Christianity with increasing explicitness—from Ursula's childlike rejection of "turn the other cheek," through Birkin's/ Lilly's/Somers' search for something beyond the anemic consolations of Christian doctrine, to "The Man who Died" 's full revaluation of Christian motives and symbols. The ideal of selflessness he had early recognized as a respectable category for self-evasion, and the ambiguities of sacrifice were painfully brought home to him through his mother's "selfless devotion" and his own later ordeal of eloping with Frieda. He writes Frieda's sister in December 1912:

> Dear Else: I was not cross with your letter. I think you want to do the best for Frieda. I do also. But I think you ask us to throw away a real apple for a gilt one. Nowadays it costs more courage to assert one's desire and need, than it does to renounce. If Frieda and the children could live happily together, I should say "Go"—because the happiness of two out of three is sufficient. But if she would only be sacrificing her life, I would not let her go if I could keep her. Because if she brings to the children a sacrifice, that is a curse to them. If I had a prayer, I think it would be "Lord, let no

one ever sacrifice living stuff to me—because I'm burdened enough." (*Letters*, 1:486)

One way of summarizing Lawrence's enterprise is to see it as an ever-renewed testing of the differences between real apples and gilt ones, between the quick and dead. Eventually he came to see the categories of the ideal, the abstract, and the permanent as three facets of Western culture's most burdensome gilt apple:

> There are no gems of the living plasm. The living plasm vibrates unspeakably, it inhales the future, it exhales the past, it is the quick of both, and yet it is neither. There is no plasmic finality, nothing crystal, permanent. . . . The ideal— what is the ideal? A figment. An abstraction. A static abstraction, abstracted from life. . . . It is a crystallized aspiration, or a crystallized remembrance: crystallized, set, finished. ("Introduction to New Poems," 85, 89)

At this level of generalization Lawrence's differences from his Victorian predecessors and his kinship with the Joyce of *Ulysses* can be stated. If Dickens and George Eliot succeed (or nearly succeed) in squaring their imaginative grasp of experience with the cultural ideals and abstractions by which they evaluate life, if Hardy and Conrad generate tragedy from the failure of those same cultural norms to harmonize with their imaginative sense of natural and human sequences, then Lawrence and Joyce come into focus as writers who tap—one for passionate liberation, the other for dispassionate comedy—the same discrepancy between the flickering givens of incarnate nature and the crystalline ideals of discarnate culture. Maggie and Gwendolen submit, Tess and Jude are destroyed, Jim and Decoud are undone in the face of this discrepancy. But Ursula and Birkin and Connie would reverse its force, while Leopold Bloom—who reverses nothing— would smilingly absorb its threat. These summary distinctions are spelled out extensively elsewhere, and I now conclude my introduction to Lawrence by returning to what he understands by "the living plasm."

"The self that lives in my body I can never finally know. . . . The me that is in my body is a strange animal to me, and often a very trying one" ("On Being a Man," 616). Housed in "the living plasm," it is a kind of daemon, ranging incessantly (as Lawrence ranged) from "things gone dead," in search of "new places," both within and without. To stay put, to repeat oneself, to fall into ritual, is to become entrapped in the idolatries of the permanent and the absolute. All living relations are, as the world implies, relative, and they hurt so long as they live. The tempting alternative to them is the shortcut of "voluptuous," machine-like, repeated relations: transforming the mobile "living plasm" into a reified and predictable instrument. What is death-dealing in the conscious will here emerges. The will is the faculty—so praised by Dickens and Eliot, Hardy and Conrad, so scrutinized by Lawrence—which anaesthetizes our living vulnerability by enabling us to become predictable, closed off, instrumentally perfected.[11]

Lawrence defines the novel as, precisely, a genre created by faculties within the writer other than the will. At its best the novel does not idealize, crystallize, abstract, or prove anything. "The novel is the highest example of subtle inter-relatedness that man has discovered. Everything is true in its own time, place, circumstance, and untrue outside of its own place, time, circumstance. . . . Morality in the novel is the trembling instability of the balance" ("Morality and the Novel," 110).

I close these remarks by emphasizing that word "trembling." It points to the vulnerability and candor of Lawrence's enterprise. Beneath the myriad shrillnesses and incoherence of Lawrence's work there remains—and this is why many of us read him—the radical undefensiveness of his grasp of "the living plasm." He exposes himself generously to error because he believes in no categories of victory or completion. "Anything that *triumphs*, perishes. The consummation comes from perfect relatedness." There can be no triumph, but there is no escape from battle. "It is wrong to make the lion lie down with the lamb. This is the supreme sin, the unforgivable blasphemy of which Christ spoke. This is the creating of nothingness . . . ("The Crown," 373).

---

[11] As Leo Bersani puts it in a provocative essay on Lawrence, the will is that "faculty by which we manage to function without interruption, to continue 'moving' as if we had severed all connections with our own disruptive desires and anxieties as well as those of other people" (40).

Battle in Lawrence's work is furious; no reader need be reminded of his novels' violence. But in his best work he knows, and makes us know, that the violence is generated from tensions which are livingly opposed but not hostile—tensions that lie at the heart of the nature that surrounds and informs us.

> No, if we are to break through, it must be in the strength of life bubbling inside us. The chicken does not break the shell out of animosity against the shell. It bursts out in its blind desire to move under a greater heavens. ("The Crown," 415)

"THE TREMBLING INSTABILITY" OF *WOMEN IN LOVE*

Women in Love has elicited more and better criticism than anything else Lawrence wrote.[1] It remains difficult, however, for the commentator faced with "the trembling instability of [its] balance" to refrain from "put[ting] his thumb in the scale, to pull down the balance to his own predilection" ("Morality in the Novel," 110). In stressing that balance this chapter attends to the novel's textural variety by exploring three different "arenas" of narrative, each concerned with the tension between a set of given cultural arrangements, on the one hand, and a cluster of latent natural impulses, on the other. The first (and the most assured) "arena" is Lawrence's dramatization of what he calls in "The Crown" the "flux of corruption," the destructive rituals of thinking, feeling, and acting that beset society as a whole, and Gerald and Gudrun in particular. The assurance of chapters like "Rabbit," "Death and Love," and "Snowed Up" contrasts markedly with the ambiguities that appear in the second "arena": the Gerald-Birkin relationship. That male pairing, on closer scrutiny, verges on incoherence. It is easy to identify (if not to articulate)

---

[1] Leavis, Vivas, and Daleski, building successively on each other, have established the main line of commentary on the novel as Lawrence's most complex and significant work. Graham Hough, George Ford, Julian Moynahan, Colin Clarke, and Roger Sale, among others, have written penetratingly of *Women in Love* in their book-length studies of Lawrence. Separate articles on the novel are legion; I have benefited especially from the recent pieces by T. H. Adamowski and Garrett Stewart.

the sinister dynamic of the scene with Bismarck: the "gleaming" Gerald beating the rabbit on the neck, Winifred crooning, Gudrun revealed, "her voice like a seagull's cry" (233). By contrast, when Birkin, "with dark, almost vengeful eyes," says to Ursula of the dead Gerald, "He should have loved me, I offered him" (471), his comment is articulate and yet, on reflection, far from clear. Would the offered love have saved Gerald? Was the love offered? What kind of love is in question? Finally, between these "arenas" of assured critique, on the one hand, and ambiguity or incoherence, on the other, there is the "arena" of Birkin's relationship with Ursula. In my reading of the novel, the rhythm of this relationship best embodies the "trembling instability of the balance" that is *Women in Love*'s finest achievement. Its unpredictable turns lie midway between the clarity of the "flux of corruption" and the confusion of *Blutbrüderschaft*.

≈

"WE ROAM in the belly of our era" ("The Crown," 367), and "Creme de Menthe" is one of the chapters in *Women in Love* that best display the era's belly. London Bohemia, with its "very thorough rejecters of the world," frequents the Café Pompadour; and though these avant-gardists seek to be free of convention, they remain, as Birkin tells Gerald, "for all their shockingness, all on one note" (53). Their repudiation of respectability has not brought freedom but merely exchanged one social code for another; Lawrence finely conveys the fixed, foreclosed quality of their motions.

Minette's affected lisp, Halliday's self-conscious histrionics—playing up to an audience attuned to his gestures—the protocol of eating and drinking ("But you can't eat oysters when you're drinking brandy," Halliday squeals): programmed moves like these fill the scene as its tension builds. Gerald is instantly placed—by Minette, by Halliday, by the crowd—as Minette's potential lover, and this easy identification stimulates in Gerald "an awful, enjoyable power over her, an instinctive cherishing very near to cruelty" (57). Halliday thrives on the pain of being ousted, and when he screams on discovering Minette in the Pompadour, "the cafe looked up like animals when they hear a cry" (58). Swiftly—as though the scene had been rehearsed before—the antagonism mounts. A few drops of brandy in Halliday's face leads to talk of blood and beetles, and then to Minette's knifing the young man's hand. The calculated sex-play and the accumulating brutality are not alternative activities; they are versions of an identical dynamic: the programmatic itching of raw nerves, sensual gratification through self-abuse and the abuse—verbal, physical—of others. Within well-ordered confines the Bohemians at the Pompadour avert the ennui that stalks their life by teasing at, toying in public with, the constitutive elements of their passional life. They know they are alive by the lacerating, self-delighting sensations thus produced.

> Minette looked at him with a slow, slow smile. She was very handsome, flushed, and confident in dreadful knowledge. Two little points of light glinted on Gerald's eyes.
> "Why do they call you Minette? Because you're like a cat?" he asked her.
> "I expect so," she said.
> The smile grew more intense on his face.
> "You are, rather:—or a young, female panther."
> "Oh God, Gerald!" said Birkin, in some disgust. (64)

The opposite of animals, these are humans playing at being animals, looking at their animal motions in mirrors. "In our nighttime, there's always the electricity switched on" (37), Birkin had told Ursula, and Minette has taken on a cat's name so as to stimulate half-conscious fantasies of animal passion in her potential lovers. Her sexuality is worked, stroked, advertised. The only spontaneous gesture in the chapter is Birkin's rising up involuntarily in disgust. "You're all right," the Russian tells Gerald: you've met the standards, you can sleep with Minette. The chapter closes, not on the mysterious note of Gerald's sexual entry into Minette's "potent darkness," but on the flatly urbane note of blasé, nihilistic Bohemia: "The men lit another cigarette and talked casually" (69).

Behavior at the Pompadour, for all its surface differences, answers to the same terms with which Birkin assesses the social rounds at Breadalby: ". . . how known it all was, like a game with the figures set out . . . the same figures moving round in one of the innumerable permutations that make up the game"

(92). Nothing is more achieved in *Women in Love* than Lawrence's scenes of intercourse among those who have a great need but no capacity for it. The conventions of this dominant background serve to silhouette nicely a relationship which reveals quite other impulses and requires for its interpretation a new vocabulary: the inchoate, abortive love between Gerald and Birkin.

❧

"YOU DON'T believe in having any standard of behaviour at all, do you?" he challenged Birkin, censoriously.

"Standard—no. I hate standards. But they're necessary for the common ruck. Anybody who is anything can just be himself and do as he likes. . . . It's the hardest thing in the world to act spontaneously on one's impulses—and it's the only really gentlemanly thing to do—provided you're fit to do it."

"You don't expect me to take you seriously, do you?" asked Gerald. . . . "You think people should just do as they like."

"I think they always do. But I should like them to like the purely individual thing in themselves, which makes them act in singleness. And they only like to do the collective thing."

"And I," said Gerald grimly, "shouldn't like to be in a world of people who acted individually and spontaneously, as you call it. We should have everybody cutting everybody else's throat in five minutes."

"That means *you* would like to be cutting everybody's throat," said Birkin.

"How does that follow?" asked Gerald crossly.

"No man," said Birkin, "cuts another man's throat unless he wants to cut it, and unless the other man wants it cutting. This is a complete truth. It takes two people to make a murder: a murderer and murderee. And a murderee is a man who is murderable. And a man who is murderable is a man who in a profound if hidden lust desires to be murdered."

"Sometimes you talk pure nonsense," said Gerald. . . .
(26-27)

207

Birkin's joining of a murderer and a murderee as requisite, each, for the other's fulfillment, goes far—farther than he knows. Immediately it proposes the latent form of Gerald's relationship with Gudrun, with each figure playing both roles. Gudrun's swoon (in "Coal Dust") at the sight of Gerald's spurs coming down on the mare's bleeding flanks is caused by the double identification. She is both mare and rider. As Freud writes in *Three Essays on the Theory of Sexuality*: "A person who feels pleasure in producing pain in someone else in a sexual relationship is also capable of enjoying as pleasure any pain which he may himself derive from sexual relations. A sadist is always at the same time a masochist . . ." (7:159). Gudrun repudiates any acknowledgment of double roles. When she later rejects Birkin's formulation by calling Gerald's killing his brother "the purest form of accident" (42), she is reserving for herself the right to "accidental" murder.

The Cain reference resonates throughout the narrative. The only major figure with a past that ultimately controls him, Gerald-as-child-murderer is the foremost exception to Lawrence's usually optimistic mode of conceiving the characters he cares for as free to become who they are. Gerald's culture has him by the throat. A useless class-molded education, a pair of frustrated and inescapable parents, lengthy immersion in a brutal and brutalizing profession: in Gerald we measure (as we will later measure it in Clifford Chatterley) the weight of cultural determinants which Lawrence must suspend if he is to free his protagonists to center on their native resources. Birkin (and later Mellors) is revealingly exempted from much of this sinister context, and one reason for Birkin's appealing mobility is his lack of the usual cultural baggage. Gerald is exempted from nothing. His movements in the present are as keyed, Conrad-like, to the fatal accumulation of his past as they are to the unfolding of any future. Joyce Carol Oates has rightly termed him "Lawrence's only tragic figure" (561). He gives the lie to Lawrence's confident assertion that "tragedy is lack of experience." When in "Water Party" he lets go "for the first time in his life . . . imperceptibly . . . melting into oneness with the whole" (170), the death that is in him—not his life potential—emerges. As David Cavitch has noted, his is the most moving death in Lawrence's work (63-66). This is so because

Birkin is complicit in that death in ways never acknowledged. "It takes two people to make a murder." It is a relational act, and Birkin is only less implicated than Gudrun. On the page following the conversation already quoted between Gerald and Birkin we read:

> There was a pause of strange enmity between the two men, that was very near to love. It was always the same between them; always their talk brought them into a deadly nearness of contact, a strange, perilous intimacy which was either hate or love, or both. They parted with apparent unconcern, as if their going apart were a trivial occurrence. . . . Yet the heart of each burned from the other. . . . This they would never admit. . . . (28)

How different that earlier interchange looks after this paragraph. The subtext rises into place, and now we really do know that "it's the hardest thing in the world to act spontaneously on one's impulses." What appeared as detached argument is reseen to be relational drama. The Bohemians at the Pompadour were incapable of spontaneous candor and so—despite his argument, *during* his argument—is Rupert Birkin. He too, in his sexual orientation, cannot get clear of "the collective thing." Tugging against the novel's overt commitment to Gerald's death—a murder waiting in the wings, "collectively" inscribed in both men's inability to transcend their culture's social/sexual mores—is the unexpressed, incompletely expressible cluster of inchoate feelings that they nevertheless bear for each other. Their relationship comes into focus as a tension between the tragic conclusion premised in the Cain symbolism and the whispered possibility, despite Cain, of *Blutbrüderschaft* that is intimated in their cryptic looks and gestures.

Frank Kermode has persuasively claimed that the most important point to note about the Prologue to *Women in Love* is that Lawrence struck it out, thus preserving the indecisiveness of his novel's treatment of male love (64). Whereas the unpublished Prologue centers almost feverishly on Birkin's unuttered feelings, the novel itself dramatizes the quandary of male love as the joint concern of both men. A private feeling has been transformed into an abortive relationship, and the moral interest of that relationship inheres in Lawrence's inability to expose its felt life to full conceptualization or assessment. Beneath the overt drama of focused ideas we find the latent drama of undelivered feelings. *Women in Love* is most provocative as a novel of ideas in just the measure that its proclaimed ideas are affected by the cluster of unarticulated feelings they emerge from and descend into.

Consider the scene between the two men "In the Train." Birkin espouses there his doctrine of "the finality of love" with a woman: perfect marriage. If we read the scene dramatically, we find, beneath the clear doctrinal positions, an ambivalent dance of feelings between the two men. Birkin concedes, under its spell, his occasional hatred—his starry hatred—of Gerald; they watch each other warily. Gerald's questions about love elicit Birkin's claim that "I do—I want to love," but to Gerald's ears "it sounded as if he were insistent rather than confident" (50). Gerald continues quietly to mock Birkin's now rather strident claim, and "Birkin could not help seeing how beautiful and soldierly [Gerald's] face was, with a certain courage to be indifferent" (51). Birkin grows angry, "You are a born unbeliever," but Gerald responds: "I only feel what I feel."

> And he looked again at Birkin almost sardonically, with his blue, manly, sharp-lighted eyes. Birkin's eyes were at the moment full of anger. But swiftly they became troubled, doubtful, then full of a warm, rich affectionateness and laughter.
>
> "It troubles me very much, Gerald," he said, wrinkling his brows.
>
> "I can see it does," said Gerald, uncovering his mouth in a manly, quick, soldierly laugh. (51)

The scene continues in another mode, one of narrative conceptualization, and now begins to stress (at Gerald's expense) the differences between the two men. "There was something very congenial to him in Birkin. But yet, beyond this, he did not take much notice. He felt that he, himself, Gerald, had harder and more durable truths than any the other man knew . . ." (51). Responding to the tension between the scene's two modes of discourse, we see that Birkin is not merely stating his views; he

210

is trying to believe them. Gerald's finer "manly" candor, his "soldierly" willingness actually to "feel what I feel," momentarily emerges in the dialogue as its center, as the unstated challenge (felt by Birkin as well) to Birkin's doctrinal position. But it quickly disappears in the conceptual prose that reminds us of Gerald's conventionality. Most critics take the reminder so well to heart that they forget the candor of Gerald that had preceded it.[2]

Two longish bedroom scenes—that they take place in bedrooms is not irrelevant—occur before the decisive wrestling match. In the first, at Breadalby, Gerald is trying to sort out his mix of feelings toward Minette. He remains in Birkin's room despite the latter's urging him to go to bed. Birkin eventually wearies of the Minette issue, and Gerald says, " 'I wish you'd tell me something that *did* matter,' looking down all the time at the face of the other man, waiting for something" (89). Nothing comes, Gerald retires, and the next morning as soon as he awakens he recommences the conversation:

> "What am I to do at all, then?" came Gerald's voice.
> "What you like. What am I to do myself?"
> In the silence Birkin could feel Gerald musing this fact.
> "I'm blest if I know," came the good-humoured answer.
> "You see," said Birkin, "part of you wants Minette, and nothing but Minette, part of you wants the mines, the business, and nothing but the business—and there you are—all in bits—"
> "And part of me wants something else," said Gerald, in a queer, quiet, real voice.
> "What?" said Birkin, rather surprised.
> "That's what I hoped you could tell me," said Gerald.
> (90)

The interchange contains a plea for recognition and intimacy. Gerald cannot identify his own feelings, and Birkin seems incapable of doing it for him. The grooved round of rituals at Bread-

---

[2] Robert Kiely is an exception: "The failure of this friendship to take root and grow in the lives of these two men is usually blamed on Gerald. . . . But Birkin is not so simple a surrogate of Lawrence as to be exempt from all culpability" (159).

alby further discourages discovery; the two men move their separate ways.

Later, during Birkin's illness after the "Water Party" disaster, Gerald visits him in his rooms. The scene is intense; they discuss Gerald's *contretemps* with Gudrun, and Birkin's conviction that "there's a long way to go, after the point of intrinsic death, before we disappear" (196). Birkin urges Gerald to "keep entirely out of the line. It's no good trying to toe the line, when your one impulse is to smash up the line" (197). The scene thus establishes Birkin as seeking to act on his unconscious impulses, while Gerald remains defensive and afraid to break out of his sterile patterns. In this posture Birkin recognizes most fully his love for Gerald—" of course he had been loving Gerald all along, and all along denying it" (198)—and he rises for the first time into utterance, proposing his pact of *Blutbrüderschaft*. Gerald is tempted but reserved; he backs off: "We'll leave it till I understand it better" (199). Birkin then reaches his often quoted assessment of Gerald: "This strange sense of fatality in Gerald, as if he were limited to one form of existence, one knowledge, one activity, a sort of fatal halfness, which to himself seemed wholeness . . . Gerald could never fly away from himself, in real indifferent gaiety" (199). Discussion of the scene usually ends here, each figure in his characteristic stance of openness and closure, but the conclusion three pages later deserves notice:

> Gerald came near the bed and stood looking down at Birkin whose throat was exposed, whose tossed hair fell attractively on the warm brow, above the eyes that were so unchallenged and still in the satirical face. Gerald, full-limbed and turgid with energy, stood unwilling to go. . . .
>
> "So," said Birkin. "Good-bye." And he reached out his hand from under the bed-clothes, smiling with a glimmering look. . . .
>
> The eyes of the two men met again. Gerald's . . . were suffused now with warm light and with unadmitted love, Birkin looked back as out of a darkness, unsounded and unknown, yet with a kind of warmth, that seemed to flow over Gerald's brain like a fertile sleep.

212

"Good-bye, then" [Gerald says]. "There's nothing I can
do for you?"

"Nothing, thanks." (202)

To take this passage into account is to see that Gerald is not
simply the denier. He has verbally retreated but physically ad-
vanced, and his "unadmitted love" emerges in his lingering over
Birkin and asking if he can do anything. "Nothing," Birkin replies, and at the least the roles of initiation and recoil shift here,
complicating our response to both men.

The wrestling scene crystallizes their mutual attraction. It is
one of the supreme things in Lawrence, and it eludes the extremes of commentary that would find in it either the clear superiority of homosexual desire or merely (in Mark Spilka's phrase)
the working through of Birkin's desire for Gerald "before he can
love Ursula 'body and soul' " ("Lawrence Up-Tight," 257). It
neither gives the lie to heterosexual love nor acts as an impediment to heterosexual love that must be worked through and beyond.[3] Rather, the wrestling scene is Lawrence's fullest expression of carnal desire between males, only thinly displaced as
wrestling, and yet inadmissible without that displacement. What
the men feel for each other is simultaneously precious and unacceptable; no one can read the scene without sensing its cathar-
tic release of tensions. As though magically freed of his fear of
sexual fusion, Birkin penetrates deeper and deeper into Gerald,

[3] The question of homosexual attraction has aroused much critical heat and
little light. Spilka and Roger Sale take positions close to mine, but they tend to
oversimplify Lawrence's dilemma by reading the male bond as malefic. "To say
that Birkin wants Gerald is to say that Lawrence wants Gerald and the want is
diseased enough to stop everything else for the sake of the want and healthy
enough to seek its own destruction" (Sale, 105). Jeffrey Meyers collapses the
issue into Lawrence's unambiguous (though unacknowledged) preference for males;
he centers on the putative act of anal intercourse in "Excurse" as proof that
Lawrence/Birkin was seeking Gerald and taking Ursula as a substitute. Vivas,
Kermode, Meyers, Emile Delevaney, and Clarke all make too much of the rare
acts of buggery in Lawrence's fiction. In both *Women in Love* and *Lady Chatterley's Lover* the crucial passionate encounters—those with the widest imaginative
resonance within the novels themselves—are heterosexual and "normal." In any
case, as Roger Sale says, the detective work in this arena has been carried out in
"a spirit of appalling vulgarity" (100).

the mind lapsed out, "there was no head to be seen, only the swift, tight limbs, the solid white backs, the physical junction of two bodies clinched into oneness" (263).

Trouble returns with consciousness, for Lawrence can endow neither man with categories that accept these feelings undisplaced. "One ought to wrestle and strive and be physically close. It makes one sane," Birkin asserts. "We are mentally, spiritually intimate, therefore we should be more or less physically intimate too—it is more whole," he repeats. "I don't know why one should have to justify oneself," he states a moment later. "One should enjoy what is given. . . . We should enjoy everything" (265). Birkin may not know why justification is required, but he manifestly requires it. His compulsive "shoulds" and his self-evasive recourse to the pronoun "one" betoken a mind seeking to overcome internal resistance, to combat the strictures of returning consciousness. Gerald, significantly, says little after the wrestling. He has had his intimacy with Birkin, mindlessly; he will never get further in the head. The chapter ends with Gerald glimpsing that he is, indeed, played out: "And mind you, I don't care how it is with me—I don't care how it is—so long as I don't feel . . . so long as I feel I've *lived*, somehow . . ." (268). Almost retrospectively, Gerald surveys his life from its imagined and inevitable terminal point.

Only once more, on the edge of a marriage decision for himself, does Gerald importune Birkin as we have seen in the preceding encounters. Birkin is about to marry, and a quietly desperate Gerald says:

> "One comes to the point where one must take a step in one direction or another. And marriage is one direction—"
> "And what is the other?" asked Birkin quickly.
> Gerald looked up at him with hot, strangely-conscious eyes, that the other man could not understand.
> "I can't say," he replied. "If I knew *that*—" He moved uneasily on his feet and did not finish.
> "You mean if you knew the alternative?" asked Birkin. "And since you don't know it, marriage is a *pis aller*."
> Gerald looked up at Birkin with the same hot, constrained eyes. (344)

214

Lawrence will not say either, and we are left to register for ourselves the meaning of those "hot, strangely-conscious eyes." The scene is deliberately cryptic; Gerald cannot verbalize what he wants from Birkin. The point is that it is Gerald who wants something, Gerald the suppliant, and that the novel refuses to assess, even to identify, what he desires.

At the end of "Continental," the half-crazed Gerald listens to Birkin's bitter reminder: " 'I've loved you, as well as Gudrun, don't forget.' 'Have you?' [Gerald] said, with icy skepticism. 'Or do you think you have?' He was hardly responsible for what he said" (431). Whoever is responsible, the words reverberate. It takes two men to make a murder, two men to produce a failed relationship. "He should have loved me, I offered him," Birkin tearfully addresses Ursula, in the presence of Gerald's frozen carcass. The tears bespeak an unacknowledged rejection lurking beneath that offer, a relationship whose failure goes deeper than any of the novel's conceptual explanations can explain. "When these feeling-patterns become inadequate . . . we are in torture," Lawrence had written in "The Good Man." "Something is inadequate in the expression-apparatus, and we hear strange howlings" (258). In the relationship of Gerald and Birkin, if we listen closely, we hear such howlings.

&

"IT IS TRUE what I say; there is a beyond, in you, in me, which is further than love, beyond the scope, as stars are beyond the scope of vision, some of them."

"Then there is no love," cried Ursula.

"Ultimately, no, there is something else. But, ultimately, there *is* no love."

Ursula was given over to this statement for some moments. then she half rose from her chair, saying, in a final, repellant voice:

"Then let me go home—what am I doing here?"

"There is the door," he said. "You are a free agent."

He was suspended finely and perfectly in this extremity. She hung motionless for some seconds, then she sat down again.

"If there is no love, what is there?" she cried, almost jeering. . . . (137)

This sequence takes place in "Mino," and it admirably captures the rhythm of the Ursula-Birkin relationship. Neither perfectly resolved at the conceptual level nor verging on incoherence beneath the argument, the passage from "Mino" shows Birkin and Ursula at a stalemate—and at the same time weathering that stalemate. Ursula repudiates her lover's arguments, even as her motions and his bear out the point he would articulate: "He was suspended finely. . . . She hung motionless . . . then she sat down again." She stays to argue, but surely the important thing is that she stays. Bonded as though gravitationally, held together by what each of them intrinsically is, Ursula and Birkin argue incessantly in *Women in Love.* Argument is for them, as it seems to have been for Frieda and Lawrence, the enduring form of their bond.[4]

Critics tend to disparage "Mino." Especially they lament the failure of its symbolism. H. M. Daleski is representative in conceding "the sad truth . . . that the 'wild cat' is very easily tamed" (174), and C. Pirenet dismisses the chapter from serious concern: "tout ceci est du domaine de la comédie" (143). We *are* dealing with comedy in "Mino": the deepest rhythm of the Birkin-Ursula relationship, symbolism and gesture, argument and embrace, is a comic rhythm. The gap between the Mino's actual behavior and Birkin's assertion of cosmic meanings is not a sign of novelistic failure but the enabling point of contention that fills the chapter. Birkin presses for a will to power, but Ursula is not having any. "There you are—a star in its orbit! A satellite—a satellite of Mars—that's what she is to be! There—there—you've given yourself away! You want a satellite. . . . You've said it—you've said it—you've dished yourself!" (142).

Birkin may be "dished" for argument (though he never *said* "satellite"), but he is anything but rebuffed as a lover. "He stood smiling in frustration and amusement and irritation and admi-

---

[4] "L'affrontement, chez eux [Ursula and Birkin], n'a pas la même gravité que chez Gerald et Gudrun: il se dépense en paroles, il est même très bavard. Gerald et Gudrun ne s'affrontent jamais au niveau des paroles; leur lutte est essentielle, muette" (C. Pirenet, 141).

ration and love. She was so quick, and so lambent, like discernible fire, and so vindictive, and so rich in her dangerous flamy sensitiveness" (142). These are not the thoughts of a disappointed man. The chapter reveals a supple dialectic between argument and feeling, each unpredictably inflecting the other. They fight, they mock, they subside in tenderness, they flare up in passion or in anger, they fight again.

> "But don't you think me good-looking?" she persisted in a mocking voice.
> He looked at her, to see if he felt that she was good-looking. (138)

A smile is as appropriate a critical response to this passage as a knowing frown. What Birkin wants is unutterable because he has never experienced it: the perfect release, through their unconventional bond, of their unconventional selves. "It is quite inhuman—so there can be no calling to book, in any form whatsoever—because one is outside the pale of all that is accepted, and nothing known applies" (138). A miracle of spontaneous good form is what he seeks, yet Ursula is no fool for not following his desire immediately. Within the dramatized scene, Birkin's argument for freedom appears as an expression of domination; his insistence on the stars, an evasion of the body. (After the encounter with Hermione one understands why he fights shy.) Ursula mocks him, he takes it for a while and then retreats into his dignity:

> "All right," he said, looking up with sudden exasperation. "Now go away then, and leave me alone. I don't want any more of your meretricious persiflage."
> "Is it really persiflage?" she mocked, her face really relaxing into laughter. She interpreted it, that he had made a deep confession of love to her. But he was so absurd in his words, also.
> They were silent for many minutes, she was pleased and elated like child. His concentration broke, he began to look at her simply and naturally.
> "What I want is a strange conjunction with you. . . ."
> (139)

217

Lawrence captures "the trembling instability" of their living relationship: his huffiness, her softening, her conviction (half-true, half-false) that he has confessed his love, his easing into intimacy, and then, refreshed, his launching into further argument. He introduces the stars. "Isn't this rather sudden?" she mocks, he laughs, and the two cats take over the scene. Nothing has been resolved, and the symbolic cats only accentuate their disagreement. The landlady enters to announce that tea is ready, their internal chemistry begins to alter, and in the midst of further bickering Ursula breaks out with "What *good* things to eat!" "Take your own sugar," he answers her.

Only an ideologue would want this changed. Lawrence is one of the few novelists (Joyce is another) to render arguing and eating as dissimilar but related activities performed by the same living subject. What is unresolved in argument is mercifully overlooked, forgotten, while eating.[5] They soon begin to argue again, each pressing for his own version of the coming relationship. Eventually, "they had talked and struggled till they were both wearied out."

> "Tell me about yourself and your people," he said.
> And she told him about the Brangwens, and about her mother, and about Skrebensky, her first love, and about her later experiences. He sat very still, watching her as she talked. And he seemed to listen with reverence. Her face was beautiful and full of baffled light as she told him all the things that had hurt her or perplexed her so deeply. He seemed to warm and comfort his soul at the beautiful light of her nature. (145)

Their differences are not superficial, but what joins them is deeper: they are already releasing each other, unconsciously, during those intervals when they forget to maintain their self-defining attributes, when they just let themselves be. The argument,

[5] Sale is the only critic I know to appreciate this interplay. "Lovely, the paradoxes brought to life in acceptance and admiration of another, and lovely too, the way this insures that after the argument makes them weary, they stay together, the bond there even though neither likes the other's terms to describe it" (85).

218

they know, cannot be won by either. "But I want us to be to-gether without bothering about ourselves—to be really together because we *are* together, as if it were a phenomenon, not a thing we have to maintain by our own effort" (242), Birkin urges in "Moony." Irresistible as this is, Ursula resists it—"No, you are just egocentric," she replies—and in her resistance she re-estab-lishes the rhythm of argument and intimacy that is the unchosen mark of their relationship.

This rhythm of unpredictable flame-life characterizes not only "Mino" but the larger form of *Women in Love* as well. Too often critics analyze individual chapters as static entities and then con-clude on the note of stalemate, cosmic despair, or equally cosmic triumph.[6] But flame-life flickers, and the career of the flicker is usually comic. In "Moony" the movement of feeling follows a similar pattern, with kindred implications.

Ursula descends to Willey Water and discovers Birkin curs-ing "Cybele . . . Syria Dea," while he hurls rocks at the moon's reflection on the water. Rather than offer another interpretation of this over-interpreted symbolic act, I would note that his action exhausts his anger.

> "Why should you hate the moon? It hasn't done you any harm, has it?"
> "Was it hate?" he said.
> And they were silent for a few minutes. (241)

He gradually draws close to her and—in a telling reversal of his former action—he says: "There is a golden light in you, which I wish you would give me" (241). The moon that had oppressed him he now desires; they each quietly reveal their sense of lack. Their lacks, of course, differ, and the scene turns from gentleness to altercation, each insisting that the other yield. They grow peaceful again; he teases her about her war-cry and concedes that he loves her.

---

[6] In a 1979 MLA discussion on *Women in Love* as a Modernist novel all three panelists insisted on the novel's apocalyptic tones—unwilling to credit its creation of a flickering, unassertive life-relationship in the midst of any number of ultimate death-scenarios.

"Are you sure?" she said, nestling happily near to him.

"Quite sure—so now have done—accept it and have done."

She was nestled quite close to him.

"Have done with what?" she murmured happily. (244)

Their intimacy increases, and he kisses her with his soft, moth-like kisses. In her difference she is kindled and wants passion. He resists and she goes home. Then, with uncanny rightness, Lawrence registers a return in Birkin's spirit toward her. He visualizes his plight of unrelatedness on a cosmic scale, and he sees that if he does not marry he will die. Filled with a vision of sacred marriage as a state of supremely balanced singleness and connection, pride and submission, he rushes to Beldover. "They must marry at once, and so make a definite pledge, enter into a definite communion. . . . There was no moment to spare" (247).

Lawrence's ability to keep his hand off the scale appears in what follows. Birkin's vision reflects, after all, his desires, not Ursula's nor the disposition of the world outside those desires. Will Brangwen enters the chapter at this point—*the* Lawrentian figure who has failed to center his life on his own desires—and he and Birkin engage in an inconsequent discussion of Ursula's upbringing and Birkin's purposes. Each man rebukes the other by saying that Ursula will please herself, and it is fine that she should, upon her entry into the scene, enrage them both by pleasing herself. They each withdraw, baffled and angry, Ursula joining Gudrun and Birkin finding the consolation of wrestling with Gerald at Shortlands.

After the wrestling scene Ursula begins to regain "ascendance over Birkin's being. . . . Gerald was becoming dim again, lapsing out of him" (266). The final ascendance is realized some fifty pages later in "Excurse," but before attending briefly to that climax I would generalize the pattern I have been following. In the imaginative world of Lawrence one centers on carbon or flame, but one neither wills the shape of one's carbon nor dictates the flow of one's flame. The union of Ursula and Birkin comes when it comes, not when one of them sees fit to make it happen. The movement of the novel from "Moony" through "Gladiatorial" follows the unpredictable career of desire, of developments beyond the aegis of the characters' will. In "Excurse" this rhythm is most pronounced.

Discussion of "Excurse" usually focuses on the climaxes and scants their sustained preparation.[7] Locally the quarrel between the lovers derives from the tea party at Hermione's the day before, with its invidious display of well-bred polylingual culture, in the shadow of which Ursula feels vulgar, dumpy, lower-middle-class. She is sure Birkin's rings will not fit her fat fingers. Beneath the local quarrel is the essential one: the passional differences between them—her wanting to engulf him, his still-lingering, sham-spiritual tie to Hermione—threaten to burst them asunder. The magnificent battle they engage in is, reasonably, followed by their magnificent love-making; no one disputes the dynamic. But whereas their anger is irrefutably alive on the page, critics have been wondering for at least thirty years what is happening in their ecstatic union.

The fight clears the air. Ursula's invective identifies and for the moment dissolves the knot of contradictions Birkin carries within himself.

> He wanted her to come back. He breathed lightly and regularly like an infant, that breathes innocently, beyond the touch of responsibility.
> She was coming back. He saw her drifting desultorily under the high hedge, advancing towards him slowly. He did not move, he did not look again. He was as if asleep, at peace, slumbering and utterly relaxed. (301)

She was coming back. The core of Lawrence's art is in his creative grasp of how we leave and return, how our flame-life flares, gutters, renews itself. There follows the gentlest love scene in Lawrence's work.

---

[7] Kermode is an exception. He sees the bicyclist who interrupts the lovers' quarrel as "very typical of Lawrence" (76). Leo Bersani also notes that "there is nothing final about the peace of 'Excurse,' " further remarking that, "for all Birkin's insistence, the dominant mode of *Women in Love* is interrogative rather than assertive" (58).

She looked up at him. The wonderful yellow light in her eyes now was soft and yielded. . . . He kissed her softly, many, many times. A laugh came into her eyes.

"Did I abuse you?" she asked.

He smiled too, and took her hand, that was so soft and given.

"Never mind," she said, "it is all for the good." He kissed her again, softly, many times.

"Isn't it?" she said.

"Certainly," he replied. "Wait! I shall have my own back."

She laughed suddenly, with a wild catch in her voice, and flung her arms around him.

"You are mine, my love, aren't you?" she cried, straining him close.

"Yes," he said softly.

His voice was so soft and final, she went very still, as if under a fate which had taken her. Yes, she acquiesced—but it was accomplished without her acquiescence. He was kissing her quietly, repeatedly, with a soft, still happiness that almost made her heart stop beating. . . . She hid her face on his shoulder, hiding before him, because he could see her so completely. She knew he loved her, and she was afraid, she was in a strange element, a new heaven round about her. She wished he were passionate, because in passion she was at home. But this was so still and frail, as space is more frightening than force. (302-303)

Roger Sale claims, without exaggeration, that "almost a thousand pages [of *The Rainbow* and *Women in Love*] lie behind that 'space is more frightening than force,' and we need almost every one to read it rightly" (98). Space is the peaceful dimension you get to without willing it, once you break away from a self-manipulated identity; force is what that instrumental identity can make happen. The quoted passage is transparent and serene, a moment of the cessation of will and the unsought achievement of intimacy. His soft kisses are now what she wants, his unabrasive closeness is the "new heaven round about her."

There is no need to discuss in any detail the remainder of

the chapter. Its passionate climaxes seem, for many reasons, less clear and assured than the scene of rebirth just quoted. In certain places, like "the immemorial magnificence of mystic, palpable, real otherness" (312), the later prose of "Excurse" is positively opaque. Garrett Stewart justifies such prose as "Lawrence's post-orgastic style, the prose not of frictional rush to climax, but of the poise and reciprocal peace that ensues. Otherness must be grammatically respected" (236). Perhaps, but what I hear in that phrasing is neither poise nor grammatical respect, but the insistent alliteration of m's: the language of force asserting a transcendent experience rather than the language of space creating the image of it.

Mystic climaxes are in any case only one part of *Women in Love*. The flame-life does not remain fixed in any supreme ecstasy.[8] The rarer achievement is not some incandescent perfection of Ursula and Birkin's relationship but its mobile, phoenix-like capacity to continue under duress. Beset by Birkin's fear of merging, shadowed by his desire for an "eternal union with a man too" (473), their intimacy is most impressive where least assertive. Not created by argument, it quietly survives the thrust of the closing argument of the novel, as it has survived other arguments. "Anything that *triumphs*, perishes," Lawrence wrote in "The Crown" (373).

At its best, this novel imagines a relationship so open to its own shortcomings and yet surviving by this very openness, that it does elude the finalities of victory or defeat. Gerald and Gudrun ride their aggression and insecurity to death or spiritual disintegration. Gerald and Birkin press each other for an alternative response that neither can articulate. But Birkin and Ursula achieve the "trembling instability of the balance," a living relationship that hurts because of its inadequacy, hurts also because it is alive.

---

[8] Cf. the letter to Gordon Campbell about the excesses of ecstasy:
But do, for God's sake, mistrust and beware of these states of exaltation and ecstasy. They send you, anyone, swaying so far beyond the center of gravity in one direction, there is the inevitable swing back with greater velocity to the other direction. . . . Besides, there is no real truth in ecstasy. All vital truth contains the memory of all that for which it is not true: Ecstasy achieves itself by virtue of *exclusion*; and in making any passionate exclusion, one has already put one's right hand in the hand of the lie. (*Letters*, 2:246-47)

The novel that can, among its other achievements, render these three modes of experience as continuous reflections of each other, is rightly seen as Lawrence's masterpiece.

CHOOSING BETWEEN THE QUICK AND THE DEAD: THREE VERSIONS OF *LADY CHATTERLEY'S LOVER*

Lawrence's last novel has the winnowed clarity of fable. No one reading any of its three versions can miss its pastoral polarity of vices and virtues, its attempt to free the quick from the dead. The movement of Connie Chatterley from the societal dead world of her husband to the wooded quick world of the gamekeeper describes the entire shape of the novel's plot.[1] That movement, though, has in each version its own accents and encounters its own obstacles. Lawrence did not succeed, in his own eyes, in "getting it out clean" the first two times; and it seems to me that the third version succeeds at a considerable price. Perfect relatedness is the highest aim of Lawrentian art, and the pages that follow explore Lawrence's dilemma with *Chatterley*: his attempts to do justice to *all* the implications of his materials, and at the same to free the "perfect statue" from its imprisoning marble context.[2]

"And what do you want? Do you want me to leave Clifford and come and live in the cottage with you?"

[1] Michael Squires ("Pastoral Patterns and Pastoral Variants in *Lady Chatterley's Lover*") and Kingsley Widmer both explore the pastoral shape of Lawrence's plot. The pastoral analogy, loosely conceived, is a commonplace of *Chatterley* criticism.

[2] The quoted phrases in the paragraph above appear in Lawrence's letter to Arthur McLeod (9 February 1914), describing his revisions of *The Rainbow*: "You know that the perfect statue is in the marble, the kernel of it. But the thing is the getting it out clean" (*Letters*, 2:146). Many critics have alluded to Lawrence's revisions, but few have studied in detail the resultant changes in meaning and implication as *The First Lady Chatterley* moves through *John Thomas and Lady Jane* and finally emerges as *Lady Chatterley's Lover*. To my knowledge, Kingsley Widmer, Emile Delavaney, R. S. Gingher, Marvin Dennis Jackson, Michael Squires ("New Light on the Gamekeeper in *Lady Chatterley's Lover*"), and John Worthen (168-82) have focused most directly on the novel's genetic history.

"No I don't!" he shook his head with distaste.

"Or do you think I can turn Clifford out, and you can come and live with me in Wragby?"

"What as, your errand boy?"

"Not at all. As Sir Oliver Parkin."

"Sir Oliver Shit!" (I, 130)[3]

And his fingertips touched the two secret openings to her body, time after time, with a soft little brush of fire.

"An' if tha shits an' if tha pisses, I'm glad. I don't want a woman as couldna shit nor piss."

Connie could not help a sudden snort of astonished laughter, but he went on unmoved.

"Tha'rt real, tha art! Tha'rt real, even a bit of a bitch. Here tha shits and here tha pisses: an' I lay my hand on 'em both an' like thee for it. I like thee for it. Tha's got a proper, woman's arse, proud of itself. It's none ashamed of itself, this isna." (III, 241).

These two passages reveal the differing assumptions in force in the first and last versions of the novel. In the early passage, class conventions are insuperable; the notion of overturning them arouses in Parkin anger and obscenity. "Sir Oliver Parkin / Sir Oliver Shit!": the first phrase as unthinkable as the second is offensive. The body's functions and possibilities have not yet received their revaluation. Parkin lashes out at Connie:

"What do you call me, in *your* sort of talk?"

"My lover?" she stammered.

"Lover!" he re-echoed. A queer flash went over his face. "Fucker!" he said, and his eyes darted a flash at her, as if he shot her. (I, 127)

My lady's fucker, Sir Oliver Shit: both phrases are signs of opprobrium, and they use obscenity in a conventional way. The elements and activities of the body are isolated and dehumanized. Reference to them expresses self-disgust by way of reducing the

[3] For purposes of economy I shall refer to the three versions of the novel as I, II, and III.

more-than-bodily-wholeness of the person to the bestiality of animal functions. He is not her "lover"; the class barrier intervenes
and categorizes the terms of their relationship as partial, carnal,
irrefragably sordid.[4]

In the later passage animal function has been reconceived.
It escapes the ignominy of its conventional assessment and establishes for the lovers a mythic geography, beyond class, constituted by the texture and potencies of their interrelated bodies.
Values are generated from within this geography rather than from
a preconceived societal code that might be applied to it. To be
in a body has become the precondition of all evaluation. To be
proud of that body is the index of one's living quickness.

The First Lady Chatterley has not grasped the primacy of this
distinction. There, class consciousness remains dominant. Virtually the first words Parkin speaks after their intercourse are the
following: "Don't you feel you've lowered yourself with the likes
of me?" (I, 51.) This refrain punctuates the novel, alternating
with his incredulity that a woman of her class could desire a man
of his. When she tells him she finds his body beautiful, he grin-
ningly reiterates her admission. Then, with "a queer little smile
on his face: even now, as if he'd been insulted," he adds, " 'But
you don't take me serious, do you? . . . Not like you would one
of your own sort?' " (I, 94-95).

Lawrence's first version does not falter because of its class
opposition. Rather, it is founded on this split. Well into her
relationship with Parkin, Connie reflects:

> She could take a little farm, and he could be a farmer. Then
> she could have her own rooms and her own life and still live
> with him.
>
> But no! The meal times! The inability to converse! She
> knew she would have to have conversation. And when Hilda
> came, and at meals they talked all beyond him, and some-
> how he looked small, a cipher at his own table! . . .

[4] John Worthen also notes that obscenity in I serves to accentuate class
barriers: "Parkin uses the obscene vocabulary primarily to emphasize his class
distinction from Constance . . . he makes her say 'fucker' for the sake of hearing
her use language so much *below* her" (172).

Then why their two bodies? Why this passion, which meant more than the rest of her life to her? —Ah, if she could be in the cottage with him now, just lighting the lamp! Perhaps they would have—she tried to think of something really common—bloaters, yes, bloaters for supper, grilled bloaters. The house simply reeked of grilled bloaters. And he sat with his elbows on the table, in his shirt-sleeves, and picked bits of bloater bones away with his fingers. And drops of a tea hung on his fierce moustache. And he said:

"These 'ere bloaters is that salty, they nowt but brine. Pour us another cup o' tea, leass." . . .

She gave it up. Culturally, he was another race. (I, 81-82)

The farm option is no sooner broached than abandoned. Their problem is not where to go, but how to live anywhere as mates as well as lovers. Stephen Gill has remarked on the "shallowness of Connie's understanding of Parkin and his class, and the continuous power over her of the assumptions of her own class" (355). Nevertheless, the bloater scenario lingers in the mind, and later in the novel we see something akin to it in the impossible afternoon tea at the Tewsons':

Constance felt breathless. On the table was tinned salmon, and boiled ham, tinned peaches and tinned strawberries, though it was fruit season: brown bread and butter, and white, and currant loaf—besides various home-made cakes and pastries. . . .

Marjory love was emptying tea and tinned salmon with a teaspoon on to the fine white cloth.

The fine white cloth, the sparkling glass bowls, the bright knives and spoons, the pretty china—it was quite wonderfully refined! Constance marvelled all the time at the queer energy that kept it all going. Only the dessert spoon, with the tinned strawberries, did taste a little of metal. (I, 190)

Tinned peaches and tinned strawberries, though it was fruit season: such commentary identifies the cultural emphasis of the scene. The lower class is not therefore nearer to nature; even more pretentions intervene between their behavior and what Birkin calls in *Women in Love* the spontaneity of "perfect good form." The Tewson interior is sniffed at by the narrative voice with an insincere blusteriness, an eye for the noxious social detail, that reminds one of Dickens. "It was quite wonderfully refined!" Parkin and his friends are, culturally, another race.

Since there are no meals between Connie and Parkin in I, the bloater fantasy remains unrealized. It should come as no surprise that, in revising his materials, Lawrence chose to delete Connie's incriminating speculation. In later versions, as though to answer its challenge, he introduced numerous light meals between the lady and the lover, none of them offensive to her sensibility. "He had begun to eat again, rather hurriedly and unwillingly. But he knew perfectly well how to use his knife and fork, and how to behave. As a matter of fact, he knew how to behave in most ways, and even how to speak correctly . . ." (II, 176). This Parkin is midway between Parkin in I, the already shaped product of his class, and Mellors in III, the uncoopted possessor of class options ranging from the local dialect at times of intimacy or derision to aristocratic refinement in matters of taste and learning.

Parkin in I never dreams of such achievements. Thus Connie finds herself in the quandary of wanting two men, one culturally, the other physically satisfactory: "She sighed wearily. Apparently it was impossible to have a whole man in any man. Her two men were two halves. And she did not want to forfeit either half . . ." (I, 71). By respecting this split, Lawrence finds, in I, an imaginative access to the two men quite different from what he can find in II and III. Clifford and Connie enjoy moments of intimacy together.

> They had a quiet happy evening together. It was raining and very dark out of doors. She thought of the other man. Then, when lamps were lit, didn't think of him any more.
>
> "Look here, Con!" said Clifford as he filled his pipe after coffee. "Do you really care a bean whether you're immortal or not?"

She looked up at him. He was in good form, and he looked well. (I, 64)

The scene continues for a few pages, Clifford pressing for some suitable form of immortality. Connie suddenly looks up at him: " 'You know I am fond of you. And I want always to be fond of you. Never mind what has happened to your legs. You are you.' 'I am I,' he repeated. 'I am I! And when I am out of the body, perhaps I shall be a real thing. Till then I'm not' " (I, 66-67). In this context Connie introduces the possibility of a child. Clifford asks who would father it, Connie replies, "why need you ask which man?" and Clifford responds: "No by God! Probably I haven't [the right to ask]. Probably I've no right to a wife at all: a wife in name and appearance. No, I've no right. I've no right to you. You can go to what man you like." "No but listen, Clifford!" Connie interjects, "I love you. You've taught me so . . ." (I, 67-68). The manuscript breaks off here, with three pages missing. When it resumes one reads, less than a page later: "She was amazed at the hard cold anger that filled her at the thought of Clifford. What a subtle, cruel tyranny he had exerted over her all the time!" (I, 68.) One would like to see the transition from tenderness to anger effected in those missing three pages, for Lawrence has created a scene whose intimacy becomes its problem.[5] A lovable Clifford dictates a tragic conclusion, and Lawrence still believes that tragedy is lack of experience and that Connie's problem has a solution.

In the second version, therefore, this interchange is shortened and toughened, Connie backing off from every move her husband makes. In the third version it is deleted altogether. In like manner, Clifford's poignant awareness in I that he could father no child becomes in II the comedy of pretending to Squire Winter that "there is every hope, Sir!" (II, 146), and finally in III the hysteria of his assertion that "I might even one day have a child of my own!" (III, 117.) A man this far gone requires nothing from Connie. His case has become clinical and needs

---

[5] There is an even more intimate scene between husband and wife later in I (99-101). I do not mean to imply, however, that their tenderness is ever unalloyed, even in I.

only the maternal, if sinister, pity of Mrs. Bolton (whose nursely role increases in revision, as Clifford's pathology is stressed).

Insofar as Lawrence can sympathetically imagine Clifford in I, he can simultaneously grant the rough inadequacy of Parkin. Parkin, not Connie, is the questioning lover here. He says things "a little awkwardly," "rather sadly, perplexedly" (I, 76, 77). He trembles and cries "What am I to do?" He "was in such evident torture, she was amazed." He "shudder[s] with conflicting desires" (I, 132). This Parkin is the more easily moved of the pair; Connie characteristically sees around him. As Lawrence devastatingly puts it, she "could simply hear his mind creaking as he pondered" (I, 131).

The resultant balance between the two men blocks the resolution Lawrence's plot requires. Such resolution will come, eventually, through the dramatized and finally irresistible strength of Connie's relationship with the gamekeeper, but in the first version the physical and emotional elements of their relationship are rendered in a detached, almost cursory manner.[6] Intercourse takes place quickly; more to the point, it leads swiftly to bliss on Connie's part ("passion came to life in her" [I, 52], and, as a lover, Parkin is thereafter irreproachable. Lawrence masterfully renders their first night together. He focuses less, however, on the play and intensity of the lovers' feelings than on the visual details of the scene.

> He quietly unlocked the door, and she entered. . . .
> He had hung up his coat and his gun and his cap, and was in his shirt sleeves. . . . He sat down in his Windsor

---

[6] A few statistical comparisons will elaborate this point. In I the gamekeeper appears on the 5th page; in II, on the 27th; in III, on the 46th. The weight of implication surrounding his appearance has increased in each revision. Another scene in each version is Connie's request for a key to the hut, followed by the keeper's resistance and later consent. In I, there are two pages of complication between Connie's seeking and receiving the key; in II, there are twenty pages; in III, there are twenty-four. The first act of intercourse follows soon upon the yielding of the key, and once again the burden of implication placed upon that act increases with each version. Mark Spilka deals briefly and aptly with these improvements ("On Lawrence's Hostility to Wilful Women: The Chatterley Solution").

armchair, and began to unfasten his leather gaiters and take off his heavy boots. The dog in the scullery was rather noisily lapping something. . . .

He lit a candle, blew out the lamp, and she followed him to the stairs.

"Shut stairfoot door," he said, "for t' dog."

Balanced on one stair, she carefully closed the stairfoot door behind her. The steep stairs creaked as he went up in stocking feet, and she followed. Probably the other woman [his first wife] had followed him like this. . . .

She slowly pulled off her stockings and garters, while he still stood there against the door, motionless and inscrutable. Then she slipped her dress over her head, and stood in her thin, delicate white nightgown. She laid her dress and stockings over the bedrail. And he still had not moved.

"Shall yer sleep agen t' wa'?"

She got quietly into bed.

And then, only then, he sat down heavily on the edge of the bed and untied his tape garters and pulled off his stockings. He stood up to push off his cord breeches, and she saw his feet white and clean but gnarled out of shape by clumsy heavy boots.

He stood in his shirt—she had known he wouldn't change it—and looked at her.

"I canna believe as yer really want me," he said. . . . (I, 117-19)

I have omitted much but retained the flavor of the scene. This man bears only a slight relation to Mellors. His social otherness is persistently noted in details that quietly establish the tenor of their relationship. A woman from one class is spending the night with a man from another class. Lawrence renders exactly the gestures and apparel and way of speaking that locate him in his class, antecedent to choice. In later versions Lawrence will alter this scene—confessional talk, intense feeling, and sexual activity will replace the centrality of silent gesture and setting—and he will achieve different effects but not finer ones. In its brief five pages the scene of their first night together in I is artistically perfect, and its very perfection attests that their union is inextricably class-bound.

As he approaches disclosure of the lovers' intimacy, Lawrence casts about for an exit from the class dilemma. He lands on Duncan Forbes, the aesthetic painter whom Connie had known in the past; the results are disastrous. Forbes is compulsively inauthentic. Lawrence can neither believe a word he says nor bring the lady and the gamekeeper together without his mediation. Once Connie has confided in him, he refers to Parkin obnoxiously as "the nice man" (seven times in four pages), and even more offensively after that as Op. (Parkin had signed an awkward letter to Connie as "your obedient servant, O.P.," and Forbes, being shown the note, leaps into wordplay: " 'O.P.' Op! Is that the nice man's name? 'Ippety 'Op!' " [I, 211].) Forbes relentlessly belittles Parkin/Op, and there develops an unpleasant sense in which Lawrence cannot dislodge the narrative from the class bias of Forbes' voice and point of view. Connie grows, as by osmosis, cool and clever. "Do you think I've made a mistake, having Op's child?" she asks Forbes (I, 212); and she treats Parkin in the dangerously arousing-controlled manner of Gudrun toward Gerald. Lawrence notes her condescension but cannot imagine Connie's getting beyond it. "And she gloated in her heart, seeing how much he had wanted to come to her, to be near her. . . . She wanted Op to herself" (I, 219).

The scene grows stranger. Connie, Duncan, and Parkin drive together in Forbes' car, she secretly stroking her lover (whom Lawrence himself now refers to as "the surprised and suspicious Op" [I, 221]). They have a "jolly lunch all three together," Lawrence noting that "Parkin was amusing in a quiet way" (I, 221, 222). Connie then departs in a fit of pique. The two men draw closer "in the unspoken sympathy of men who have suffered from the same woman. Duncan and Parkin liked one another instinctively" (I, 228). There follows some rather vulgar intimacy between them, a suggestive swapping of scarves (Parkin wearing Forbes' instead of Connie's), then dinner, drinking, and further confession. It is all quite wrong. Forbes' bitchy aestheticism is the deepest layer in him (as Lawrence will acknowledge in III), and the cryptic attempt to establish a male aristocratic camaraderie in the closing pages cannot reconcile the more deeply seated class antagonism between the two men. Sixteen pages before the novel ends, Lawrence wildly has Parkin reveal himself (to Duncan, not to Connie) as a Communist; but Connie, when she learns of this, remains unmoved: "Let no one disturb her. Particularly let no man try to disturb her or lay his thoughts on her. She felt she could tear him open with one stroke of her paw if he tried. Parkin or Duncan—*à la bonne heure!*" (I, 243.)

The equivalence of the two men—"Parkin or Duncan"—reveals how disoriented the narrative has become. Lawrence has lost his imaginative grasp of the living relationship between Connie and the gamekeeper. She suddenly rouses herself, on the penultimate page of the novel, to a furious resentment against Clifford and Wragby. She realizes "she had accepted Wragby as as good as she could get" (I, 252), but now she has learned better. "Till she had loved Parkin—her Op. Yes, she loved him. He was a man, if he wasn't a gentleman" (I, 253). It is a shrill and unprepared finale. The opposed class terms of man and gentleman remain in force, and reference to Parkin as "her Op" does not instill confidence. The last time she saw him was twenty-six pages earlier, in a scene of angry departure. Lawrence closes the novel with Connie's thoughts: "My lady's fucker, as he called himself so savagely! How he had hated her for not taking him fully seriously in his manly fucking! Ah well! The future was still to hand!" (I, 253.)

If the sentences are inappropriate to the narrative they conclude (in the first version Parkin does not take fucking with greater seriousness than Connie), they nevertheless reveal what is to come. Fucking will itself be the way out. It is to be asserted by the lovers, explored and approved by the writer. It will then become the intercourse between two free beings in which they achieve their "flame life" not so much by resolving the class issue as by transcending its terms: "My soul softly flaps in the little pentecostal flame with you, like the peace of fucking. We fucked a flame into being. Even the flowers are fucked into being between the sun and the earth" (III, 327-28).

❧

IN WRITING *John Thomas and Lady Jane* Lawrence transforms his narrative, almost doubling its length. The materials of the first 183 pages in I occupy 362 pages in II. Further, whereas the remaining twenty percent of I seeks a solution after Connie's visit to the Tewsons, only ten pages follow the scene at the Tewsons in II. Lawrence omits the Tewsons altogether in III. As he gains possession over his materials he sees, first, that Duncan Forbes cannot resolve his dilemma and, second, that the Tewsons cannot either. The implicit resolution of his materials must begin in the Bertha Coutts scandal and must be completed by the revelation to Clifford, made only in III, that the gamekeeper is Lady Chatterley's lover.

The narrative of the second version is the most grave, psychologically nuanced, and patient of the three. It is the slowest-moving narrative, lacking the rapid and highly selective focus of I, and lacking as well the jaunty, hardboiled assurance—the power of summary invective—of III. It lacks other traits of III as well, but the relevant point is that it has jettisoned Duncan Forbes (and with him Op), as well as the suggestion of a Communist resolution to the struggle. "The weakness of the Communism episodes," Stephen Gill remarks, "is that they relate to nothing but the class struggle" (355): they are not empowered by the same energies released in the love relationship. There, in the love relationship, Lawrence makes his great advance, but that advance can be understood only in relation to the most perplexing aspect of *John Thomas and Lady Jane*: its treatment of the class issue.

On the one hand, class is transcended.

> There was no longer any such thing as class. The world was one vast proletariat. . . . But Parkin wasn't. He was hot-blooded and single, and he wasn't at all absorbed in himself. She had held back from him with a certain grudge, because he was lower class. Now the barrier broke, and her soul flooded free. Class is an anachronism. It finished in 1914. Nothing remains but a vast proletariat, including kings, aristocrats, squires, millionaires and working-people, men and women alike. And then a few individuals who have not been proletarianised. (II, 288-89)

In terms of this global fiat, the problem is resolved. Clifford becomes the proletarian: egoistic, cold-blooded, possessive, identified with the machine. Parkin emerges as Connie's appropriate match. The trouble is that II believes in class as fully as it disbelieves in it. *John Thomas and Lady Jane*, alone of the three versions, presents a tragic gamekeeper: a man inextricably enmeshed in class, and yet superior to class, isolated within its confines. The earlier Parkin has the consolation of mates like Bill Tewson and a workers' movement like Communism. The later Mellors is so gifted that he has—and needs—no class ties at all.

Lawrence expands the scene at the Tewsons from fifteen pages in I to twenty pages in II. All that seemed equivocal before is now frankly obnoxious. The busy house is now grotesquely crowded; Connie bumps into coats, hats, and pegs everywhere. The barely restrained children of I are now ill-behaved brats. The hearty facade of the Tewson marriage reveals here its cracks; Mrs. Tewson "hisses" her words, bosses her husband, jealously watches Connie. Bill Tewson had earlier claimed: "Everybody knows what we are. We're just decent working-class people. What would be the good of pretending anything else" (I, 192). Now he says, " 'You see what we are—working people; decent working people, it's no good pretending anything else—' he added deprecatingly,—as if he *might* have been mistaken for an archangel in disguise" (II, 354). Lawrence no longer maintains a veneer of Dickensian good-humor. These people are impossible.

Significantly, Parkin in II is absent or silent during most of the Tewson chapter. Like Birkin at the Pompadour, he is a suffering presence; unlike Birkin, he cannot get free. The Tewsons see themselves as his mates, but he writes Connie: "I can understand what you feel about Wragby. I feel a bit that way about Bill's house, I can't breathe in it, something shuts me up so I can't breathe" (II, 364). "I wish you and I was on a desert island" (II, 365), he says to Connie plaintively in the same letter, the faulty grammar underscoring their plight.

He is more vulnerable, this Parkin, and the fight that comically erupts after the Bertha Coutts scandal in I becomes serious in II. He is almost killed, and Connie realizes that he can be destroyed by an increase of violence.[7] Lawrence focuses in II on

---

[7] A curious connection develops in Lawrence's mind between Ted Bolton

Parkin's frailty at the Tewsons', his inability to do the deforming tasks demanded of him, his wounded thumb, face, and spirit. And even though Lawrence complicates Parkin's childhood background in II, he cannot spring the gamekeeper free. He is not actually a Parkin, we learn, but Oliver Seivers instead. Parkin is his stepfather's name. But this margin of separateness avails nothing; Seivers is no advantage over Parkin. The tangle of former relationships—with his mother, his stepfather, his siblings, his wife, her brothers—just holds him down the more.

John Thomas and Lady Jane accepts its own impasse, and the last ten pages contain some of Lawrence's most powerful prose. With nowhere to go, unaided by Connie's abstract denials of the meaning of class, the lovers meet outside their own turf (their pastoral seclusion has been ended by scandal) at Hucknall Church, where Byron's heart lies buried. The ending is lyrical and almost hopeless; Byron's heart haunts these pages with its implication of passion gone to waste. The lovers walk toward Annesley "into a little hollow of a wood" (II, 369); they are at the mercy both of other walkers and of gamekeepers who would send them away. "I must touch you! I must touch you, or I shall die!" (II, 369) Connie implores. At this point a gamekeeper arrives and the scene becomes exquisite: Parkin protecting Connie's exposed face and body, the gamekeeper, fascinated, trying to get a glimpse of her, while he warns that "Squire an' some of 'is folks is walkin' a bit down the 'coppy" (II, 370), Parkin stroking Connie's hair and soothing her, Connie saying she knows the old squire here. Class, class, class—the scene reiterates the unshakable social roles of a squire and his possessiveness, a gamekeeper paid to enforce his

---

and the gamekeeper. In I, Mrs. Bolton relates simply the mining accident that killed her husband; in II, Lawrence gives the miner some rather unpersuasive symbolic speech. It seems that his wife's suffering during childbirth killed something essential in his spirit ("I dunna reckon much o' life, Ivy, 'xcept fr thee!" [II, 173]). Mrs. Bolton tells Connie that "when he lay there dead, you'd almost have said he *wanted* to die" (II, 173). Both men are working stock and somehow too fine to live in the demeaning conditions imposed on their class. In III, Lawrence deletes this sacrificial aspect of Bolton, but maintains the connection through Mrs. Bolton's earlier crush on Mellors, as well as through a strange commingling, "in her half-sleep [of] thoughts of her Ted and thoughts of Lady Chatterley's unknown lover" (III, 150).

employer's directives, a pair of frustrated lovers on someone else's
land. On this note, followed by Connie's "You'll come to me if
I can't bear it?" and Parkin's quiet response, "Yes," *John Thomas
and Lady Jane* ends.

I have stressed the second narrative's contradictory insistence that class confines are both an illusion and an inescapable
trap. I turn now to the breakthrough in this version: the re-
seeing of the love relationship. Two scenes—the lovers' first act
of intercourse and their first night together—reveal the direction
of the changes Lawrence wrought. In I Connie watches the baby
chicks, helps to feed them, and then bursts into tears. Parkin sees
her weeping and, "almost without knowing what he did," crouches
near and touchs her.

> And the touch of her soft, bowed back, breathing heav-
> ily with abandoned weeping, filled him with such boundless
> desire for her that he rose and bent over her, lifting her in
> his arms. All that could ever be that was desirable, she was
> to him then. And she, lifted up, for one moment saw the
> brilliant, unseeing dilation of his eyes. Then he was clasping
> her body against his. And she was thinking to herself: "Yes!
> I will yield to him! Yes! I will yield to him." (I, 50-51)

Notation is brief and in places not particularly felicitous ("such
boundless desire . . . all that could ever be that was desirable").
The chicks are barely present. Connie's willful decision to yield
to Parkin emerges in awkward contrast to the unconscious flowing movements that give rise to it.

In the revised version, all has been deepened and extended.[8]
The hens and their chicks are described at length. As Connie's
heart warms in watching them grow, so Parkin begins to thaw
in his relation to her. She tries to touch one of the chicks, the
hen pecks at her, Parkin softly draws forth the baby bird, and
she holds it in her hand. The trembling vitality of the chick reaches,

---

[8] Spilka, in the article noted above, remarks that Lawrence virtually pens a
sermon in II (just prior to their first intercourse) on the inability of the will to
force emotional issues. "Life is so soft and quiet, and cannot be seized. It will
not be raped . . ." (II, 107). Spilka also places Mellors precisely as a figure of
unwilled "creaturely tenderness" (203): the reverse of Michaelis.

beneath her conscious class-identity, into Connie's unconscious center of feeling, and she begins to cry. What follows is, like the movement of life through the birds, "blind," "unconscious," "uncertain." There is no "boundless desire," no clasping of bodies, no exultant decision to yield. " 'Shall yer come?' he asked, in a quiet, colorless voice" (II, 113). It is a quiet scene, "she seemed to go to sleep." Her gestures and feelings are described in terms of somnolence, of ceasing to battle. Parkin takes the lead, but Lawrence renders his movement in such a way as to show the unconscious desire in him reaching expression, the "groping, soft, helplessly desirous caress" (II, 114) of one body upon another: spontaneous good form.

The relationship takes on mystery and passional complexity as Lawrence explores it further. Bliss is not achieved at first, nor the next day either. In fact, Connie retains in II a fear that his interest in her is passional only. "Kiss me because you like me, not because you want me" (II, 78), she pleads later. I turn now to their first night together.

The silence of I is replaced by discourse in II, and the couple of I are replaced by a trio in II. Bertha Coutts, vestigially present in the photograph and Connie's brief questions of I, has now entered massively into the lovers' relationship. Parkin has an erotic past as well as an erotic present; intimacy with him requires knowledge of this past. In revising his manuscript, Lawrence seems to have realized that Bertha Coutts would affect the new relationship in more ways than merely as an obstacle to its future bliss. He thus has Connie seek out, delicately, the cluster of meanings the earlier woman held for her lover. All talking and no fucking, so runs the cliché version of Lawrence's attack on his cerebral culture, but the truth is that he never sees them simply as opposed activities. Intimacy in talking increases with physical intimacy. As the lovers' intercourse grows more complex, as its physical and emotional range becomes enlarged, so too does their capacity to release themselves in speech.

The tale Parkin tells is remarkable. He had been an early playmate of the Coutts boys, and he had endured, when a boy of eleven or twelve, a traumatic sexual experience with their older sister Bertha. She had lifted up her skirts and shown him her vagina. Its hairiness shocked and repelled him; for the next ten years he avoided her entire sex. At twenty-one he met her again. She courted him, and they married. But the marriage was consummated only when, on his finally admitting his trauma, she had him shave her. Thereafter, for a brief time, they were compatible lovers; then she overmastered him. "An' then she began to play tricks on me—an' wouldn't cook my dinner—an' wouldn't sleep with me—an' when she did sleep with me, she wanted it all her own way, I was nowhere: as if she was the man, an' me the woman" (II, 226).

This vignette suggests that Lawrence has in some respects invested himself more intimately in the Parkin of II than in Mellors later.[9] Whatever its smaller details may mean, the episode is suffused with sexual fear and vulnerability. This man may reach climax four times with Connie during the present night and following morning, but he carries ghosts within him. A vagina frightened him, especially its resemblance to the male genitals. Like men, Bertha Coutts has a developed sexual apparatus and aggressive sexual desire; she runs over him like a man as well. The vignette is suggestive, and one can be sure that the twenty-one-year-old virginal Parkin who suffers in it will not reappear in the experienced and unflappable Mellors of III.

The confessional interchange depresses Connie, and when she rises to go upstairs he notes her half-heartedness: "I don't want to force you in any way" (II, 230). She goes nevertheless. He embraces her; she begs him to love her and he says he will. They attempt to work through their bodily shyness in each other's presence (space is more frightening than force); they remove their shirt and nightgown. She looks at his roused body:

[9] Lawrence's accomplishments and "biographical data" are of course more evident in the creation of Mellors. But Parkin of II reveals something of the fearful incapacity, the latent impotence, that recurrently shadowed his creator's psychic life. Parkin of II supplies, as it were, the missing ingredient that would link Mellors with the more complex and troubled figure of Birkin. For further discussion of the gamekeeper's vulnerability, see Squires, "New Light on the Gamekeeper," 237-40.

"Tell me it isn't only fucking," she said, pleading.

He was breathless for a moment. But the tense phallus did not change. It was like another being.

"I don't know what you mean by only!" he said, baffled. . . . "What is there more? What is there more than fucking?" came his puzzled voice like an unknown voice out of the night. And for the moment she submitted, and was gone. (II, 231)

During the night she reflects that for him "there could never be 'only fucking' " (II, 233). She begins to see that the act of intercourse is for him no "sensational excitation, worked from the ego and the personality" (II, 233), but an expression of his unconscious self and therefore a risk of his being. She sleeps nestled in the circle of his arm, and the next morning she says, "You don't want me shaved or anything, do you?" (II, 235.) He answers "No—no!" (II, 236), and one believes it, for Lawrence has rendered the living quality of the relationship—its quickness—with considerable authority. They go through moments of passion and insecurity and then passion and peace. She leaves before breakfast, passes some bluebells on the path, and thinks:

They too knew it, the fulness of the beauty of being in the flesh. . . . There was a hint of night in them too, and in their bodily blossom, fulness from the night.

She felt still and full and hyacinthine as they were, on the cool stem of flesh. The body! It was a greater mystery and complexity than anything. It was not even physical. It was like the hyacinths, a thing of bloom, the love body. A thing of bloom. (II, 239)

That "greater mystery" is beyond class and within nature. In II, by more fully imagining the love relationship between Connie and the gamekeeper, Lawrence discovers the mystery. In III he taps to the full its potential. *Lady Chatterley's Lover* lacks the intellectual richness and emotional range of *The Rainbow* and *Women in Love*, lacks as well the raw psychological realism of *Sons and Lovers*. But there, more than anywhere else, Lawrence succeeded in dramatizing the love body as a thing of bloom.

240

ϡ

BY FURTHER retarding the union of his lovers in III, Lawrence thickens its range of implications. For the first time he devotes space to Clifford and Connie's first years of marriage—not merely stating them as a *donnée*—and he shows that this frightened man was "in some paralysing way, conscious of his own defenceless-ness" (III, 7) even before he married, entered the war, and received his wound. His insentient hopelessness sounds as a motif throughout the novel. As Clifford's pathology is more fully developed, so is Connie's emotional history expanded. Lawrence extends the hint of a "cultured-unconventional upbringing" (II, 2) into carnal relationships with German students in III: carnal, but "it was the talk that mattered supremely" (III, 3). Most significantly, Lawrence alters the entire chemistry of the final version by introducing Michaelis.[10]

Made "plausible" by the new Clifford's lust to become a best-selling novelist, Michaelis the writer enters Wragby as a young-old man, utterly detached, ready for anything and dead, at his passional center, before he begins. Lawrence relates his affair with Connie in a passage as brisk as it is assured.

> "Am I altogether a lonely bird?" he asked, with his queer grin of a smile, as if he had toothache; it was so wry, and his eyes were so perfectly unchangingly melancholy. . . .
>
> "Why?" she said, a little breathless, as she looked at him. "You are, aren't you?" . . .
>
> He looked up at her with the full glance that saw every-thing, registered everything. At the same time, the infant crying in the night was crying out of his breast to her in a way that affected her very womb. . . .
>
> "May I hold your hand for a minute?" he asked sud-denly, fixing his eyes on her with almost hypnotic power . . .
>
> She stared at him, dazed and transfixed, and he went over and kneeled beside her, and took her two feet close in

[10] Spilka touches on the effect of introducing Michaelis in III ("On Law-rence's Hostility to Wilful Women," 201-202).

241

his two hands, and buried his face in her lap, remaining motionless. She was perfectly dim and dazed, looking down in a sort of amazement at the rather tender nape of his neck, feeling his face pressing her thighs. In all her burning dismay, she could not help putting her hand, with tenderness and compassion, on the defenceless nape of his neck, and he trembled with a deep shudder. . . .

He was a curious and very gentle lover, very gentle with the woman, trembling uncontrollably, and yet at the same time detached, aware, aware of every sound outside. . . .

When he rose, he kissed both her hands, then both her feet . . . and in silence went away to the end of the room, where he stood with his back to her. . . .

"And now, I suppose you'll hate me!" he said in a quiet, inevitable way. She looked up at him quickly.

"Why should I?" she asked.

"They mostly do," he said; then he caught himself up. "I mean . . . a woman is supposed to."

"This is the last moment when I ought to hate you," she said resentfully.

"I know! I know! It should be so! You're *frightfully* good to me . . ." he cried miserably.

She wondered why he should be miserable. . . .

"But we needn't let Clifford know, need we?" she pleaded. . . .

"Me!" he said, almost fiercely; "he'll know nothing from me! You see if he does. Me give myself away! Ha! Ha!" He laughed hollowly, cynically at such an idea. She watched him in wonder. He said to her: "May I kiss your hand and go? I'll go run into Sheffield I think, and lunch there if I may, and be back to tea. May I do anything for you? May I be sure you don't hate me?—and that you won't?"—he ended with a desperate note of cynicism.

"No, I don't hate you," she said. "I think you're nice."

"Ah!" he said to her fiercely, "I'd rather you said that to me than said you love me! It means such a lot more. . . .

Till afternoon then. I've plenty to think about till then." He kissed her hands humbly and was gone. (III, 24-26)[11]

I have quoted the scene at length because it constitutes the novel's single physical contrast to the love relationship that will follow. Lawrence seems to have realized that the way out of his lovers' dilemma lay within the quality of their relationship itself, that the index of quality would be the depth of physical and emotional notation he could provide, and that the first step toward the expression of consummate good form would be the example of consummate bad form: Michaelis.

Michaelis never for a moment deviates into spontaneity. He bounds up those stairs intent on the seduction of Clifford Chatterley's wife, but even as his words and moves are calculated and hackneyed, Connie does discover the deepest thing in him: his childlike helplessness and inadequacy. At his core he wants to cry, and throughout the scene—both beneath his strategy and incorporated within it—he is crying for a breast. That, rather than the calculation, is the appeal she cannot resist, as Mrs. Bolton will not resist later when it comes from Clifford.

As Connie maternally strokes him, he releases further gestures, and we see throughout a sad, separate, cunning child-man, whose body never moves in time with hers, who enacts a ritual performance, and who succeeds (so he will view it) in enlisting her aid. Were he to cry, as he almost does, it would be an expression of uncontrollable self-pity; he is choked inside with the sense of his abused vulnerability. He has learned, though, to exploit his inadequacy by making others pay for it. The scene captures beautifully the flurry of motions he makes in the absence of spontaneity, and no one is surprised when he later snarls at her for pushing him too hard. Incapable of yielding, miserable when near tenderness even though he seeks it, Michaelis will stay with Connie only so long as the thrill of cuckolding Clifford outweighs the demands of intimacy. Thereafer he will bolt. We are thus prepared to appreciate, as in neither of the former versions,

[11] Ellipses within Michaelis' speech are Lawrence's; the other ellipses are mine.

what is spontaneous and fulfilling in the major relationship about to be unfolded.

The crucial alteration in III is of course the shift from humble Parkin to lordly Mellors. At his first appearance, he makes Connie "a slight bow, like a gentleman" (III, 47). His character-formation owes more to an implausible devotion to an aristocratic officer in India than to any English class upbringing. Mrs. Bolton remembers him not as the Oliver Seivers who spoke "bad language" but as "a clever boy [who] had a scholarship . . . and learned French and things . . . quite the gentleman, really quite the gentleman!" (III, 154-55). In each version he is a lover for Connie whom Mrs. Bolton would never have guessed, but only in III is he "the one man I might have thought of" (III, 155). Perhaps the simplest index of the change in the gamekeeper's status appears in his introduction to Hilda. In I Lawrence does not allow them to meet; in II Connie says, "This is my sister Hilda! Hilda, this is Parkin!" (II, 265); in III she says, "This is my sister Hilda. Won't you come and speak to her? Hilda! This is Mr. Mellors" (III, 262).

Lawrence insists on Mellors' escape from his class origins in other ways. There are no Tewsons here. Further, Mellors is not a man one lays hands on with impunity. The first Parkin had been in fights earlier, the second Parkin was nearly killed, but Mellors is untouched. The revelation of the scandal, which so disorients Parkin in I and II (sending him, beaten, to brutalizing work in Sheffield), spares Mellors. Connie, about to be exposed as "the other woman," comes under pressure instead. Mellors retains his self-assurance, abusing Hilda as he sees fit, joining Sir Malcolm at the club in an impossibly vulgar drinking fest in which the older man dilates in praise of the younger man's putative sexual potency.

Finally, Mellors speaks dialect when and if he pleases, sometimes as invective, sometimes as tenderness. Lawrence has created exquisite passages of dialect between the lovers, but one may still wonder if the issue of Mellors' speech is fully resolved. Julian Moynahan offers a fine reading of this novel, yet he remains unbothered by Lawrence's reconception of the gamekeeper. "Parkin [of I] is a short, homely man, ill-educated and emotionally identified with the working class. Mellors is a tall slender, well-favored man who looks like a gentleman when dressed up, has been an army officer, reads books, and has severed his ties of loyalty to his proletarian background" (142n.). Can the transformation be so complete: are class ties simply severed? To what extent is one's style of speech a matter of choice? Does not the capacity to speak either dialect or the king's English at will suggest that one speaks them "at will"? Beneath the asserted superiority to class standards one may still hear the criteria of a class standard:

> There he stood, tall and slender, and so different, in a formal suit of thin dark cloth. He had a natural distinction, but he had not the cut-to-pattern look of her class. Yet, she saw at once, he could go anywhere. He had a native breeding which was really much nicer than the cut-to-pattern class thing. (III, 297)

Connie's claims notwithstanding, class values have not been transcended; rather, Mellors is (unlike most of her class) the genuine article. "Distinction . . . he could go anywhere [i.e., he is presentable] . . . breeding . . . really much nicer"—these phrases and tones are invidious, socially valorized, depending for their force on an upper-class standard of sartorial elegance and well-bred nonchalance which he alone meets.[12] The greatest flaw in *Lady Chatterley's Lover* is Mellors insofar as he remains, in contradictory ways, a class-conceived figure. Within the private relationship he is more credible, and the scenes between him and Connie represent Lawrence's most sustained attempt at "perfect relatedness" (which is something other than perfect happiness) in matters of passion.

Most of the expansions and complications of erotic feeling developed in II are retained in III. The course of their intimacy becomes even less predictable, however, and those critics who attack the novel as a simplistic record of pneumatic bliss can

---

[12] Cf. the following: "The three ate in silence. Hilda looked to see what his table manners were like. She could not help realizing that he was instinctively much more delicate and well-bred than herself . . ." (III, 264).

hardly have attended to Lawrence's text. Further, Lawrence provides, infamously, explicit physical notation in III. The results can be found throughout the novel. I shall focus on them only in Chapter 12, a daytime visit by Connie to Mellors which has no earlier counterpart.

When she arrives at the hut he is not there, so she seeks him out at the cottage. They are both slightly wrought up, she at not finding him, he at having to get summonses for two poachers. She officiates at his tea—its difference from her tea (to which she will return that afternoon) is neither sentimentally ignored nor made a jagged obstacle—and she tells him she is going to Venice next month. She seeks assurance that he loves her; he is unwilling to give it. They rehearse the motive of her going to him merely to get a child. He asks her to go upstairs. She declines, saying that she wants him at the hut instead and that she wants to touch him as he touches her. He mocks gently her making use of him and thanks her ironically for "doing me the honours of my teapot" (III, 182). She returns to Wragby "downcast and annoyed" (III, 183).

After tea she goes again, frustrated, to the hut and—speaking dialect now—he invites her in. Each is terse. As though to prove something, they remove their clothing, he tells her to "lie down there!" (III, 184), and they have intercourse.

> And this time the sharp ecstasy of her own passion did not overcome her; she lay with her hands inert on his striving body, and do what she might, her spirit seemed to look on from the top of her head, and the butting of his haunches seemed ridiculous to her, and the sort of anxiety of his penis to come to its little evacuating crisis seemed farcical. Yes, this was love, this ridiculous bounding of the buttocks, and the wilting of the poor insignificant, moist little penis. . . .
>
> Cold and derisive her queer female mind stood apart, and though she lay perfectly still, her impulse was to heave her loins, and throw the man out, escape his ugly grip, and the butting over-riding of his absurd haunches. (III, 184-85)

I do not see how one can fault this prose. The lingering tensions between them do not magically dissolve but reappear in the intercourse.[13] Nothing less than the visualized notation Lawrence provides can convey Connie's feelings of scorn and detachment. She had wanted to touch him and now, suffering from "her own double consciousness and reaction" (III, 285), she begins to weep.

> "Ay!" he said. "It was no good that time. You wasn't there." So he knew! Her sobs became violent.
> "But what's amiss?" he said. "It's once in a while that way."
> "I . . . I can't love you," she sobbed, suddenly feeling her heart breaking.
> "Canna ter? Well, dunna fret! There's no law says as tha's got to. Ta'e it for what it is." . . .
> His words were small comfort. She sobbed aloud.
> "Nay, nay," he said. "Ta'e the thick wi' th' thin. This wor' a bit o' thin for once."
> She wept bitterly, sobbing: "But I want to love you, and I can't. It only seems horrid."
> He laughed a little, half bitter, half amused.
> "It isna horrid," he said, "even if tha thinks it is. An' tha canna ma'e it horrid. Dunna fret thysen about lovin' me. Tha'lt niver force thysen to 't. There's sure to be a bad nut in a basketful. Tha mun ta'e th' rough wi' th' smooth." (III, 185)

Connie's thoughts about a disgusting function—her sex in the head—begin to alter; Lawrence notes the sadness that overtakes her scorn. The scene has moved from action to reflection, and it now moves into talk. On the next page it will move into more action; meanwhile, the talk is wonderful. With an understanding far less cosmic than Birkin's balanced stars, Mellors

[13] A less developed version of this passage occurs in II some fifty-five pages after their initial intercourse (II, 167). The sense of melancholy alienation thus expressed has no counterpart in I (where sexual bliss comes swiftly and remains), whereas in III it appears twice: both here and earlier (III, 133-34), some ten pages after their first intercourse. Early and late, the physical relationship in III achieves greater intensities and is subject to greater vicissitudes.

comforts Connie with a dialect wisdom that is wrought into the texture of *Lady Chatterley's Lover*: that passional life is not dictated by the will, that when intercourse is good it's marvelous, and when it's bad it may not be tragic, that tenderness can sooth the rough moments and enable the magic ones. By the time of his last novel Lawrence knows little more for certain than this, but he renders it with a confidence he had never mustered in the past.

On the next page, after her tears, Connie watches Mellors rise and button his breeches; she thinks of Michaelis, who "had had the decency to turn away" (III, 186). This is the moment of her own turning—the Michaelis comparison rescues Connie's vision of Mellors from her own ironies—and she suddenly clings to him. There follows the often cited, fullest description of intercourse in Lawrence's work, and I need to say about it only three things. It has been ushered in, involuntarily, by the tension and separateness of the act that preceded it, its character as an experience depends on Lawrence's capacity to render both gesture and feeling with as much fullness as he can manage, and during it—as well as after—she touches him as he had touched her. Immediately afterwards they break into dialect together, she comically imitating him whereas, just minutes earlier, she had "hated the dialect: the *thee* and the *tha* and the *thysen*" (III, 185). He tells her she's good cunt, and when she equates cunt with fuck, he says: "Nay, nay! Fuck's only what you do. Animals fuck. But cunt's a lot more than that. It's there, dost see: an' tha'rt a lot beside an animal, aren't ter? even ter fuck! Cunt! Eh, that's the beauty o' thee, lass!" (III, 191.) She asks if he loves her, his answer is a kiss.

"The descriptions of sex are either too fabulous (the unfailing potency, the absence of loveplay); or they are too specific to carry the weight of significance demanded of them," Mark Kinhead-Weekes argues in a very suggestive article on "Eros and Metaphor" in Lawrence (119). I have tried to show that the lovers' intercourse is a good deal less programmatically "fabulous" than Kinhead-Weekes claims, and I can close this discussion by articulating the connection in the novel between the "specific" acts and the "significance" they bear. Only in the third version of his story did Lawrence realize that the general significance had to be inscribed in the specific acts. "We fucked a flame into being," Mellors writes Connie. What he stands for, finally, is his capacity to acknowledge his vulnerable bodiness and to commit himself in a living relationship. Connie asks him "the point of your existence" (III, 300), and by the third version of the novel the gamekeeper has an answer: his touch, his tenderness. "Sex is really only touch, the closest of all touch" (III, 301). In *Lady Chatterley's Lover* that touch is described in its unpredictable variations, and the bodies that touch and are touched are likewise rendered in all their parts. Lawrence must honor their incarnate, moment-by-moment intimacy, for, as Moynahan puts it, "the only reality and the only marvel is to be alive in the flesh" (152).

That marvel is rendered specifically or not at all; this version is the only one to give the discrete body its full due. Mellors, unlike Connie's earlier lovers, is kind "to the female in her" (III, 129); through him Lawrence joins as strenuously as he can the generalities of the mind and the specifics of the body. Thus we hear of sanity and the balls, the phallus rooted in the soul, Connie's pretty tail connected with Mellors' tenderness, the four-letter words that bring the mind into an uncurried encounter with the body's humble and sublime functions.[14] The trembling chicks, the soughing forest, the hyacinthine bluebells, and the pulsing blood are kindred elements in a world of living relatedness. "What had been an emphasis on the largely unconscious power of sensate and responsive 'touch' in the first version has become an avowed politics in the final version" (Widmer, 303).

Confidence in this "politics" allows Lawrence to complete his novel. Only in the third version do the specifics of touch attain their full significance for the plot. Only here does Connie seek out Clifford and tell him (after an attempt at hedging) that she loves the gamekeeper and that she is carrying his child. In

---

[14] The body-language is playfully pervasive. When Clifford quotes to Connie, late in the novel, that " 'The universe shows us two aspects: on one side it is physically wasting, on the other it is spiritually ascending,' " she retorts: "And if it spiritually ascends, what does it leave down below, in the place where its tail use to be?" (III, 252-53). One knows what tail-pleasures she is remembering.

the earlier versions this denouement—an ineradicable given of the materials—is avoided or postponed. Even here it is too briefly, too thinly and picturesquely, narrated. Clifford's face turns yellow, his eyes bulge, he gazes "at her like a cornered beast" (III, 322). His words for Mellors repeat the clichés of his class: "That scum! That bumptious lout! That miserable cad!" (III, 322.) From the biased stance of class antagonism, Lawrence draws a Clifford who is merely pathological, who speaks "idiotically" and with "imbecile obstinacy" (III, 322, 323). For one moment, however, and then unintentionally, Lawrence suggests the deeper measure of Clifford's torment. On hearing Mellors' name, "if he could have sprung out of his chair, he would have done so" (III, 321). If he could have sprung out of his chair, who knows how many things might have been different?

Finally, as Henry James says, ". . . we must grant the artist his subject, his idea, his *donnée*; our criticism is applied only to what he makes of it" (60). The *donnée* of *Lady Chatterley's Lover* includes in every version a crippled husband, an emotionally repressed wife, a gamekeeper of creaturely tenderness. This discussion has attempted to identify the various things Lawrence "makes of it"—some of them imaginatively compelling, others willed and inert—as he moves through the three versions of his novel, seeking both to relate his materials perfectly and to free the quick from the dead.

≈

LAWRENCE'S aims in *Women in Love* and *Lady Chatterley's Lover* are clear enough: to give nature its due, to get free of those cultural injunctions that impede self-discovery and self-release. Each narrative, however, comes upon its own intransigent obstacles.

Desire itself, in *Women in Love*, emerges as an enigmatic force. Susceptible to pathology (in Gerald and Gudrun's sadomasochism), inadmissible when not heterosexual (in Birkin and Gerald's tortured longings), unpredictable when most appealing (in Birkin and Ursula's turbulent relationship), desire waxes and wanes, seeks to escape societal repression but can find no place of its own. Further, in Lawrence's most thoroughly meditated attempt to celebrate desire—*Lady Chatterley's Lover*—he finds that (despite two complete revisions) the class matrix cannot be simply transcended. He is able to imagine the union of Connie and Mellors only upon condition that Clifford be deprived of human complexity, reduced to the status of a reified impediment. (Think how Conrad might have approached this figure of pathos and psycho-cultural victimization. Conrad is as tender toward men paralyzed by their unworkable projects as Lawrence is impatient with them, drawn instead to protagonists seeking to break away.) Not only must Clifford be vilified; more urgently, Mellors' class background must be expunged from his present history. Not surprisingly, lines of stress continue to show through: though both novels are open-ended, one concludes in unresolvable quarrel, the other in separation and wistfulness, "a little droopingly, but with a hopeful heart" (III, 328).

By contrast, Joyce knows that the journey of escape from one's matrical culture is as futile as it is imperative. Futile because there is "no known method from the known to the unknown" (*Ulysses*, 701); imperative because the known reveals its savor—indeed its novelty—only to him who has voyaged beyond its ideological confines. Detached from ideology and restored to its status as phenomenon, the known becomes capacious. First experienced, Dublin is a Cyclopean prison. Retrospectively visited, purged of belief and reprojected from the human imagination, it can become an inexhaustible universe.

Six &. New Heaven, New Earth: Joyce and the Art of Reprojection

BORN INTO a church, family, and country that devour their own progeny, Joyce spent the first twenty years of his life doing something that others in less inimical circumstances do with less urgency and self-consciousness. He spent those years finding and then defending his identity from his culture's claims upon it.[1] His culture conspired to make him other, to coerce him into signing its testimonials. He was to be the child of the Catholic Church, the son of an Irish gentleman, the citizen of a ghostly Gaelic community. Each of these identities reinforced the others, and together they proposed for him a world in stark opposition to his immediate perceptions. To a degree unapproached by the other writers in this study, Joyce inhabited a world in which things-as-they-are-actually-encountered constituted a parody of things-as-they-have-been-named-by-the-authorities.[2] His greatest novel lives precisely in the space between the immediate experience of things and the range of cultural paradigms into which experience has been patterned so as to take on meaning and importance.

Exile, as Hélène Cixous has argued, is the enabling condi-

[1] I wish to acknowledge here a general indebtedness to Richard Ellmann's indispensable biography of Joyce and to Hugh Kenner's two most recent books on Joyce (*Joyce's Voices, Ulysses*). Their commentary has everywhere enabled my own, and if *Ulysses* had a key they would possess it.

[2] Joyce's well-known insistence on calling things by their actual names—to the despair of his early publishers—is a function of this razor-keen alertness to the gradations between fiction and fact.

tion of Joyce's art.[3] He must break radically from allegiances that deform experience by cloaking it in the wrong names. From *Dubliners* at least midway through *Ulysses*, his is an art of exposure. With God-like detachment he seeks to recover the "whatness" of experience—its hidden banality or pathos—by removing the conventional paradigms of swollen purpose and importance that conceals its lineaments.

"I fear those big words which make us so unhappy," Stephen tells Deasy (*Ulysses*, 31). As much as Hemingway, Joyce suspects the propagandistic intent behind aggressive rhetoric. Unlike Hemingway, however, Joyce increasingly deploys the big words, and by the time of *Finnegans Wake* he is himself crafting bigger and more portentous words than any the dictionary can supply. But these huge words are doctrinally weightless, freed from their propagandistic charge as describers-of-reality. For Deasy, reality answers fully to the cluster of verbal labels he uses to map it. History moves, "per vias rectas," "toward one great goal"; moral behavior means "I paid my way"; and evil exists incarnate in the Jews. Such facile commerce between label and experience has been suspect for Stephen since his days at Belvedere:

> While he was still repeating the *Confiteor* amid the indulgent laughter of his hearers and while the scenes of that malignant episode were still passing sharply and swiftly before his mind he wondered why he bore no malice now to those who had tormented him. He had not forgotten a whit of their cowardice and cruelty but the memory of it called forth no anger from him. All the descriptions of fierce love and hatred which he had met in books had seemed to him therefore unreal. . . . (*Portrait*, 82)

Stephen is discovering that earlier crises, once survived, change their character: they shed their deforming charge of subjective malice. On being replayed in the theater of the detached mind, they take on their objective wholeness. As Stephen finds his way to the center of his earlier experience, divested from its mislead-

[3] Cixous argues brilliantly, confusingly, and at great length a thesis already present in more moderate form in Ellmann's biography.

ing cloak of "suddenwoven anger," he hides his discovery behind the cloak of another of those big words, the *Confiteor*. Pretending to confess, he is preserving his privacy beneath the rubric of Confession. At the same time he registers internally the duplicity of those other big words—"fierce love and hatred"—which he had met in books.

A paradox emerges which Joyce will exploit throughout *Ulysses*. The immediacy of experience is lost in the language and concepts habitually used to assess it; but the hidden contours of experience, freed from emotional and ideological bias, are accessible only to the detached and revisiting mind. June 16, 1904, is to be repossessed in its minute and passed-over particulars. Yet it can be adequately repossessed only when approached from the spatial and temporal detachment of "*Trieste-Zürich-Paris*, 1914-1921" (783).

The Joycean career is shaped decisively by this dual allegiance. Experience is first endured, then remembered, and thereafter—with increasing lavishness—"reprojected from the human imagination" (*Portrait*, 215). Joyce painfully suffers his childhood, then sidesteps it in the abstract sketch of "A Portrait of the Artist," then defensively narrates it in the incomplete *Stephen Hero*, then grasps it synoptically (tenderly and ironically) in the finished *Portrait*, then parcels it out magisterially into both Stephen Dedalus and the Dublin scene in *Ulysses*, and finally reprojects it into the myriad mythical encounters that make up *Finnegans Wake*. As Joyce's temporal distance increases, he finds more—eventually finds everything—in the discrete story of his own childhood. He remains loyal to its dual character—as moment-by-moment process, as temporally completed form—but, unlike Proust, he grants no characters in his work such a privileged perspective. They are not allowed to repossess their experience, to become retrospectively wise.[4] They must enact eighteen

---

[4] I do not wish to overstate the point. Stephen muses on his past in "Proteus," and Bloom does so, fleetingly, throughout the book (in "Ithaca" he goes so far as to recognize the shallowness of his earlier scorn for his father's religious practices [724]). But these wiser thoughts enjoy no special status. Stephen and Bloom neither rise to them nor linger on them. Rather, they are immersed in a stream of perceptions that moves overwhelmingly forward. *Ulysses* does indeed "Hold to the now, the here, through which all future plunges to the past" (186).

hours of their moment-by-moment lives, while their godlike creator exploits at his leisure the gap between the immediacy of endured experience (much of it formerly his) and the mediated possibilities of experience recollected, recomposed, and reprojected.[5]

This contrast helps to account for one of *Ulysses'* notable paradoxes, its way of narrating immediately affecting experiences within a rhetoric of detachment, indeed of insouciance. Bloom in the Ormond bar at four-thirty is a pitiable figure, but, as Frank Budgen remarks, "this is the brightest and gayest episode in the whole book" (133). In like manner the theme of execution is the sinister keynote both of Stephen's history and of Irish history as a whole. "Habemus carneficem" (482)—we have an executioner—has been an appropriate gloss on "habemus pontificem"—we have a Pope—ever since Adrian's Bull in the twelfth century.[6] Stephen's hangman god is another name for the cannibalizing adult world—the insatiable old sow—that consumes its young. Gummy Granny, Edward VII, May Dedalus, Horace Rumbold, and Private Carr are all death-wielders; their preemptive paradigms have shaped the nightmare of history from which Stephen is trying to escape. Yet the elaborate mock-execution in "Cyclops," like the numerous executions in "Circe," is conceived mainly in the spirit of play. The writer, like God, has already endured, then escaped, and then pondered the menace that stalks his creation. His creative gesture is enabled by the aesthetic calm of reprojection, not the vengeful bias of judgment.

The following discussion of *Ulysses* proceeds, then, from these premises: that the immediacy of experience is comically at odds with the variety of moral and meaningful paradigms used to assess experience; that mental and emotional life are best expressed, in their wholeness, both from the immediate perspective of subjective consciousness itself and from the mediated perspective of

---

[5] Ellmann proposes Vico as a general source for this pattern of experience repossessed imaginatively and reprojected. He quotes Croce on Vico: "Man creates the human world, creates it by transforming himself into the facts of society: by thinking it he recreates his own creations, traverses over again the paths he has already traversed, reconstructs the whole ideally, and thus knows it with full and true knowledge" (*Ulysses on the Liffey*, 141-42).

[6] I owe this point to Hugh Kenner, *Ulysses*, 120-21.

an ever-present, never-visible god; and, finally, that the artist who emulates such a god will take as his task the creation of a world, not the parceling out of judgment. The bearing of these premises upon the rendering of desire and value is massive, and comparisons with the other novelists in this study will be undertaken as appropriate.

٨

"My patience are exhausted" (78)

I would not know how to prove this, but I believe that *Ulysses* receives and repays more attention than any work of literature written in English since Wordworth's *Prelude*. Anyone who has taught it knows, afresh each year, its impenetrability. It is one of those rare texts that continue, even after the tenth or twentieth reading, to reveal facets of their coherence not earlier glimpsed. *Ulysses* first signals through its difficulty that it will serve awkwardly as a ground for comparison with other novels.

So much is different here that many hesitate to call it a novel at all.[7] Its interest in character is intense but intermittent, its sense of a governing rhetorical decorum is non-existent or undiscoverable. It arouses expectations for a plot sequence that never takes place. It alludes to and incorporates other written materials to an unheard-of degree. Page by page, at any given moment, it is liable to subvert the hermeneutic norms it has seemed to establish. In Fritz Senn's words, "the verbal, situational, and narrative texture is too polytropic for our customary inertia" (41).

The extent to which we fail to master the book, despite diligent application, would be monstrous, were it not that this word should be reserved for *Finnegans Wake*, where the dilemma increases exponentially. Robert Boyle, writing of one of the two most important pairings in a book of 783 pages, concedes: "It is not possible, it seems to me now, to determine which of the two, Molly or Poldy, is more responsible for their unsatisfactory sexual relationship" (416). The concession is based on scrutiny, not ignorance; earlier Boyle had known, but further study has revealed a finer mesh of opposed explanations. I know of no

---

[7] Kenner characterizes Goldberg's magisterial study of *Ulysses* as "how *Ulysses* would read if it were a novel" (*Ulysses*, 177).

other novel in which, discussing an inexplicable narrative shift in "Sirens," Hugh Kenner could appropriately comment: "We deduce, for what good it may do us, that such a manoeuver is permitted in this chapter" (*Joyce's Voices*, 76).

It would be fatuous to "psychoanalyze" such a text. One must have reasonable control over the manifest connections before delving into latent ones, and the surface of Joyce's novel does not explain all of its connections. This is obviously the case with the last six pages of "Oxen of the Sun" and with discrete phrases in "Circe," but it is also pervasively true of the more accessible stream-of-consciousness early chapters. "The stream of consciousness techniques, by permitting the maximum play between the elements of experience juxtaposed by the characters, enlarge the possible ways in which we may view that experience. The relative thinness of plot . . . can be regarded as the avoidance of any over-committed syntax of event . . . The elaborate but unsystematic repetition of words and images constitutes . . . a pervasive suggestion of an *un*apprehensible order beyond any actually perceived" (Goldberg, 266). *Ulysses* is a deliberately centrifugal novel, its echoing words and phrases radiating heuristically into the reader's consciousness and suggesting paradigms that exceed their textual sources. The result, in S. L. Goldberg's happy phrase, is "a pervasive suggestion of an unapprehensible order beyond any actually perceived."

That ultimate order is unapprehensible, but the unusual satisfaction this novel provides comes from the progress one continues to make, Moses-like, toward the promised land. Although M'Intosh remains unidentifiable, the novel is strewn with brief Pisgah glimpses of its center. As David Hayman says, "Our movement through [*Ulysses*] is its own reward and virtually endless, for the object will never be fully perceived. *Ulysses* can be seen as a collection of skillfully arranged vibrations whose intensity will depend on our awareness of them . . ." (101).

The key to our response is patience, and if our "patience are exhausted," the novel will resemble the cerebral construction and callous arrangement it is often taken for.[8] Static contemplation was Joyce's aesthetic desideratum from the Paris notebook of

[8] I am paraphrasing Senn, "Book of Many Turns," 30.

1903 through the writing of *Finnegans Wake*. He is not a writer for readers on the run, and on the run means, for *Ulysses*, a refusal to devote upwards of a hundred hours.[9] The first reading is suffered; the second involves tantalizing scraps of memory; the third, fourth, fifth, and so on proceed with increasing authority, as the reader projects from his stocked memory and trained imagination the context needed to bestow on those cryptic phrases their human resonance. I have deliberately echoed the phrases I used to describe Joyce's use of his own experience, for the reading reenacts the career which the life underwent as it entered successive phases of Joyce's art. Appreciation and a sense for implication increase with distance; disciplined imaginative projection is possible only after the most patient rehearsal of the materials. At first it is largely cacophonous; melodies surface in the early rereadings; chamber music later; symphonies thereafter. . . .

No one need accept these humbling terms of approach, but I have come to believe that *Ulysses* rewards no other approach. The legitimate alternative is to reject Joyce's later work, and every year many critics do so in print.[10] It is a rare critic who stays with *Ulysses* and yet retains a sense of it as an equivocal achievement: we tend to love what we have come to recognize so well. Recognize, not reduce to theme; as the book grows more real,

[9] This estimate is of course subjective. Two complete readings would take at least sixty or seventy hours, and the finer pleasures begin on the third reading. My Honors students at Swarthmore College put about fifty hours into the book, and at least half of them do not feel cheated: *Ulysses* offers considerable rewards early on. Joyce wrote Harriet Weaver that he had spent almost 20,000 hours writing his book (*Selected Letters*, 282); one hundred seems a not unreasonable number to ask of his readers.

[10] The classic rejection remains Wells's 1928 letter to Joyce, refusing to support *Finnegans Wake*: "You have turned your back on common men, on their elementary needs and their restricted time and intelligence and you have elaborated. What is the result? Vast riddles. Your last two works have been more amusing and exciting to write than they will ever be to read. Take me as a typical common reader. Do I get much pleasure from this work? No. Do I feel I am getting something new and illuminating as I do when I read Anrep's dreadful translation of Pavlov's badly written book on Conditioned Reflexes? No. So I ask: Who the hell is this Joyce who demands so many waking hours of the few thousands I have still to live for a proper appreciation of his quirks and fancies and flashes of rendering?" (Quoted in Ellmann, *James Joyce*, 621.)

it escapes more readily thematic recuperation. Richard Ellmann's commentary may be quoted to illustrate this point. In 1959 he wrote: "The theme of *Ulysses* is simple. . . . Casual kindness overcomes unconscionable power" (*James Joyce*, 390). While this is true, it is not the simple truth, and when Ellmann edited the *Letters* seven years later he achieved a more telling formulation: ". . . the method of his prose books is a kind of absorption of the universe rather than a facing up to it; he seems to draw it bit by bit inside him, and conceives of the imagination as a womb. . . . His work is not conceived as a blow in the face, but, these letters help us to perceive, as a matrical envelopment" (*Letters*, 2:xlvi, lii).

An "absorption of the universe," "a matrical envelopment," a world: gradually, *Ulysses* reveals its wholeness, its incomparable resonance. We must be patient enough to become enveloped, to submit to its matrical authority. Even so, it eludes critical possession. "Its universe," as Kenner claims, "is Einsteinian, non-simultaneous, internally consistent but never to be grasped in one act of apprehension: not only because the details are so numerous but also because their pertinent interconnections are more numerous still" (*Ulysses*, 20).

Pertinent interconnections and echoing phrases may be an appealing description to puzzle-solvers but a cold formula for novel-readers. Does the book's tireless network of salient verbal motifs empty it of the illusion of human experience? At first this might seem the case, and for the bulk of the book's readers (those who are defeated by it) it remains the case, but it is not true for readers with sufficient patience. The relation of words on a page to an illusion of human experience is itself unpredictable. Joyce makes the most of the transparency of words (their status as invisible carriers of thought and feeling), but he exploits as well their opacity: their status as visible counters in a sign-system. The word "key," for example, refers at various times (and on later readings simultaneously) to the object that opens the doors of the Martello Tower and the house at 7 Eccles Street, the symbol of ecclesiastic power (St. Peter's keys), the emblem of a political institution (House of Keys), a man's name (Alexander Keyes), a musical notation, a verb of sexual innuendo ("properly keyed up"), and a metonymy for rootedness (Bloom and Stephen: key-less). Here, as elsewhere, Joyce draws on "the polytropic potential that [he] found in everyday language" (Senn, 42).[11]

It skills not to declare at exactly what point this literary practice forfeits its freight of human experience and rises into the rarefied atmosphere of self-reflexive word-games. Rather, the relations between word-play and human feeling are plastic and reciprocal; the coolest chapter in the novel, "Ithaca," breaks abruptly into the pathos of Bloom remembering his father's suicide letter:

> What fractions of phrases did the lecture of those five whole words evoke?
>
> Tomorrow will be a week that I received . . . it is no use Leopold to be . . . with your dear mother . . . that is not more to stand . . . to her . . . all for me is out . . . be kind to Athos, Leopold . . . my dear son . . . always . . . of me . . . *das Herz* . . . *Gott* . . . *dein* . . . (723, Joyce's ellipses)

This letter caps a sequence that includes, among others, Deasy's to the newspapers, Milly's to Bloom, Boylan's to Molly, Martha's to Bloom, and Bloom's to Martha, as well as the fantasy letters of Bloom to the horsey women and of H. Rumbold to the High Sheriff of Dublin. The playful context thus established only deepens the local effect. Likewise, the ubiquitous motif of kindness to animals—a motif played out in a range of fanciful forms—in no way subverts the sincerity of the dying man's care for his dog. Finally, the shift to inarticulate feeling—expressed in a reversion to German—simultaneously contributes to the novel's polylingual texture and reveals, beneath the layer of Christianized English-speaking Irishman, the homeless European Jew. Form and feeling are reciprocal.

ᔒ

"The epic of the human body"

"The epic of the human body" (Joyce's phrase for *Ulysses*, noted by Budgen) suggests the well-known Linati schema, in which Joyce identified some seventeen organs in the body as symbolic entities woven into the texture of fifteen chapters, each

[11] I owe this dazzling example of polytropic keys to Senn.

organ stressed in its appropriate chapter (81). No organ is assigned to the first three chapters, on the grounds that Telemachus is not yet embodied. The premise seems to be that, as the novel progresses, the body acquires its epic fullness. The organ for "Penelope" is, not inappropriately, "fat."[12]

The chapters do reveal, in an uneven way, this organic emphasis, but the more compelling rendering of the body occurs unschematically. "In my book the body lives in and moves through space and is the home of a full human personality" (Budgen, quoting Joyce, 21): here is Joyce's achievement. In this respect the opposite of Lawrence, for whom the body is revered as the locus of passional energy, Joyce is drawn to the body as living matter. Though he may be cleared from Wells's charge of a "cloacal obsession," there is no denying his fondness for "adipose posterior female hemispheres, redolent of milk and honey and of excretory sanguine and seminal warmth" (734).[13] Mellors' "Here tha shits and here tha pisses: an' I lay my hand on 'em both an' like thee for it" (*Lady Chatterley's Lover*, 241) sounds by contrast the slightly defiant note of disgust overcome. He affirms Connie's "proper, woman's arse" enough to affirm its baser functions too. Mellors also maintains a distinction between fuck and cunt ("Animals fuck. But cunt's a lot more than that" [191]), and we know that Lawrence never ceased to distinguish between the seminal and the excretory.[14]

In *Ulysses*, such gradations are of little moment. Seminal and

---

[12] Ellmann reprints the Linati schema as an appendix to *Ulysses on the Liffey*.

[13] Wells used the quoted phrase ("cloacal obsession") in a review of *Portrait*. Unperturbed, Joyce repeats the phrase in *Ulysses* (131), to identify a leading characteristic of the Romans and the English.

[14] Lawrence writes in 1929: "The sex functions and the excrementory functions in the human body work so close together, yet they are, so to speak, utterly different in direction. Sex is a creative flow, the excrementory flow is towards dissolution, de-creation, if we may use such a word. In the really healthy human being the distinction between the two is instant, our profoundest instincts are perhaps our instincts of opposition between the two flows" ("Pornography and Obscenity," 39). Lawrence goes on in the same essay to excoriate masturbation as "the one thoroughly secret act of the human being . . . [in which] there is nothing but loss. There is no reciprocity. . . . The body remains, in a sense, a corpse, after the act of self-abuse" (41-42). It is not surprising that Joyce and Lawrence thoroughly repudiate each other's work.

excretory are not just contiguous but indistinguishable. And the essential point about copulation is that animals and humans, when so engaged, resemble each other.[15] Molly is aroused to the intercourse that produces Rudy by the sight of "the two dogs up in her behind in the middle of the naked street" (778). "Circe" spells out in a dozen dazzling ways the implications of humans doubling as animals in their sexuality. If desire is holy for Lawrence and the body must be revered, then desire is comic for Joyce and the body must be acknowledged. The guilt that the soul suffers by being housed in a body can be overcome, Lawrence believes, by mental candor and by ecstatic physical intercourse. That same guilt is for Joyce comically inextinguishable. The soul is never wholly at home in its material precincts; the body's appetites are permanently and delightfully outrageous.[16]

Excretory and seminal are extremes that for Stephen Dedalus never meet. He conducts in *Portrait* and *Ulysses* a war against his body, "this dogsbody to rid of vermin" (6). Despite the awareness that he must fall, his symbol of creativity remains flight, soaring, imaginative transcendence of the body's laws rather than seminal intercourse. When Stephen's imagination fails—as in the misquotation of Nash's line in *Portrait*—his body falls to its animal captors: "He had not even remembered rightly Nash's line. All the images it had awakened were false. His mind bred vermin. His thoughts were lice born of the sweat of sloth" (*Portrait*, 234). To be embodied is for Stephen to be impotent in Dublin (the failure of the Paris flight) and exposed to the ills that flesh is heir to. Matter is alien to him—he has no home in the realm of the known—and he projects his outcast condition vividly in the specter of the drowned man risen to the surface in "Proteus":

[15] This is not to say that humans appreciate the resemblance. Even Molly, who welcomes Blazes Boylan's ardor, "didn't like his slapping me behind . . . I'm not a horse or an ass am I . . ." (741).

[16] Joyce's notorious letters of 1909 to Nora make it clear that precisely the grossest activities of her body provoke him, and that the provocation is accompanied by a delicious sense of shame. His feelings are bestial and exalted at the same time: "Nora, my faithful darling, my sweet-eyed blackguard schoolgirl, be my whore, my mistress, as much as you like (my little frigging mistress! my little fucking whore!) you are always my beautiful wild flower of the hedges, my dark-blue rain-drenched flower" (*Selected Letters*, 181).

A corpse rising saltwhite from the undertow, bobbing land-
ward, a pace a pace a porpoise. There he is. Hook it quick.
Sunk though he be beneath the watery floor. We have him.
Easy now.

Bag of corpsegas sopping in foul brine. A quiver of
minnows, fat of a spongy titbit, flash through the slits of his
buttoned trouserfly. God becomes man becomes fish becomes barnacle goose becomes featherbed mountain. Dead
breaths I living breathe, tread dead dust, devour a urinous
offal from all dead. Hauled stark over the gunwale he breathes
upward the stench of his green grave, his leprous nosehole
snoring to the sun. (50)

Here is the ultimate violation to which the body is exposed,
the sentence to which—as a body—it is condemned.[17] Lycidas
and Shakespeare's Alonso may rise from the water's embrace intact and even reborn, but they are idealized literary fictions. Stephen, by contrast, is subject to the "law of falling bodies" (72),
and his Newtonian mind tells him that a body in the water nine
days will no longer be itself. No longer being himself is his greatest fear. He takes the cycle of becoming as a continuous insult.
He lives in a ubiquitous cemetery, ingesting dead breaths. The
body he envisages has been invaded; its orifices have been ran-
sacked and become diseased, transformed. In place of genitals, a
quiver of minnows; the nose a leprous hole; the entire body
reduced to its latent essentials: urine, offal. In a body, he sees
himself as waste, wasting, wasted. June 16, 1904, means for Stephen, inevitably, twenty-four more hours of entropy. To find out
what else can happen in time, we must turn to Bloom, and the
best initial portrait is his envisaging himself, like Stephen, in the
water:

Enjoy a bath now: clean trough of water, cool enamel,
the gentle tepid stream. This is my body.

He foresaw his pale body reclined in it at full, naked,
in a womb of warmth, oiled by scented melting soap, softly

[17] When Paddy Dignam and May Dedalus emerge in "Circe" from the rat-
infested cemetery, they have likewise been mutilated and are both noseless.

laved. He saw his trunk and limbs riprippled over and sustained, buoyed lightly upward, lemonyellow: his navel, bud of flesh: and saw the dark tangled curls of his bush floating, floating hair of the stream around the limp father of thousands, a languid floating flower. (86)

This is my body. In the Mass the statement testifies to the mystery of transsubstantiation, the bread and the wine becoming the substantial body and blood of Christ. Bloom's use of the phrase is free of transactions; his phenomenal body is itself the source of the mystery. He lives within its confines, enjoying its propensities. Exposed to the form-dissolving element of water, he sees himself floating, sustained by its touch, imagining the sexual pleasure of masturbation and the sanitary one of a sensuous bath. The "grey sweet mother" which Stephen finds threatening, Bloom likens to a womb. His delight in its matrical embrace conveys the crucial difference between them; he remains unconstrainedly himself in the presence of invasive elements most unlike him.[18] "Touch, touch me" (49), Stephen muses, but his more urgent need is to keep at bay all contact that would alter him: "As I am. As I am. All or not at all" (49). Whereas, for Bloom, contact is usually a non-abrasive encounter that does not so much alter self or other as minutely illuminate, in the self, the otherness of the other: moments of infinitesimal metempsychosis.[19]

Examples abound. "Bantam Lyons' yellow blacknailed fingers unrolled the baton. Wants a wash too. Take off the rough dirt. Good morning, have you used Pears' soap? Dandruff on his shoulders. Scalp wants oiling" (85). The picture is unsentimental, precise, hygienically angled. Later, next to the maudlin de-

[18] The point needs qualification. Under great duress (as in "Cyclops") he will break into abrasive quarrel. And there are many critics who find his normally "limp" and "languid" posture a sign of impotence rather than flexibility.

[19] Cf. Robert Kiely's formulation: "Metempsychosis, the exchange of souls, occurs within Bloom's imagination. His ambivalence is not mere confusion or passivity, but the personification of dramatic displacement, an act of perception and sympathy that does not lose touch with the self but connects it with the larger network of human experience beyond the individual" (201).

scription of the deceased Paddy Dignam—"As decent a little man as ever wore a hat" . . . "Breakdown . . . Heart" (95)—Bloom's laconic thoughts are welcome and explanatory: "Blazing face: redhot. Too much John Barleycorn" (95). Looking around at the cemetery, Bloom notices a team of funeral horses: "Horse looking round at it [the coffin] with his plume skeowways. Dull eye: collar tight on his neck, pressing on a bloodvessel or something. Do they know what they cart out here every day?" (101) Such perceptions could hardly be sharper, and they accumulate discreetly throughout the book to generate the sense of Bloom's considerable acumen. He sees his world with the crisp authority of a man who lives in his body and discerns daily the state of others—healthy or sick—by their unconscious bodily posture.

It is an authority capable of generosity and wonder as well. He spots pigeons overhead in "Lestrygonians" and thinks: "Their little frolic after meals. Who will we do it on? I pick the fellow in black. Here goes. Here's good luck. Must be thrilling from the air" (162). *Must be thrilling from the air*: those six words transform a whimsical perception of victimization into a genuine (albeit humble) act of sympathetic imagination. That it comes from a man who enjoys the release of his own bowels enables rather than disqualifies his sense of the "whatness" of the pigeons. In like manner, musing on a bat in "Nausicaa," he reflects: "Like a little man in a cloak he is with tiny hands. Weeny bones. Almost see them shimmering, kind of a bluey white" (378). Perhaps the most charming speculation occurs as well in "Nausicaa": "Do fish ever get seasick?" (379) These perceptions share an immediate grasp of the object as a creature of bodily life, its vitality glimpsed and enjoyed through the minute construction of its material parts.

Stephen imagines in "Proteus" what it would be like to be blind, and he succeeds in hearing better the "crackling wrack and shells" (37). What he mainly registers, though, is his continuing stream of personal thoughts. He gets no closer to the subjective reality of blindness than "My ash sword hangs at my side. Tap with it: they do" (37). By contrast, here is Bloom helping a blind stripling cross the street:

Stains on his coat. Slobbers his food, I suppose. Tastes all different for him. Have to be spoonfed first. Like a child's hand his hand. Like Milly's was. Sensitive. Sizing me up I daresay from my hand. Wonder if he has a name. Van. Keep his cane clear of the horse's legs tired drudge gets his doze. That's right. Clear. Behind a bull: in front of a horse.
—Thanks, sir.
Knows I'm a man. Voice. . . . Poor young fellow! How on earth did he know that van was there? Must have felt it. See things in their foreheads perhaps. Kind of sense of volume. Weight. Would he feel it if something was removed? Feel a gap. Queer idea of Dublin he must have, tapping his way round by the stones. Could he walk in a beeline if he hadn't that cane? . . . Look at all the things they can learn to do. Read with their fingers. Tune pianos. Or we are surprised they have any brains. . . . Sense of smell must be stronger too . . . (181)

Much of Bloom is captured in this still shot: his generosity, his curiosity, his practicality, his quickness. Bloom reads the scene for its potential obstacles—the van that is not moving, the cane clear of the horse's legs—and he sees details in a variety of frames. Food stains first reveal the blind man's plight, but soon suggest the strangeness of a blind man eating. The tiny hand, childlike in size and in trust, leads Bloom to memories of Milly, and these memories perhaps energize his further (one is tempted to say inexhaustible) speculations about perception, orientation, thought process, and activity. The speculations are both astonishing and quotidian; for this reader at least, they put Stephen's kindred ones in "Proteus" to shame. Throughout, the living otherness of the blind man engages Bloom's attention, but whatever the reaches of that attention, it is founded on the senses of sight, touch, taste, and hearing that are common to living creatures. Focused on the play of these common faculties, Bloom's mind can make unpredictable leaps. At any turn he may find, embodied, himself, his history, and his family in anyone he confronts.

Bloom reads the bodies of others; he also takes surreptitious pleasure in the resources of his own. Stroking his belly (182), scratching the sole of his foot (369), smelling his spilled semen (375) as well as his lacerated toenail (712), he reveals the incarnate ground of his values—the frame within which he assesses his world—in a myriad humble details. Likewise, his grandest scenarios are sanctioned by the body. He conjures up cosmic schemes before bedtime because such meditations "when practiced habitually before retiring for the night alleviated fatigue and produced as a result sound repose and renovated vitality" (720).

The same scruple that led Joyce to research the exact distance between the railings at 7 Eccles Street and the area pavement leads him to feature the digestive tract in his portrait of Bloom. Motive and behavior are constrained by the body's shape and functions. And not just Bloom's motives and behavior. Paddy Dignam, returned from the grave in a "Cyclops" fantasy, has only one request: "a quart of buttermilk [which] was brought and evidently afforded relief" (301). Despite the esoteric aura of the scene, it is not surprising that, when pressed, Dignam remembers of the other world mainly its "modern home comfort[s] such as tālāfānā, ālāvātār, hātākāldā, wātāklāsāt" (301). Ghosts in *Ulysses* have bodies; they must eat like others, and like others they must void after eating. When Dignam returns again, in a "Circe" fantasy, he has another request: "A lamp. I must satisfy an animal need. That buttermilk didn't agree with me" (473).

Everyone in *Ulysses* has bowels; only the gods and goddesses operate on other principles.[20] The book is therefore strewn with refuse, but, whereas Stephen recoils from such "urinous offal," Bloom takes delight in it. He knows that manure is fertilizer, that life feeds on death, and that excretory and seminal are extremes that meet. One of his more delectable schemes for acquiring great wealth involves "the utilisation of waste paper, fells of sewer rodents, human excrement possessing chemical properties, in view of the vast production of the first, vast number of

[20] So they claim. It is true that the statues have no anuses and that the bullying nymph in "Circe" brags that "We eat electric light" (551). However, once Bloom calls the nymph's bluff, her plaster cast cracks and "a cloud of stench" escapes (553).

the second and immense quantity of the third, every normal human being of average vitality and appetite producing annually . . . a sum total of 80 lbs. . . . to be multiplied by 4,386,035 the total population of Ireland according to the census returns of 1901" (718). Matter-laden, answering to the census, obeying the "law of falling bodies," characters in *Ulysses* enact their eighteen-hour irreversible movement through time. Simultaneously—and this is what we must now examine—they are placed within a profusion of mythic systems that soar above, in their gaudy significance, the mundane facts of dung and urine.

ᕗ

The "dance of the hours" (69)

On the second page of "Lestrygonians" Blooms throws into the Liffey a crumpled throwaway he had just been handed, with "Elijah is coming" written on it. As the paper ball descends, he thinks: "Elijah thirtytwo feet per sec is com" (152). The paradox is succinct. On the one hand, Elijah the precursor of Christ, coming to redeem the humdrum word of dung and urine, space and time. On the other, Elijah a figment of words on a sheet, an advertisement crumpled and thrown away, falling at the inescapable Newtonian rate for all matter: thirty-two feet per second. Is he the promise of transcendence or one more instance of sublunary trumpery? Joyce does not answer, but his book delights in raising the question. We see Elijah in other suggestive contexts—Elijah J. Dowie, ben Bloom Elijah, Elijah the Throwaway, crumpled skiff, making his journey down the Liffey—and we also measure him here, as the gulls gauge the descending throwaway's value as nourishment: "They wheeled lower. Looking for grub. . . . Not a bit. The ball bobbed unheeded on the wake of swells, floated under by the bridge piers. Not such damn fools" (152). Whereupon Bloom, ever kind to animals, buys a penny's worth of Banbury cakes, throws them into the water, and watches the gulls swoop upon them: "They never expected that. Manna" (153).

"Manna" engages "Elijah" nicely. For the moment the true miracle is the generously given cakes, from one animal to another. (Bloom's kindness to animals is polytropic: he is kind to other animals, he is kind to the animal in himself, he recognizes that he and other animals are of the same *kind*.) Banbury cakes lack the sanction of the divine wafer, however; they are matter subject to terrestrial conditions. The guarantee of their authenticity is that they are corruptible in time. In "Lestrygonians" Joyce renders Bloom's relationship with Molly through the related terms of matter, time, and appetite. Created under the aegis of appetite, that relationship suffers the fate of appetite. And the activity of appetite, at its starkest, is a kind of murderous consumption and ejection: "Eat or be eaten. Kill! Kill!" (170)

In the light of this pattern several motifs come into focus: Plumtree's Potted Meat, with its implications of an abode of bliss, an act of intercourse, and an obituary column; Josie Breen's report of the U.P. conundrum; Bloom's cryptic memory of the MacTrigger limerick; his peripheral awareness of his wife's coming adultery, keyed to the recurrent question "Who's getting it up?" (172) Blazes Boylan is getting it up—indeed it gets "bigger and bigger and bigger"—while Bloom is incomplete, without the meat, buried in the obituary column. He has "been eaten and spewed" (164). Even the recall of his first intercourse with Molly on Howth Hill is introduced by the image of "Stuck on the pane two flies buzzed, stuck" (175), and concludes with the melancholy notation: "Me. And me now. Stuck, the flies buzzed" (176). The memory itself is surpassingly lyrical, but it was founded on appetite—the warm seedcake, mawkish pulp, soft warm gumjelly lips—and it offers no remedy against appetite's bondage to time. Desire waxes then wanes; the moment is unrepeatable. The relentless pressure of time dissolves bodies, makes them throwaways: "No one is anything" (164).

Hugh Kenner has elegantly shown that space and time are the gods of *Ulysses*; it dances to their tune (*Ulysses*, 13-17, passim). Within that dance there is no stillness, and all attempts to impose transcendental stasis are doomed. Bodies "all fall to the ground" (72), and when they enter the ground they continue to fall. Bloom could not go to Dignam's funeral in a light suit because that would "make a picnic of it" (57), but crumbs are spotted in the funeral carriage: "—Someone seems to have been making a picnic party here lately, Mr. Power said" (89). A funeral is a picnic. Bloom sees the huge rat enter Paddy's crypt, and he imagines the post-mortem communications: "Regular square feed for them. Flies come before he's well dead. Got wind of Dignam" (114). In the midst of death we are in life: "One born every second somewhere. Other dying every second" (164). *Ulysses* responds to this premise obviously, with a birth chapter to match a death one, and with the extensive awareness (by way of Bloom: no one else) that "the cells or whatever they are go on living. Changing about. . . . Nothing to feed on feed on themselves" (108-109). The same premise operates casually, as in the "Lotus Eaters" vignette in which M'Coy's maudlin report of the death of Paddy Dignam is counterpointed by Bloom's surreptitious maneuvering to catch sight of a woman exposing her thigh as she climbs into a carriage. Both strands of the vignette come together in the capacious concluding phrase, "Another gone" (74).

Stream of consciousness, in Joyce's hands, is protean, unpredictable, irreverent. Recent critics have warned against making too much of this strand in *Ulysses*, but it remains the decisive source of movement and vitality in over half the book's chapters.[21] By juxtaposing the moment-by-moment play of the mind against august cultural scripts of meaning and importance, Joyce does incessantly what Buck Mulligan's Mrs. Cahill warns against: he makes tea and water in the one pot (12). Mulcahy and the statue of our Savior can be mistaken for each other (107)—as Mary Shortall and Jimmy Pidgeon can be mistaken for Mary and the Holy Ghost (520)—only in the spirit of play. The comedy derives from the gap, perceived by Joyce since early childhood, between the flux of actual experience and the wide range of schematic paradigms into which experience has been patterned so as to take on authority and significance.

Phillip Herring, after a painstaking edition of *Joyce's Notes*

[21] David Hayman, Marilyn French, and Hugh Kenner represent the current tendency to downplay Joyce's reliance on stream of consciousness technique. But their view that this technique becomes minor after "Hades" is open to objection. Stream of consciousness remains crucial in "Lestrygonians," "Nausicaa," and "Penelope"; and it plays a critical role in "Scylla and Charybdis" and "Sirens."

and Early Drafts for "Ulysses," warns "that schema and text are by their nature incongruent, and readers who wish to interpret *Ulysses* by means of such plans of necessity encounter the temptation to distort the one to fit the other" (122-23). On the other hand, a veteran Joycean like Walton Litz declares that he has "long since abandoned the notion—always a reductive one—that the novelistic elements in *Ulysses* can be separated from the *schema* and claimed as the true line of the work's meaning" (405).

Litz and Herring might agree, however, that to superimpose the *schema*—as a master key—upon the narrative plane would be as ill-advised as to discard it altogether. *Ulysses* has no master key. The book is generated by the inexhaustible space between the paradigmatic scripts of cultural self-understanding and the welter of fluid perceptions that move through the mind on a given day in 1904. Joyce's genius is to have crafted his materials in such a way that the realm of Meaning and the realm of phenomena continuously, provocatively, engage each other. Sometimes the engagement is harmonious, at other times parodistic, but it is rarely complacent enough to warrant critical pontification. Joyce feared the big words too—he and his country had both been made too unhappy by them—and so his work reveals a variety of orders but not Order, a range of purposes but not that Purpose in the service of which all data may be recuperated and one may confidently separate the sheep from the goats, the saved from the damned.

The chapter in which Meaning and phenomena are most aggressively juxtaposed is "Ithaca." The father and the son have finally achieved homecoming, and the long-awaited terms of relationship may now be unfolded. As though to maximize the ensuing points of symbolic kinship, Joyce narrates the chapter through the technique of catechistical question and answer. Catechism is not only the heavy-weight form for soul-searching endorsed by the Catholic Church; it was also, as Walton Litz and others have discovered, a pedagogic device in service throughout the nineteenth century in secular textbooks. "Questions that any child might ask are phrased in simple form, while a voice of hectoring authority responds with a surfeit of information and misinformation" (Litz, 405).

271

"Hectoring authority," I have been claiming all along, is the inadmissible principle in Joyce's aesthetics. It is right that this chapter of "resolution" should exploit the paradigm within which, throughout his childhood, Joyce heard the church and school wrap up the multiplicity of phenomena and deliver them over into packages of ordained Significance. The nineteenth-century passion for relationship is here displayed, and the latent comedy of comparison emerges. Stephen and Bloom do resemble each other (each sees the effect of electric light on adjoining trees as baneful [667]), but in the way that, if pushed hard enough, any two phenomena can be said to resemble each other. The form, oblivious to the "whatness" of the objects under scrutiny, supplies the resemblances it requires.

The questions posed tend either to be delightfully irrelevant to the comparison, or to turn the comparison into a plastic exercise. A middle-aged man having a drink of cocoa in the middle of the night with a rather battered youth whom he has befriended—both of them keyless, one of Catholic, the other of Jewish background, both urinating before the young man departs into the darkness: this set of casual circumstances would answer to a request for casual meaning, a request appropriately reduced for the events of a single day.[22] But to subject their meeting to the biggest rhetorical guns in Joyce's repertory, to press it tirelessly for minute and elaborate points of connection that have become available during the previous 665 pages—this is to reveal the paucity of objective resemblance and the ingenuity of the subjective drive for kinship.

Recurrently the procedure seems to announce its own playful inconsequence. A man whose name is susceptible to at least five anagrams, whose age can be computed, for comparative purposes, from 38 to 83,000—such a man can be likened to anything and in himself is nothing. Beneath the parade of possible

[22] Drawing on the work of Georg Simmel (especially "The Metropolis and Mental Life"), Philip Fisher discusses *Ulysses* as a work whose typical relationships follow the urban model of secondary (superficial and fleeting) rather than primary (profound and permanent) contact. One may say that the bond between Stephen and Bloom is a secondary contact that countless critics (treating *Ulysses* as a Victorian novel) have interpreted as primary.

significances lies the unaltered actual circumstances: "the irreparability of the past" and "the imprevidibility of the future" (696). Human life would be "infinitely perfectible," could one eliminate, by means of selective paradigms,"the generic conditions imposed by natural, as distinct from human law" (697). But these conditions are permanent. The law of falling bodies applies to all; even Elijah descends at thirty-two feet per second. Does *Ulysses* propose any escape, except in play, from the moment-by-moment movement, entropic and unsanctioned, of human bodies through time?

&

"If we were all suddenly somebody else" (110)

Natural law is irresistible, and *Ulysses* everywhere acknowledges its sway. What needs to be reconceived is human law. Joyce here joins Lawrence—and differs from Dickens and Eliot, Hardy and Conrad—in his radical response to the inadequacies of human law. His mode of response is comic and detached—Lawrence's is urgent and partisan—but they share a sense of the unreformable unsoundness of their culture's assumptions. Dickens and Eliot oppose their culture as well, but their critique is incremental and in behalf of established values. Their fictions enact the integration of an unruly self into an imperfect society: it is the paradigm of the Victorian novel. Socially inadmissible impulses are outgrown, deflected onto peripheral or villainous figures, or retained in the guise of other names. In rare cases where the self remains incorrigible, it must be denatured (Gwendolen) or destroyed (Maggie).

In Hardy and Conrad this dilemma has become commonplace. Societal injunctions retain their primacy within the protagonists' sense of identity and options, but they are incompatible with the givens of human nature. Norms of aspiration and identity continue to appeal, but they cannot be maintained. How many of Hardy's and Conrad's novels could be described as the commitment (often involuntary) of the protagonist to social contracts he can neither sustain nor disown? Nature is for both of these novelists anathema to culture, and neither nature nor culture can be changed. Is it any wonder that their finest work is cautionary?

Lawrence, as I have tried to show, rebels in behalf of native quickness, the living plasm. The self he would release into flame-life is unconscious and hidden beneath the overlay of culturally sanctioned traits. Joyce, perhaps more audacious yet, probes the possibility that there is no single self, that we survive the constraints of natural law both by yielding to our plural selves and by accommodating (by meeting obliquely) the manifold indignities that (according to the paradigms of human law) are beyond accommodation. Ulysses polytropos, man of many turns, twisting and maneuvering through a narrative even less predictable than he is: Joyce more than Wilde supplies the antidote to Victorian single-minded earnestness.[23]

Earnestness, as I argued earlier, is the paramount virtue in *David Copperfield*. "By co-ordinating the self's energies in the prosecution of self-transcending, socially esteemed work, earnestness is a means of generating and maintaining self-respect" (see above, 30f.). "Never to put one hand on anything on which I could throw my whole self" (*David Copperfield*, 464), David exalts as his "golden rule." The rationale for my chapters on Dickens and Eliot could be described as the attempt to chart the movement of that disowned hand, for "my whole self" is an illusory construct that their best work exposes.

David, Esther, and Arthur; Adam, Maggie, and Daniel; Clym, Angel, and Jude; Jim, Gould, and Heyst: these are single-minded figures, morally on one key, with little capacity for their own contradictions. They are, moving from Dickens to Conrad, exceedingly humorless, and the subject on which they concentrate their greatest earnestness is themselves. They construe themselves as an ideal which either preexists or which they can will into being. Their apotheosis, the figure who seems to summarize their accumulating self-engrossed, condition-spurning non-adaptability, is an "impossible" young man named Stephen Dedalus.

[23] Kenner is wonderfully alert in both of his books to this dimension of *Ulysses*. The best brief treatment of *Ulysses'* cunning unpredictability is Fritz Senn's "Book of Many Turns."

These protagonists share a concern with immaculateness. They are cleaners-up; they all want a clean slate. Uninterested in their own obscurities, they insist on making distinctions, on defining themselves as transcendentally incorrupt against a background of alien and inimical arrangements. They know with mounting precision the tainted situations in the larger society to which they have said "No," and by the time of Joyce there are no untainted situations yet to be colonized. Dickens' and Eliot's heroes could remain intact in London, Hardy's and Conrad's collapse on discovering that the new arrangements are the old ones recomposed. Lawrence's protagonists are in permanent transit, while Stephen Dedalus languishes in Dublin, his escape to Paris a fiasco.

Each option Stephen ponders in "Proteus" is a false option. Joachim Abbas, Columbanus, and Swift; Simon Dedalus, Richie Goulding, and the Egans; saint, sage, gentleman, and wild goose: "Houses of decay, mine, his and all. . . . Come out of them, Stephen. Beauty is not there" (39). Each of these identities is a pose, all too common (as Buck Mulligan demonstrates) in an Ireland that is a "Paradise of pretenders then and now" (45). So Stephen would run out of the nightmare of history altogether, into the unconditioned future. Bloom shares this fantasy, but knows it to be fantastic:

> The new I want. Nothing new under the sun. . . . Think you're escaping and run into yourself. Longest way round is the shortest way home. (377)[24]

The drama of transcendent escape is played out both because the roles have all been played before and because the escapee in any case carries himself along, wherever he goes. The self he carries, however rebellious, is stained with inexpungeable social traces.

Nothing new under the sun: sons are born into families,

[24] Stephen is moving "syllogistically from the known to the unknown," while Bloom proceeds "energetically from the unknown to the known" (697). The one moves "upon the incertitude of the void"; the other moves "through" that incertitude. It is as inevitable that Stephen must disappear into the unknown outer darkness as that Bloom must come to rest upon Molly's all-too-well-known bottom.

churches, countries. Others have always been there first and established the scene. Stephen's true enemy is sonship itself. He
desires to create the world out of himself, not to submit to its
ubiquitous priority. Not for nothing does he muse throughout
Ulysses over the heresies of Arius and Sabellius. Arius would sun-
der the Trinity into separable parts; Sabellius would fuse the
parts into indistinguishable unity. Neither heretic can tolerate
the trinitarian poise in which separateness and union co-exist,
each entity itself, each implied by the others, the Father dominant over all.[25]

If immaculate escape (engineered by the will) is impossible,
there remains only acceptance.[26] In place of the pure transcendence of Non Serviam, there is the stained immanence of the "key-
less citizen" (697). Keyless because nothing that he has may be
said to belong to him, Bloom is nevertheless a citizen of Dublin.
In him exile is compatible with citizenship—inescapable cultural
scripts can be acknowledged without being endorsed—and because this is so *Ulysses* is the greatest celebration of presence in
modern fiction. Joyce has created an image of experience in which
Yes accommodates No without ceasing to be Yes.[27]

[25] Edwin Lewis claims that the idea of the Trinity means that "none of the
Three Persons can exist or act save in relation to the other two. . . . [This notion]
makes God a perfect Personal Fellowship; He is social rather than solitary" (785).

[26] Cf. Cixous: ". . . the leap towards the unknown is replaced by a dive
into the known. . . . The lesson which Stephen has learned in the time between
Portrait and *Ulysses* boils down to the discovery that the Universe awaiting him
beyond the known, beyond the limits of the city and of time present, beyond the
nets and the traps, is *the same* universe still; the same, but recognised, caught in
the bounds of the artist's imagination and in the net of his awareness, it is 're-
flected' and experienced *within*. The belief in a completely different unknown, in
a transcendence, in the possibility of being the first to gaze upon a beauty that
had not yet come into the world, in the existence of some virgin territory not
yet named by anyone else—this vague but exhilarating belief that bore up Stephen's soul throughout *Portrait* . . . has now disappeared" (668). It seems to me
that this is indeed the lesson Joyce learned, but I see no evidence that Stephen
learns it too.

[27] Kenner rightly reminds us that Molly's final Yes is no sentimental affirmation, and he quotes (from Ellmann) Joyce's 1938 comment to Louis Gillet:
"In *Ulysses*, to depict the babbling of a woman going to sleep, I had sought to
end with the least forceful word I could possibly find. I had found the word

No still obtains. All problems broached in *Ulysses* remain unresolved. Clive Hart is surely correct in saying that "In the Dublin of *Ulysses*, aspiration is rarely matched by achievement, perception fails to confirm intuition, actions do not lead to expected results, hopes remain velleities. Despite the many pleas for the contrary view . . . nothing much has happened by the end of the book" (183). To justify the paucity of achievement on the grounds that nothing much usually happens in eighteen hours misses the point: Joyce has chosen a time frame in which, except through fabulous intervention, nothing much *can* happen.

He has assaulted the notion of "happens"; he has underminded the cultural conventions that underpin it. A cohesive self moving through public time and space and, eventually, either achieving the social career that he has personally willed or failing (for carefully documented reasons) to do so: this, the generic plot *donnée* of the nineteenth-century novel, is what Joyce has spurned. Even by the time of *Jude the Obscure*, the notions of self, will, and social career that enable such a plot have become badly bruised and started to unravel.

Lawrence and Joyce exploit this plot in their early Bildungsromane, then discard it. Neither writer can imagine the subjective experience of freedom within its terms. For Lawrence, such a protagonist represents the smugly sanctioned fiction of an earlier period: "a spurious, detestable product. . . . This is the self-conscious ego, the entity of fixed ideas and ideals, prancing and displaying itself like an actor" ("Democracy," 711). Lawrence conceives a self in essential opposition to this model, a self that is not self-conscious, not performed through the exercise of will, and not interested in a career defined by lengthy apprenticeship

---

'yes,' which is barely pronounced, which denotes acquiescence, self-abandon, relaxation, the end of all resistance" (Ellmann, *James Joyce*, 725n., as quoted in Kenner, *Ulysses*, 147). The corrective is useful but excessive. Joyce at fifty-six is a tired man, and he brings up the "Yes" (as further quotation would show) only to compare it with the utterly unemphasized last word of the book he was just ending, *Finnegans Wake*. The last thoughts of Molly, penned some seventeen years earlier, vibrate with assertion. Joyce himself said in 1922: "The book must end with yes. It must end with the most positive word in the human language" (quoted in Ellmann, *James Joyce*, 536). The Yes is unsentimental because of its immeasurable inclusiveness, not because of its "lack of all resistance."

to and eventual mastery over culturally approved forms of work. (David and Arthur, Adam and Daniel, Clym and Jude, Jim and Gould: these protagonists are as eager to get on with their work as Paul, Ursula, Birkin, Somers, and Mellors are unable to stay with theirs.) Lawrence's subjects are in search of something else— the flame-life within—for which the Victorian model of identity (and the plot it assumes) is simply an impediment.

Joyce repudiates this model for more oblique and complicated reasons. Like Lawrence he has no interest in a culturally sanctioned career, but unlike Lawrence—and this may be their essential difference—he finds a life free of cultural determinants a contradiction in terms. In his own experience, in his *Portrait* of that experience, he found his freedom (personal and artistic) through the range of reprojective stances he was able to take toward necessities that (he saw in retrospect) could not be escaped. His creative direction is homeward. His story is the voyage back, even as Lawrence's is the voyage out.

Stephen is the second figure of *Ulysses* because he is still on the voyage out. Joyce shows in every way why that is a doomed trip, and why freedom is a matter of homecoming. There is no getting clear of church, family, and country; there is only getting into relationship with them. A career conceived in cultural terms remains ludicrous—accepting sonship does not entail believing in the scenarios proposed for sons—but it is fantasy to imagine some transcendent activity beckoning elsewhere in the beyond. No methods exist for getting "from the known to the unknown" (701). There is only the known; freedom inheres in the reprojection of given terms, not the invention of new ones.

Nothing new under the sun: *Ulysses* supremely demonstrates that what is novel is not the new but the daily. It dramatizes neither the plot of societal reintegration nor the plot of societal escape. Beneath both plots are all the quotidian materials overlooked by the institution of plots. These materials become visible insofar as there is no intent to get somewhere else. By rejecting the intent to get somewhere else, Joyce bypasses the assumptions of self, will, and career that make up the Victorian novel. Going beneath purpose, he comes upon process. In Pound's words, he abandons "the tiresome convention that any part of life, to be interesting, must be shaped into the conventional form of a story" (28).

Though not bound by them—in the sense of trusting them as reliable maps for experience—Joyce (unlike Lawrence) does not attempt to discard conventional plots. Instead, he collects them by the score and puts them to his own use. Rather than the chosen forms that house his work's meaning, conventional stories become the fictive models against which he everywhere juxtaposes his sense of the momentary feel and shape of experience. Disbelief in his models permits Joyce to use them with verve and impunity, for he escapes all charges of imitation. *Ulysses* concedes priority on every page, beginning with its title. It ransacks—on a greater scale than *Tristram Shandy*, indeed almost indiscriminately—the cultural scripts that precede it. "The [first spoken] words . . . are imitation, resounding for the millionth time, as prologue to the book whose characters play parts, whose actions often consist in acting, and many of whose words are quotations to an extent that the author never even attempted to single out individual quotes by customary typographical marks. A quotation also links the present occasion with a former one; it is a strand-entwining chord back in time. So the first words uttered aloud in *Ulysses* take us even beyond the Roman Catholic Mass to the Hebrew Psalms of the Old Testament. They span several millenia" (Senn, 33).

The extent to which *Ulysses* absorbs and acknowledges prior configurations is less well known than the book's originality, but equally telling. Joyce always deprecated his own inventive faculty; he thought of himself as primarily an arranger. Proposing no original plot of its own, *Ulysses* manipulates an array of plots first arranged by others. Likewise, it attains its originality of language largely through massive deployment of phrases first penned by others. To these two arenas of filiation may be added a third. It features a central character in no way created by his own will, immaculate, separable, thrusting. Bloom represents sonship with a vengeance.

"As I am. As I am. All or not at all," which poses the question of Stephen's career, yields to "Never know whose thoughts you're chewing" (171), which proposes the company of Bloom's antecedents. Stephen's doomed bid for originality is replaced by the walking plagiarism that is Bloom. As in Joyce's book, so in Bloom's mind: tireless cliché after cliché. Neither is burdened by a salvational urge or a lust to colonize unknown territories. Both respond with interest to the welter of refuse around them. (I am suggesting not that Bloom could have created *Ulysses*—though he is nearer than Stephen to its germinal pulse—but rather that he shares his author's extraordinary receptivity to the look and feel of prior arrangements.) Bloom's mind is a sieve through which everything passes: what he has read, remembered, seen, thought, fancied—supplemented by all the motley perceptions of June 16. Many of his speculations are based on error. They add up to no pronounced philosophy; Bloom pronounces on nothing. What he knows is almost beyond words: "He bore no hate. Hate. Love. Those are names. Rudy. Soon I am old" (285). Names, places, desires, regrets—none is original. All have been established or felt before, and all language for expressing them has been used before.

Though linked in countless ways with others' lives, Bloom does not therefore avert "the soul's incurable loneliness" (suffered by Mr. James Duffy in "A Painful Case"). "The painful character of the ultimate functions of separate existence" (697) remains in force. But immaculate separateness is equally illusory. When Ned Lambert mockingly asserts that, by Bloom's fuzzy definition, he is himself a nation (331), the joke is in part on Lambert. He is a nation in the sense that Bloom is, saturated through and through by the experience of a life lived in Dublin. He has absorbed its institutions into his body and mind, and the fact of absorption is prior to considerations of endorsement or rejection. He is *there* before he is for or against. So far as I know, Bloom is the first protagonist in literature for whom being there is prior to being for or against. (This is why the plot does not matter, also why the book, by accommodating in Bloom all the stains—cultural and natural—that earlier protagonists had sought to disown, can celebrate presence.)

If Bloom had smiled at the notion of Molly's lover (the "if" is poignant), he would have been reflecting that "each one who enters imagines himself to be the first to enter whereas he is always the last term of a preceding series even if the first term of a succeeding one, each imagining himself to be first, last, only and alone, whereas he is neither first nor last nor only nor alone in a series originating in and repeated to infinity" (731). Each is inscribed in innumerable series. It is only the rigidity of our paradigms that insists on separate emphases, on this but not that.

The insistence "on this but not that" is at the core of Stephen Dedalus, and it is a core composed of will, seeking immaculateness. To seek immaculateness, Joyce eventually saw, is to court betrayal. Bloom emerges as a figure whose maturity is conceived on an opposed model: the relaxation of will, the acceptance of betrayal. If betrayal is unavoidable, it is not necessarily beyond accommodation. This is so because betrayal, like other human stances toward experience, is a partial reading, accompanied by others (equally partial) that complement and defuse it. Situations themselves may accommodate a host of contradictory stances: Bloom is for Molly first and last, married and truant, as well as all the positions in between.[28] It is beyond sorting out into binary distinctions.

For example, what is his religion? All and none. Born Protestant, baptized into the Catholic Church prior to his wedding, vestigially (but ineradicably) Jewish, Bloom accommodates and yet eludes each attribution. Our discovery in "Nausicaa" that he has a foreskin, coming just after the anti-Semitic attack in "Cyclops," is suggestive. He may be doctrinally and "organically" free of Judaism, but these marks of independence have failed to liberate. The father's decision not to have his son circumcised tells us less of successful conversion than of the alienation that this transplanted family has suffered, its hopeless attempt to become racially invisible. The foreskin suggests this much to us, but to the cronies in Barney Kiernan's pub it would only prove that Bloom is an even stranger Jew than they had taken him for.

---

[28] Fisher notes (in "Torn Space") that *Ulysses* would be an elegiac novel if it attends exclusively, in the manner of Victorian novels, to the cleanly aspiring will of its protagonists, a will that cannot achieve satisfaction. But the novel also provides, in addition to these doomed attempts to achieve "this but not that," the richest context of trans-personal, unsought, and "unimportant" traffic: the inexhaustible transactions of city life.

So he wears his Judaism as he wears his other endowments: unchosen, imposed by others for dubious reasons, contingent yet unchangeable, deforming but not uncomfortable.

"In effect, Bloom is a diffused personality—not merely dim and hazy around the edges, but with chunks of other personalities incorporated with his . . ."[29]—Robert Adams describes Bloom thus in "Hades," as a warning that later he will begin to dissolve into hetrogenous parts: "if we were all suddenly somebody else" (110). It is true that later Bloom does alter spectacularly, but Joyce's conception of identity—if I have it right—posits latent heterogeneity at all times. Helplessly porous, the self is heterogenous. Out of Stephen Dedalus leaps the crabbed and fanged May Dedalus. Stephen does not turn into her (as Bloom turns into his internal companions), but this may be a sign of his deeper non-adaptability. He can only be attacked by the company he keeps inside; Bloom is more adroit.

He is perhaps too adroit, and in "Circe" his internal governing mechanism cedes its control. The parts he can imagine playing begin to play him. Hugh Kenner claims that Joyce's single connection with Shakespeare is their common view "that things are done in the world as they are done in the theater, by changing garb and diction: that different persons merely play different parts . . ." (*Joyce's Voices*, 52). Taking "part" as a pun, we can view "Circe" as the chapter in which the subsidiary parts, precariously controlled during the day, take their turns at the dominant role.

The rhythm of "Circe" is "Locomotor ataxy" (521): a pathological confusion of the walking system, caused by syphilis. Bloom and Stephen have trouble staying on their feet throughout the chapter. The vertical posture is the human signature, testifying to our single-selved autonomy and coherence, but we relinquish it several hours each day. The posture exacts a price and cannot be indefinitely sustained; it is a strain to remain oneself. In "Circe" the twin attacks upon Bloom's vertical identity are fatigue and

---

[29] "Hades," in *James Joyce's Ulysses: Critical Essays*, 110. Cf. C. H. Peake's view of Bloom as "not a single self, capable of revealing himself through interior monologue, but a multiplicity of selves, often conflicting . . ." (231).

sexual susceptibility. Ever since Homer, the myth has expressed a failure of sexual discipline by way of transmogrification; men mastered by sexual appetite become swine. So long as they stand they remain men, and Joyce nicely connects the toppling to the animal position with syphilitic symptoms. Syphilis is itself the mark of the beast, testifying to the human animal's continuing struggle with his own flesh.

At night the body's stresses become irresistible. Univocal earnestness recedes and polymorphous impulses, seeded in the body and unacted during the day, come to the fore. Exhausted, Bloom begins to collapse into his latent selves. To prevent arrest by the watch, he pretends to be dental surgeon Bloom, then a card falls from his hat identifying him as Henry Flower, then he takes on the jovial military tone of Major Tweedy, then he tries to pass through by saying "Shibboleth" (but can only manage "Shitbroleeth"), and finally is reduced to: "Gentlemen of the jury, let me explain. A pure mare's nest. I am a man misunderstood. I am being made a scapegoat of. I am a respectable married man, without a stain on my character. I live in Eccles street. My wife, I am the daughter of a most distinguished commander . . . (457).

Out it slips. Gears that were never firm have shifted, and preparation for the Bella confrontation is underway. The parts he plays are mainly his, but tics become monsters; daytime fluidity is nighttime incoherence. At the "bip" of a button he finally resumes control. In a letter to Budgen Joyce described the Homeric Moly—the herb that protected Ulysses from Circe's magic—as follows:

> Moly is the gift of Hermes, god of public ways, and is the invisible influence (prayer, chance, agility, *presence of mind*, power of recuperation which saves in case of accident. This would cover immunity from syphilis—swine love). . . . In this special case his plant may be said to have many leaves, indifference due to masturbation, pessimism congenital, a sense of the ridiculous, sudden fastidiousness in some detail, experience. (Budgen, 230-31)

Two points may be noted. Joyce's Ulysses, unlike Homer's, is unprotected; he must fall into every trap to which his body of fears and desires is liable. And Joyce's description of Moly is whimsically plural. It translates into no specific remedy for a specific dilemma, returning the beleaguered Ulysses to his formerly unambiguous identity; rather, the way back up is for Bloom as casual and chancy as the way down. His marriage has certainly not been healed (by him it has not even been faced), yet all readers of "Circe" come away with an indelible sense of the contours of that bond—its strengths as well as its weaknesses.[30] A brief discussion of their marriage and of Molly Bloom will bring this chapter to a close.

Molly overturns customary ways of thinking. Normal distinctions fail, not because she escapes them but because she occupies all the intermediary positions. She is not amenable to selective focus:

> I wouldnt lower myself to spy on them the garters I found in her room the Friday she was out. . . . (739)

> anyhow its done now once and for all with all the talk of the world about it people make its only the first time after that its just the ordinary do it and think no more about it why cant you kiss a man without going and marrying him first you sometimes love to wildly when you feel that way so nice all over you you cant help yourself I wish some man or other would take me sometime when hes there and kiss me in his arms theres nothing like a kiss long and hot down to your soul. . . . (740)

> he must have eaten oysters I think a few dozen he was in great singing voice no I never in all my life felt anyone had one the size of that to make you feel full up he must have eaten a whole sheep after whats the idea making us like that with a big hole in the middle of us like a Stallion driving it

[30] French, Peake, and especially Kenner have helped me to understand the ways in which "Circe" is and is not a chapter of hallucinations. Whatever our finer awareness of his strengths and weaknesses, Bloom himself never refers later to the trials "undergone" at Bella Cohen's brothel. They form no part of his consciousness.

up into you because thats all they want out of you. . . .
(742)

Id just go to her and ask her do you love him and look her
square in the eyes she couldnt fool me but he might imagine
he was and make a declaration with his plabbery kind of a
manner to her like he did to me though I had the devils
own job to get it out of him though I liked him for that it
showed he could hold in and wasnt to be got for the asking.
. . . (743)

Each of these passages (and there are dozens of others) enacts turns of thought and feeling that are the despair of logical
assessment. She doesn't spy, but she does; it's all over and unimportant after the first kiss, but there's nothing in the world
like a kiss long and hot; with that huge organ he filled her full
up, but what's the idea of having a hole to be plunged into like
that; he is "plabbery" enough to make a declaration, yet he has
a man's restraint and isn't to be got for the asking. Insofar as
consciousness moves in this moment-by-moment contradictory
fashion—and a fortiori nighttime consciousness, the mind self-
propelled and spinning, no goal in a sight—the artifice of argument becomes apparent. Joyce has constructed *Ulysses* in a way
that exploits both these premises.

He has put together a book that finds (actually creates) the
spaces that exist between and prior to paradigms of coherent
identity, consistent purpose, and incremental sequence by which
we normally orient ourselves. When Kenner describes *Ulysses'* appeal as "the novel fascinations of watching the perfectly commonplace take its course in an unfamiliar medium," he under-
states Joyce's achievement (*Ulysses*, 46). The perfectly commonplace, on being observed, is almost incredible; it is exactly what
slips through our mind every minute of the day. We are sieves
as much as Bloom is; we cannot hold the shape and color of our
momentary experience. Joyce brings to our consciousness the
strangeness of consciousness. And he refreshes our awareness of
(among others) the following quotidian realities that are foreign
to normal thinking:

285

1) A man walking through a city all day long is simultaneously alone and accompanied at every minute: his mind is a nation.

2) A man and a woman sixteen years married, both of them sexually interested, have not had intercourse for eleven years, and yet their marriage is not in disarray.[31]

Bloom is himself alone; he is a social world. Molly is a promiscuous lover; she is a faithful wife. The marriage is a disaster; the marriage will endure. These things all make sublunary sense, but our modes of assessing are usually eager to thin them out into their logically opposed parts. We usually prefer simply to oppose subject to object, and to measure their encounter in terms of a successful or failed imposition of the conscious will upon its conditions. Drawing on Platonic models, we tend to denature such plotless phenomena as *Ulysses* presents, or to call them incomprehensible:

> *First proposition.* The reasons for which "this" world has been characterized as "apparent" are the very reasons which indicate its reality; any other kind of reality is absolutely indemonstrable.
> *Second proposition.* The criteria which have been bestowed on the "true being" of things are the criteria of notbeing, of *naught.* . . . (*Twilight of the Idols,* 484)

Nietzsche is blunt, but he states this book's essential case for the movement of English fiction from Victorian to Modernist premises. Dickens and Eliot create fictive universes in which slippage of the protagonists' beliefs, goals, and behavior from "the 'true being' of things" constitutes a fall into error. Such slippage is acceptable on condition that it be (as in Dickens) disguised. Otherwise it meets with admonishment, penalty, or death. For the faltering protagonists of Hardy and Conrad, slippage is the

---

[31] I join those critics who see the marriage as neither bad-but-improving nor bad-and-degenerating, but instead as an incalculable mixture of strengths and weaknesses, and likely to remain so. Robert Kiely's comment is apt: "The Blooms' marriage seems to have nearly everything wrong with it, except that both appear to take comfort from it and will it into surviving through their intense awareness of and involvement in one another's being and modes of expression" (102).

order of the day, but the unitary idols of "true being" remain in place, impotent but unforgiving. Lawrence and Joyce, faithful to the conditions of incarnate life, begin the job of dismantling the idols, one through attack and the other through play.

Nietzsche had hoped that this dismantling would initiate a revaluation of all values—the end of metaphysical ideals and the beginning of a life both modeled and assessed in accordance with the conditions of the earth itself: "Noon; moment of the briefest shadow; end of the longest error; high point of humanity; IN-CIPIT ZARATHUSTRA" (*Ibid.*, 486).

It seems, though, that there is nothing new under the sun, that the need of supremely clarifying fictions is perennial, and that idols must always be drafted to stabilize the scene. The new idols differ of course from the old ones, seem (at least for a time) to be truer to the innumerable conditions of felt experience and to bring a measure of grace and order into our daily sense of who we are and what we can do. Eventually they too will be "revealed" as myths and will need to be replaced.[32] Such a passage of imaginative convictions—the altering premises about what makes up subjective identity, how it accommodates the givens of incarnate nature and the sanctions of historical culture—has informed this study of the novel from *David Copperfield* to *Ulysses*.

In retrospect it certainly seems fair to describe Lawrence's restless career as the quest for new gods—immanent rather than transcendental—to replace the inhospitable ones provided by his culture. And Joyce's art—the two books that devoured twenty-five years of his life—constituted the supreme fiction (at once liberating and tyrannical) within whose coordinates he playfully de-mythologized all other fictions within his reach. Bloom and Molly, Mellors and Connie—they are no happier than Arthur and Amy. Nor are they freer. But they enjoy a different relation to their bodies, and this relation entails a different cluster of values, allegiances, and pitfalls: a different reciprocity between culture and nature, a different semantics of desire.

[32] The relations between myths and fictions, and the kinds of belief appropriate to each, are acutely discussed in Frank Kermode's *The Sense of an Ending*.

Afterword

If you mean speculation, sir, said Stephen, I also am sure that there is no such thing as free thinking inasmuch as all thinking is bound by its own laws. (Joyce, *A Portrait of the Artist as a Young Man*)

STEPHEN DEDALUS is right. All thinking *is* bound by its own laws, but those laws are neither given nor known in advance. I knew when I began, roughly, what I hoped to show, as well as, in each chapter, where I wanted to come out. Yet this book was essentially created twice: once when it first came into being, again when (through several revisions) I sought to find out more fully the bearing of what I had originally written.

The central lines of inquiry, as well as the further implications, came into focus only gradually. The issue of desire (repressed or endorsed) eventually revealed itself to be an issue of identity, of how a protagonist sees himself in his world. The relation between desire and value became the relation, within a protagonist, between the stresses of nature and the constraints of culture. "Within a protagonist" because there the novelist imagines most intimately what it is to be a desiring subject in a world of others. How much of himself can this subject manage to know? bear to know? What are his culture's norms, and what is his posture towards them? What does he want from his world? fear in it? How does he move through his world, and in what ways is it constituted so as to fulfill or deny his fears and desires? These questions enable each chapter, and I saw finally that they circle a common center: they all bear on the author's imagination of freedom.

Freedom involves not an escape from conditions but a coherent activation of them, and of oneself within them. It means, within the scope of this study, achieving a satisfactory relation to the matrical systems of nature and culture. Mid-Victorian and Modernist writers imagine this relation more readily than do their late-Victorian counterparts. Dickens and Eliot seek to square the natural with the cultural; Lawrence and Joyce, the cultural with the natural. But Hardy and Conrad's protagonists absorb the alien force of both systems. The sway of nature is as irresistible in their work as the sanctions of culture are unavailing. The result is tragic impasse.

If this study were more directly historical, other authors would require attention; a greater attempt at coverage would be in order. Coverage without depth would be pointless, however. My object is the writer's imagination, and that faculty cannot be cursorily or peremptorily brought into view. Most of this book's contentions could, I believe, be sustained in a more comprehensive study. The development of imaginative models of identity traced here is demonstrably part of a larger movement in English culture between its mid-Victorian and its high-Modernist phases. How a novelist conceives of a protagonist—what he imagines his protagonist wanting to do and being able to do—is never a matter of purely private choice. Although the historical dimension remains oblique, this study has posed in its own way the question that, according to Irving Howe, Lukács considered decisive: how does a historical consciousness become embodied in a work of art? Within the wide range of inquiries that this question may legitimately command, the imaginative dimension of the writer's work—its character as art—must remain essential.

ॐ

MY CHAPTER on Joyce provided one form of summary by glancing at the progression of idealistic males that began with earnest David Copperfield and ended in "impossible" Stephen Dedalus. This study may now come to a close by offering—as another form of summary—a brief review of its gallery of virginal, violated, and adulterous women.

Little Em'ly and Lydia Glasher (different though they be) are representatively Victorian versions of the fallen woman.

Whatever sympathies they evoke, they serve mainly as cautionary disasters, nodal points within their narratives of uncontrolled and illicit desire. They are culturally beyond recuperation. Annie Strong and Gwendolen Harleth are sternly urged to escape a kindred fate, whereas heroines like Agnes Wickfield and Amy Dorrit are conceived so fully within their culture's altruistic norms as to be immune, if not to desire, then to desire's dangers.

George Eliot means Maggie Tulliver to follow the same discarnate, self-transcending model—to be a creature of her own superego—and Maggie breaks her heart in the attempt. A sensuous woman who both arouses and responds to desire, Maggie writhes under an image of herself that cannot tolerate the feelings with which her creator has so confusingly invested her. *The Mill on the Floss* founders on this confusion, as Eliot insists simultaneously on her heroine's complicity and virginity, her guilty desire and her innocent aspiration.

The important turning occurs with Tess. Natural law begins to supersede human law as an imaginative priority. Unlike Eliot, Hardy is interested in the fact, not the sin, of Tess's intercourse (he leaves its "sinfulness" to others). Tess is not virginal. Hardy's world does not accommodate immaculateness of any kind. Her story, the reverse of Maggie's, is of encounters undergone, not narrowly avoided, of adulterations poignantly sustained, not maliciously asserted. She is as guilty of the charges against her as Maggie is technically innocent. Fully inscribed within opposing natural and societal systems, she accretes and then accepts her own destruction. Her story poses, though in no way resolves, the question of guilt itself.

Connie Chatterley and Molly Bloom are, within the terms germane to this study, Modernist versions of sexual emancipation. They have largely gotten beyond the guilt prescriptions of the superego. Nature flourishes in both women; their identity is inscribed in their bodies and on their impulses. Yet Lawrence must still struggle, in each version of his novel, to resolve the conflict between nature and culture, to release the lovers' desire from the molestations of class. The marks of imaginative stress within each version testify to the rooted recalcitrance of the problem. Recalcitrant not only because class inflects identity beyond conscious reckoning, but also because desire makes in all three versions a broader and more audacious claim: to begin anew, to transcend the orientations (inner and outer) that culture has already established. Desire is optative, lives in the future tense: the drama of *Lady Chatterley's Lover* is Lawrence's attempt, never quite successful but never relinquished, to create for his lovers a new slate.

Molly Bloom provides perhaps the most intriguing perspective on these issues. In Dickens and Eliot's terms she is guilty, but that word has little purchase upon her. Guilt implies transgression; transgression requires commanding distinctions between good and evil; Molly absorbs and finally overpowers such distinctions. Nature is maculate and nature governs her, but not more than culture does. She is bonded in countless ways: unconsciously scripted by society (she revels in its clichés), likewise shaped without consultation by nature (a big hole in her middle, menstruation, flatulence, a tendency to overweight, approaching middle age: she never asked for any of these). Her powers and her problems are inseparable: desire itself creates society, has led her through Mulvey and Gardiner to Bloom, then (with Bloom) to Milly and the haunting memory of Rudy, now (still with Bloom) to Boylan. She is scripted up to her neck, has a stake in a dozen contradictory positions, acts on her desires and yet is incomplete, frustrated beyond resolving.

Yet Molly Bloom is free, in the measure that human beings can be free. She has not created her conditions, nor can she escape them. Nor would she. She is free because she takes the conditions as her own; she actualizes herself through them. Her body, mind, and language have come to her shaped and manipulated by many other sources. She is a creature of stain. All the more wonderful then—both liberating and trouble-making—are the things she does with and through that body, mind, and language. Molly Bloom's Yes is not the Yes of victory, the Yes of some achieved idea of herself. It is instead the Yes of unthinking acceptance—both of her desires and their complications, of her husband and his alternatives, of her bounded life and its unforeclosed options. It is the Yes that makes her present in her own life, a model for no one else as she engages in the daily activity of becoming who she is.

List of Works Cited

Acton, Lord. "George Eliot's Life." In *A Century of George Eliot Criticism*. Ed. Gordon Haight. London: Methuen, 1966, 151-60.

Adamowski, T. H. "Being Perfect: Lawrence, Sartre, and *Women in Love*." *Critical Inquiry*, 2 (1975): 345-68.

Adams, Robert. "Hades." In *James Joyce's Ulysses: Critical Essays*. Ed. Clive Hart and David Hayman. Berkeley: University of California Press, 1974, 91-114.

Alvarez, A. "The Poetic Power of *Jude the Obscure*." Afterword to *Jude the Obscure*. New York: New American Library, 1961. Rpt. in *Jude the Obscure*. New York: Norton, 1978, 414-23.

Auerbach, Nina. "The Power of Hunger: Demonism and Maggie Tulliver." *Nineteenth-Century Fiction*, 30 (1975): 150-71.

Bakhtin, Mikhail. *Problems of Dostoevsky's Poetics*. Trans. R. W. Rotsel. Ann Arbor: Ardis, 1973.

Barthes, Roland. *S/Z*. Paris: Seuil, 1970.

Bayley, John. *Essay on Hardy*. Cambridge: Cambridge University Press, 1978.

Bedient, Calvin. *Architects of the Self: George Eliot, D. H. Lawrence, and E. M. Forster*. Berkeley: University of California Press, 1972.

Benvenuto, Richard. "Modes of Perception: The Will to Live in *Jude the Obscure*." *Studies in the Novel*, 2 (1970): 31-41.

Bersani, Leo. "Lawrentian Stillness." *Yale Review*, 65 (1975): 33-60.

———. *Marcel Proust: The Fictions of Life and Art*. New York: Oxford University Press, 1965.

Blake, William. *The Poetry and Prose of William Blake*. Ed. David B. Erdman and Harold Bloom. Garden City, New York: Doubleday, 1970.

Boyle, Robert. "Penelope." In *James Joyce's Ulysses: Critical Essays*. Ed. Clive Hart and David Hayman. Berkeley: University of California Press, 1974, 407-33.

293

Brown, Janet H. "The Narrator's Role in *David Copperfield*." In *Dickens Studies Annual, 2*. Ed. Robert B. Partlow, Jr. Carbondale, Illinois: University Press, Southern Illinois, 1972, 197-207.

Buckley, Jerome H. *Season of Youth: The Bildungsroman From Dickens to Golding*. Cambridge: Harvard University Press, 1974.

Budgen, Frank. *James Joyce and the Making of Ulysses*. Bloomington: Indiana University Press, 1960.

Burstein, Janet. "The Journey Beyond Myth in *Judge the Obscure*." *Texas Studies in Language and Literature*, 15 (1973): 499-515.

Carlisle, Janet. "*Little Dorrit*: Necessary Fictions." *Studies in the Novel*, 7 (1975): 195-214.

Cavitch, David. *D. H. Lawrence and the New World*. New York: Oxford University Press, 1969.

Chase, Cynthia. "The Decomposition of the Elephants: Double Reading: *Daniel Deronda*." *PMLA*, 93 (1978): 215-27.

Cixous, Helene. *The Exile of James Joyce*. Trans. Sally A. J. Purcell. New York: David Lewis, 1972.

Clarke, Colin. *River of Dissolution: D. H. Lawrence and English Romanticism*. New York: Barnes and Noble, 1969.

Conrad, Joseph. *Heart of Darkness*. Ed. Robert Kimbrough. New York: Norton, 1971.

———. Letter to *The New York Times* (1901). Rpt. in Lawrence Graver, *Conrad's Short Fiction*. Berkeley: University of California Press, 1969.

———. *Lord Jim*. Ed. Thomas C. Moser. New York: Norton, 1968.

———. *Nostromo*. Harmondsworth, England: Penguin, 1963.

———. *A Personal Record*. London: Dent, 1946.

———. *Typhoon*. In *The Portable Conrad*. Ed. Morton D. Zabel. New York: Viking, 1947.

Crews, Frederick. *Out of My System: Psychoanalysis, Ideology, and Critical Method*. New York: Oxford University Press, 1975.

Croce, Benedetto. *The Philosophy of Giambattista Vico*. Trans. R. G. Collingwood. London, 1913.

Culler, Jonathan. *Structuralist Poetics: Structuralism, Linguistics, and the Study of Literature*. Ithaca: Cornell University Press, 1975.

Daleski, H. M. *Dickens and the Art of Analogy*. New York: Schocken, 1970.

———. *The Forked Flame: A Study of D. H. Lawrence*. London: Faber and Faber, 1965.

———. *Joseph Conrad: The Way of Dispossession*. London: Faber and Faber, 1977.

Delany, Paul. *D. H. Lawrence's Nightmare: The Writer and his Circle in the Years of the Great War*. New York: Basic Books, 1978.

Delevaney, Emile. "Les trois amants de Lady Chatterley." *Etudes anglaises*, 29 (1976): 46-63.

De Man, Paul. *Blindness and Insight: Essays in the Rhetoric of Contemporary Criticism*. New York: Oxford University Press, 1971.

Descombes, Vincent. *Le même et l'autre*. Paris: Minuit, 1979.

Dickens, Charles. *David Copperfield*. Ed. Nina Burgis. Oxford: Clarendon Press, 1981.

———. *Little Dorrit*. Ed. Harvey Peter Sucksmith. Oxford: Clarendon Press, 1979.

Donoghue, Denis. " 'Till the Fight is Finished': D. H. Lawrence in his Letters." In *D. H. Lawrence: Novelist, Poet, Prophet*. Ed. Stephen Spender. New York: Harper and Row, 1973, 197-209.

Drabble, Margaret. "Hardy and the Natural World." In *The Genius of Thomas Hardy*. Ed. Margaret Drabble. London: Weidenfeld and Nicholson, 1976, 162-69.

Eagleton, Terry. *Criticism and Ideology: A Study of Marxist Literary Theory*. London: NLB, 1976.

Eliot, George. *Daniel Deronda*. Ed. Barbara Hardy. Harmondsworth, England: Penguin, 1967.

———. *The Mill on the Floss*. Ed. Gordon Haight. Oxford: Clarendon Press, 1980.

———. "The Natural History of German Life." In *Westminster Review* (1856). Rpt. in *Essays of George Eliot*. Ed. Thomas Pinney. London: Routledge and Kegan Paul, 1963, 266-99.

Eliot, T. S. "Little Gidding." In *T. S. Eliot: Collected Poems, 1909-1962*. London: Faber and Faber, 1963.

Ellmann, Richard. *James Joyce*. New York: Oxford University Press, 1959.

———. *Ulysses on the Liffey*. New York: Oxford University Press, 1972.

Emerson, Ralph Waldo. "Self-Reliance." In *The Selected Writings of Ralph Waldo Emerson*. Ed. Brooks Arkinson. New York: Random House, 1940, 145-69.

Ermarth, Elizabeth. "Maggie Tulliver's Long Suicide." *Studies in English Literature*, 14 (1974): 587-601.

Faulkner, William. *The Sound and the Fury*. New York: Random House, 1956.

Fisher, Philip. "Torn Space: Joyce and Theories of Spatiality in the City." Lecture given at *The English Institute*. Cambridge, Mass., September, 1981.

Ford, George. *Double Measure: A Reading of the Novels and Stories of D. H. Lawrence*. New York: Holt, Rinehart and Winston, 1965.

Foucault, Michel. *Les Mots et les choses*. Paris: Gallimard, 1966.

———. *L'Ordre du discours*. Paris: Gallimard, 1971.

French, Marilyn. *The Book as World: James Joyce's Ulysses*. Cambridge: Harvard University Press, 1976.

Freud, Sigmund. *Civilisation and its Discontents*. In *The Standard Edition of the Complete Psychological Works of Sigmund Freud*. Gen. ed. and trans. James Strachey. 24 vols. London: The Hogarth Press, 1953-1974, 21: 57-146.

———. "The Ego and the Id." In *The Standard Edition of the Complete Psychological Works of Sigmund Freud*. Gen. ed. and trans. James Strachey. 24 vols. London: The Hogarth Press, 1953-1974, 19: 1-59.

———. *Five Lectures on Psychoanalysis*. In *The Standard Edition of the Complete Psychological Works of Sigmund Freud*. Gen. ed. and trans. James Strachey. 24 vols. London: The Hogarth Press, 1953-1974, 11: 1-55.

———. *Interpretation of Dreams*. In *The Standard Edition of the Complete Psychological Works of Sigmund Freud*. Gen. ed. and trans. James Strachey. 24 vols. London: The Hogarth Press, 1953-1974, Vols. 4-5.

———. *Three Essays on the Theory of Sexuality*. In *The Standard Edition of the Complete Psychological Works of Sigmund Freud*. Gen. ed. and trans. James Strachey. 24 vols. London: The Hogarth Press, 1953-1974, 7: 123-244.

Friedman, Alan. "The Other Lawrence." *Partisan Review*, 37 (1970), 239-53.

Garis, Robert. *The Dickens Theatre: A Reassessment of the Novels*. Oxford: Clarendon Press, 1965.

Gilbert, Sandra, and Susan Gubar. *The Madwoman in the Attic: The Woman Writer and the Nineteenth-Century Literary Imagination*. New Haven: Yale University Press, 1979.

Gill, Stephen. "The Composite World: Two Versions of *Lady Chatterley's Lover*." *Essays in Criticism*, 21 (1971): 347-64.

Gingher, R. S. "The Three Versions of *Lady Chatterley's Lover*." *DAI*, 39 (1978): 294A-295A.

Girard, René. *Desire, Deceit, and the Novel: Self and Other in Literary Structure*. Baltimore: Johns Hopkins University Press, 1965.

Glassman, Peter J. *Language and Being: Joseph Conrad and the Literature of Personality*. New York: Columbia University Press, 1976.

Goldberg, S. L. *The Classical Temper: A Study of James Joyce's Ulysses.* London: Chatto and Windus, 1961.

Gottfried, Leon. "Structure and Genre in *Daniel Deronda.*" In *The English Novel in the Nineteenth Century.* Ed. George Goodin. Urbana: University of Illinois Press, 1972, 164-75.

Graver, Lawrence. *Conrad's Short Fiction.* Berkeley: University of California Press, 1969.

Gregor, Ian. *The Great Web: The Form of Hardy's Major Fiction.* London: Faber and Faber, 1974.

Guerard, Albert. *Conrad the Novelist.* New York: Atheneum, 1967.

———. *The Triumph of the Novel: Dickens, Dostoevsky, Faulkner.* New York: Oxford University Press, 1976.

Hagan, John. "A Reinterpretation of *The Mill on the Floss.*" *PMLA*, 87 (1972): 53-63.

Haight, Gordon. *George Eliot: A Biography.* Oxford: Oxford University Press, 1978.

Harari, Josue V. "Critical Factions/ Critical Fictions." In *Textual Strategies: Perspectives in Post-Structuralist Criticism.* Ed. Josue V. Harari. Ithaca: Cornell University Press, 1979, 17-72.

Hardy, Barbara. "*The Mill on the Floss.*" In *Critical Essays on George Eliot.* Ed. Barbara Hardy. London: Routledge and Kegan Paul, 1970, 42-58.

———. *The Novels of George Eliot.* London: The Athlone Press, 1963.

———. "Introduction" to *Daniel Deronda.* Ed. Barbara Hardy. Harmondsworth, England: Penguin, 1967, 7-30.

Hardy, Florence E. *The Life of Thomas Hardy.* London: Macmillan, 1962.

Hardy, Thomas. *Jude the Obscure.* New Wessex Edition. London: Macmillan, 1975.

———. *A Pair of Blue Eyes.* New Wessex Edition. London: Macmillan, 1975.

———. *The Return of the Native.* New Wessex Edition. London: Macmillan, 1975.

———. *Tess of the d'Urbervilles.* New Wessex Edition. London: Macmillan, 1975.

Hart, Clive. "Wandering Rocks." In *James Joyce's Ulysses: Critical Essays.* Ed. Clive Hart and David Hayman. Berkeley: University of California Press, 1974, 181-216.

Hartman, Geoffrey H. *Wordsworth's Poetry: 1787-1814.* New Haven: Yale University Press, 1964.

Hayman, David. *Ulysses: The Mechanics of Meaning.* Englewood Cliffs, New Jersey: Prentice-Hall, 1970.

Heilman, Robert. "Hardy's Sue Bridehead." *Nineteenth-Century Fiction*, 20 (1966): 307-23.

Herring, Phillip. *Joyce's Notes and Early Drafts for "Ulysses."* Charlottesville: University of Virginia Press, 1977.

Hirsch, E. D. *Validity in Interpretation.* New Haven: Yale University Press, 1967.

Holloway, John. "Introduction" to *Little Dorrit.* Ed. John Holloway. Harmondsworth, England: Penguin, 1967, 13-29.

Hough, Graham. *The Dark Sun: A Study of D. H. Lawrence.* New York: Capricorn, 1959.

Howells, William Dean. "Review of *Jude the Obscure.*" In *Harper's Weekly* (7 December 1895). Rpt. in *Jude the Obscure.* New York: Norton, 1978, 379-81.

Jackson, Marvin Dennis. "The Progression Toward Myth in the Three Versions of D. H. Lawrence's *Lady Chatterley's Lover.*" In *DAI*, 40 (1970): 1459A-1460A.

James, Henry. "The Art of Fiction." In *Selected Literary Criticism: Henry James.* Ed. Morris Shapira. New York: McGraw-Hill, 1965, 49-67.

Johnson, Bruce. *Conrad's Models of Mind.* Minneapolis: University of Minnesota Press, 1971.

Johnson, Edgar. *Charles Dickens: His Tragedy and Triumph.* 2 vols. New York: Simon and Schuster, 1952.

Johnson, Lionel. *The Art of Thomas Hardy.* London: Bodley Head, 1923.

Jones, R. T. *George Eliot.* Cambridge: Cambridge University Press, 1970.

Joyce, James. *Letters of James Joyce.* Ed. Stuart Gilbert and Richard Ellmann. 3 vols. New York: Viking, 1966.

———. *A Portrait of the Artist as a Young Man.* New York: Viking, 1964.

———. *Selected Letters.* Ed. Richard Ellmann. New York: Viking, 1975.

———. *Ulysses.* New York: Random House, 1961.

Kaufmann, Walter. *Nietzsche: Philosopher, Psychologist, Antichrist.* New York: Random House, 1968.

Kenner, Hugh. *Joyce's Voices.* Berkeley: University of California Press, 1978.

———. *Ulysses.* London: Allen and Unwin, 1980.

Kermode, Frank. *D. H. Lawrence.* New York: Viking, 1973.

———. *The Sense of an Ending: Studies in the Theory of Fiction.* New York: Oxford University Press, 1967.

Kiely, Robert. *Beyond Egotism: The Fiction of James Joyce, Virginia Woolf, and D. H. Lawrence.* Cambridge: Harvard University Press, 1980.

Kinhead-Weekes, Mark. "Eros and Metaphor: Sexual Relationship in the Fiction of D. H. Lawrence." In *Lawrence and Women*. Ed. Anne Smith. New York: Barnes and Noble, 1978, 101-21.

Knoepflmacher, U. C. *Religious Humanism and the Victorian Novel: George Eliot, Walter Pater, and Samuel Butler*. Princeton: Princeton University Press, 1965.

Kristeva, Julia. *Desire in Language: A Semiotic Approach to Literature and Art*. Ed. Leon S. Roudiez. Trans. Thomas Gora, Alice Jardine, and Leon S. Roudiez. New York: Columbia University Press, 1980.

Lang, Andrew. "Review of *Tess of the d'Urbervilles*." In *Longman's Magazine* (November, 1892). Rpt. in *Tess of the d'Urbervilles*. New York: Norton, 1979, 384-87.

Lawall, Sarah. *Critics of Consciousness: The Existential Structures of Literature*. Cambridge: Harvard University Press, 1968.

Lawrence, D. H. "The Crown." In *Phoenix II*. Ed. Warren Roberts and Harry T. Moore. New York: Viking, 1970, 365-415.

———. "Democracy." In *Phoenix: The Posthumous Papers of D. H. Lawrence*. Ed. E. D. McDonald. New York: Viking, 1936, 699-718.

———. *The First Lady Chatterley*. Harmondsworth, England: Penguin, 1973.

———. "The Good Man." In *D. H. Lawrence: Selected Literary Criticism*. Ed. Anthony Beal. New York: Viking, 1966, 254-60.

———. "Introduction to New Poems." In *D. H. Lawrence: Selected Literary Criticism*. Ed. Anthony Beal. New York: Viking, 1966, 84-89.

———. *John Thomas and Lady Jane*. New York: Viking, 1974.

———. *Lady Chatterley's Lover*. New York: Bantam, 1968.

———. *The Letters of D. H. Lawrence*. Ed. James T. Boulton. Cambridge: Cambridge University Press, 1979-.

———. "Morality and the Novel." In *D. H. Lawrence: Selected Literary Criticism*. Ed. Anthony Beal. New York: Viking, 1966, 108-13.

———. "The Novel." In *Phoenix II*. Ed. Warren Roberts and Harry T. Moore. New York: Viking, 1970, 416-26.

———. "On Being a Man." In *Phoenix II*. Ed. Warren Roberts and Harry T. Moore. New York: Viking, 1970, 616-22.

———. "On Human Destiny." In *Phoenix II*. Ed. Warren Roberts and Harry T. Moore. New York: Viking, 1970, 623-24.

———. "Pornography and Obscenity." In *D. H. Lawrence: Selected Literary Criticism*. Ed. Anthony Beal. New York: Viking, 1966, 32-51.

Lawrence, D. H. *Psychoanalysis and the Unconscious and Fantasia of the Unconscious.* New York: Viking, 1960.

———. *Selected Literary Criticism.* Ed. Anthony Beal. New York: Viking, 1966.

———. "The Study of Thomas Hardy." Rpt. in *D. H. Lawrence: Selected Literary Criticism.* Ed. Anthony Beal. New York: Viking, 1966, 166-228.

———. *Women in Love.* New York: Viking, 1960.

Leavis, F. R. *D. H. Lawrence, Novelist.* London: Chatto and Windus, 1955.

———. *The Great Tradition: George Eliot, Henry James, Joseph Conrad.* London: Chatto and Windus, 1948.

Leavis, F. R. and Q. D. *Dickens the Novelist.* London: Chatto and Windus, 1970.

Lentricchia, Frank. *After the New Criticism.* Chicago: University of Chicago Press, 1980.

Levine, George. *The Realistic Imagination.* Chicago: University of Chicago Press, 1981.

Lewis, Edwin. "Trinity." In *The New Harper's Bible Dictionary.* Ed. Madeleine S. Miller and J. Lane Miller. New York: Harper and Row, 1973.

Librach, Ronald. "The Burdens of Self and Society: Release and Redemption in *Little Dorrit.*" *Studies in the Novel,* 7 (1975): 538-51.

Litz, A. Walton. "Ithaca." In *James Joyce's Ulysses: Critical Essays.* Ed. Clive Hart and David Hayman. Berkeley: University of California Press, 1974, 385-405.

Martin, Graham. "*Daniel Deronda*: George Eliot and Political Change." In *Critical Essays on George Eliot.* Ed. Barbara Hardy. London: Routledge and Kegan Paul, 1970, 133-50.

May, Rollo. *Love and Will.* New York: Dell, 1973.

Merleau-Ponty, Maurice. *La Phénoménologie de la perception.* Paris: Gallimard, 1945.

Meyer, Bernard. *Joseph Conrad: A Psychoanalytic Biography.* Princeton: Princeton University Press, 1967.

Meyers, Jeffrey. "D. H. Lawrence and Homosexuality." In *D. H. Lawrence: Novelist, Poet, Prophet.* Ed. Stephen Spender. New York: Harper and Row, 1973, 135-46.

Miller, J. Hillis. *Charles Dickens: The World of his Novels.* Cambridge: Harvard University Press, 1959.

———. *The Disappearance of God: Five Nineteenth-Century Writers.* Cambridge: Harvard University Press, 1963.

———. *Poets of Reality: Six Twentieth-Century Writers*. Cambridge: Harvard University Press, 1965.

———. *Thomas Hardy: Distance and Desire*. Cambridge: Harvard University Press, 1970.

Millhauser, Milton. "*David Copperfield*: Some Shifts of Plan." *Nineteenth-Century Fiction*, 27 (1972): 339-45.

Moser, Thomas. *Joseph Conrad: Achievement and Decline*. Cambridge: Harvard University Press, 1957.

Moynahan, Julian. *The Deed of Life: The Novels and Tales of D. H. Lawrence*. Princeton: Princeton University Press, 1963.

Needham, Gwendolyn. "The Undisciplined Heart of David Copperfield." *Nineteenth-Century Fiction*, 9 (1954): 81-107.

Nietzsche, Friedrich. *Beyond Good and Evil*. In *Basic Writings of Nietzsche*. Ed. and trans. Walter Kaufmann. New York: Random House, 1968.

———. *The Birth of Tragedy*. In *Basic Writings of Nietzsche*. Ed. and trans. Walter Kaufmann. New York: Random House, 1968.

———. *The Gay Science*. Ed. and trans. Walter Kaufmann. New York: Random House, 1974.

———. *On the Genealogy of Morals*. In *Basic Writings of Nietzsche*. Ed. and trans. Walter Kaufmann. New York: Random House, 1968.

———. *Twilight of the Idols*. In *The Portable Nietzsche*. Ed. and trans. Walter Kaufmann. New York: Random House, 1954.

Oates, Joyce Carol. " 'The Immense Indifference of Things': The Tragedy of *Nostromo*." *Novel*, 9 (1975): 5-22.

———. "Lawrence's Götterdämmerung: The Tragic Vision of *Women in Love*." *Critical Inquiry*, 4 (1978): 559-78.

Paris, Bernard J. *Experiments in Life: George Eliot's Quest for Values*. Detroit: Wayne State University Press, 1965.

Peake, C. H. *James Joyce: The Citizen and the Artist*. London: Edward Arnold, 1977.

Pirenet, C. "La structure symbolique de *Women in Love*." *Etudes anglaises*, 22 (1969): 137-51.

Poulet, Georges. *The Interior Distance*. Trans. Elliot Coleman. Baltimore: Johns Hopkins University Press, 1959.

———. *The Metamorphoses of the Circle*. Trans. Carley Dawson and Elliot Coleman. Baltimore: Johns Hopkins University Press, 1966.

———. *Studies in Human Time*. Trans. Elliot Coleman. Baltimore: Johns Hopkins University Press, 1956.

Pound, Ezra. " 'Dubliners' and Mr. James Joyce." In *Pound/Joyce*. Ed. Forrest Read. New York: New Directions, 1967, 27-30.

Pritchett, V. S. "George Eliot." In *A Century of George Eliot Criticism*. Ed. Gordon Haight. London: Methuen, 1966, 210-14.

Proust, Marcel. *Remembrance of Things Past*. Trans. C. K. Scott Moncrieff. 2 vols. New York: Random House, 1934.

Putzell, Sara M. " 'An Antagonism of Valid Claims': The Dynamics of *The Mill on the Floss*." *Studies in the Novel*, 7 (1975): 227-44.

Redinger, Ruby. *George Eliot: The Emergent Self*. London: Bodley Head, 1976.

Richard, Jean-Pierre. *Littérature et sensation*. Paris: Seuil, 1954.

Ricoeur, Paul. *Le Conflit des interprétations: Essais d'herméneutique*. Paris: Seuil, 1969.

———. *Freud and Philosophy*. Trans. Denis Savage. New Haven: Yale University Press, 1970.

Rieff, Philip. *Freud: The Mind of the Moralist*. Garden City, New York: Doubleday, 1961.

Robinson, Carole. "The Severe Angel: A Study of *Daniel Deronda*." *English Literary History*, 31 (1964): 278-300.

Rutland, William R. *Thomas Hardy: A Study of his Writings and their Background*. Oxford: Blackwell, 1938.

Sagar, Keith. *The Art of D. H. Lawrence*. Cambridge: Cambridge University Press, 1966.

Said, Edward. *Beginnings: Intention and Method*. New York: Basic Books, 1975.

Sale, Roger. *Modern Heroism: Essays on D. H. Lawrence, William Empson, and J.R.R. Tolkien*. Berkeley: University of California Press, 1973.

Schopenhauer, Arthur. *The World as Will and Idea*. In *Schopenhauer: Selections*. Ed. Dewitt H. Parker. New York: Scribner's 1928.

Senn, Fritz. "Book of Many Turns." In *Fifty Years: Ulysses*. Ed. Thomas F. Staley. Bloomington: Indiana University Press, 1974, 29-46.

Showalter, Elaine. *A Literature of Their Own: British Women Novelists from Brontë to Lessing*. Princeton: Princeton University Press, 1977.

Spilka, Mark. "Lawrence Up-Tight, or the Anal Phase Once Over." *Novel*, 4 (1971): 252-67.

———. "On Lawrence's Hostility to Wilful Women: The Chatterley Solution." In *Lawrence and Women*. Ed. Anne Smith. New York: Barnes and Noble, 1978, 189-211.

Squires, Michael. "New Light on the Gamekeeper in *Lady Chatterley's Lover*." In *D. H. Lawrence Review*, 11 (1978): 234-45.

———. "Pastoral Patterns and Pastoral Variants in *Lady Chatterley's Lover*." In *English Literary History*, 39 (1972): 129-46.

Steig, Michael. "Anality in *The Mill on the Floss*." In *Novel*, 5 (1972): 42-53.

Stewart, Garrett. "Lawrence, 'Being,' and the Allotropic Style." *Novel*, 9 (1976): 217-42.

———. *Dickens and the Trials of Imagination*. Cambridge: Harvard University Press, 1974.

Stewart, J.I.M. *Joseph Conrad*. London: Longman, 1968.

———. *Thomas Hardy: A Critical Biography*. London: Longman, 1971.

Sudrann, Jean. "*Daniel Deronda*: The Landscape of Exile." *English Literary History*, 37 (1970): 433-55.

Tanner, Tony. "Colour and Movement in Hardy's *Tess of the d'Urbervilles*." In *Critical Quarterly*, 10 (1968): 219-39.

Thorburn, David. *Conrad's Romanticism*. New Haven: Yale University Press, 1974.

Van Ghent, Dorothy. *The English Novel: Form and Function*. New York: Harper, 1961.

Vivas, Eliseo. *D. H. Lawrence: The Failure and Triumph of Art*. Evanston: Northwestern University Press, 1960.

Watt, Ian. *Conrad in the Nineteenth Century*. Berkeley: University of California Press, 1979.

———. "Joseph Conrad: Alienation and Commitment." In *The English Mind*. Ed. Hugh Sykes Davies and George Watson. Cambridge: Cambridge University Press, 1964, 257-78.

Wells, H. G. "James Joyce." In *New Republic*, 10 (1917): 159.

Welsh, Alexander. *The City of Dickens*. Oxford: Clarendon Press, 1971.

Widmer, Kingsley. "The Pertinence of Modern Pastoral: The Three Versions of *Lady Chatterley's Lover*." *Studies in the Novel*, 5 (1973): 298-313.

Williams, Raymond. "Dickens and Social Ideas." In *Dickens 1970*. Ed. Michael Slater. London: Chapman and Hall, 1970, 77-98.

Wilson, Angus. "Dickens on Children and Childhood." In *Dickens 1970*. Ed. Michael Slater. London: Chapman and Hall, 1970, 195-227.

Worthen, John. *D. H. Lawrence and the Idea of the Novel*. Totowa, N.J.: Rowman and Littlefield, 1979.

Index

305

LIBRARY OF CONGRESS CATALOGING IN PUBLICATION DATA

Weinstein, Philip M.
The semantics of desire.

Bibliography: p.
Includes index.
1. English fiction—19th century—History and criticism. 2. English fiction—20th
century—History and criticism. 3. Identity (Psychology) in literature. 4. Mind
and body in literature. I. Title

PR878.I3W4 1984   823'.8'09353   83-43098
ISBN 0-691-06594-2 (alk. paper)